Asian Economic and Political Issues

Volume II

Asian Economic and Political Issues
A Series Edited by Frank Columbus

Volume II   ISBN 1-5672-688-1

Volume I   ISBN 1-5672-598-2

ASIAN ECONOMIC AND POLITICAL ISSUES

VOLUME II

FRANK COLUMBUS
EDITOR

Nova Science Publishers, Inc.

Commack, New York

Editorial Production: Susan Boriotti
Office Manager: Annette Hellinger
Graphics: Frank Grucci and John T'Lustachowski
Information Editor: Tatiana Shohov
Book Production: Donna Dennis, Patrick Davin, Christine Mathosian
and Tammy Sauter
Circulation: Maryanne Schmidt
Marketing/Sales: Cathy DeGregory

Library of Congress Cataloging-in-Publication Data

ISBN 1-56072-688-1

Copyright © 1999 by Nova Science Publishers, Inc.
6080 Jericho Turnpike, Suite 207
Commack, New York 11725
Tele. 516-499-3103   Fax 516-499-3146
e-mail: Novascience@earthlink.net
e-mail: Novasci1@aol.com
Web Site: http://www.nexusworld.com/nova

Printed in the United States of America

CONTENTS

PREFACE   VII

CHAPTER 1 JAPAN'S POLITICAL LEADERSHIP: THE PRIME MINISTER'S POWER,
           STYLE AND CONDUCT OF REFORM   1

           TOMOHITO SHINODA

CHAPTER 2 VIETNAM'S TRANSITION TO A MARKET ECONOMY   33

           RAYMOND J. AHEARN

CHAPTER 3 EAST ASIA AND THE PACIFIC   39

           ROBERT SUTTER

CHAPTER 4 TAIWAN'S ECONOMIC POLICY-MAKING IN THE DEMOCRATIC
           TRANSITION   55

           GERALD A. MCBEATH

CHAPTER 5 CHINA-U.S.-TAIWAN ECONOMIC RELATIONS   83

           WAYNE M. MORRISON AND WILLIAM COOPER

CHAPTER 6 CHINA AND THE MULTILATERAL DEVELOPMENT BANKS   137

           JONATHAN SANFORD

CHAPTER 7 THE EFFECTIVENESS OF THE PRC'S ECONOMIC MEASURES FOR
           FOREIGN DIRECT INVESTMENT, THE ASIAN FINANCIAL CRISIS, AND
           THE REFORM OF STATE-OWNED ENTERPRISES   151

           DANIEL K. T. LI, MIKE GOLDSTEIN AND GORDON WALKER

CHAPTER 8 BUSINESS, BUREAUCRATIC REFORM, AND THE EU IN TURKMENISTAN   195

           ROBERT C. RICKARDS

INDEX   217

PREFACE

This series is intended to provide a forum for substantial research contributions dealing with current political and economic developments in Asia. The papers have been selected for their quality, relevance and timeliness. The coherence of this book rests in its fit within the larger framework of the series and its goals. In this volume, the emphasis is on economic and trade developments. We also examine the inner workings of the office of prime minister of Japan.

Chapter 1

JAPAN'S POLITICAL LEADERSHIP: THE PRIME MINISTER'S POWER, STYLE AND CONDUCT OF REFORM

TOMOHITO SHINODA
International University of Japan
Niigata, Japan

SUMMARY

This study provides an analytical framework for the prime minister's role in Japan's decision making. There exist two dimensions of fraction within the government and the ruling party, inter-agency rivalry and intra-party factions, with which the leader must confront when pursuing a major policy. Despite of these obstacle as well as limited legal authority, the prime minister has at his disposal various sources of power with which he can play an imperative role to achieve a major policy goal. His leadership style can be defined, depending on what kind of sources of power they utilize in the policy process. After examining three case studies -- Hashimoto's administrative reform, Takeshita's tax reform and Nakasone's administrative reform -- this study introduces four types of leadership: the political insider, the grandstander, the kamikaze fighter and the peace lover.

INTRODUCTION

Since 1993, the Japanese political scene has witnessed a series of drastic changes. These changes have not only provided different political environments surrounding the Japanese prime minister, but also have significantly increased public interest in his political leadership. This is the first study which provides an analytical framework for the prime minister's role in Japan's decision making.

Numerous political resources are available to a Japanese prime minister. As head of the cabinet that is vested with executive power, the prime minister is at the top of the executive branch. He leads the political party or a coalition of parties that holds the majority of seats in the powerful lower house. The prime minister handles both administrative and political affairs as the leader of the government and the ruling party or coalition.

In spite of these responsibilities and authorities, the prime minister is often considered weak. Lack of leadership is a reoccurring theme in many analyses of Japanese politics. Japan scholars have long argued that political leaders depend on Japan's strong bureaucracy for the formulation and execution of policies. Some argue that the bureaucracy is so strong that political leaders, including the prime minister, have a very limited role in policymaking.

Karel van Wolferen, for example, describes the Japanese policymaking mechanism as "The System," which is made up of elite in the political, bureaucratic, and business world who as a unit somehow make decisions. According to van Wolferen, Japan's system has no political peak and thus no political leadership.[1]

Is the Japanese prime minister an ineffective national leader as van Wolferen suggests? This study provides an answer to this question by first examining the limits of his legal authority. Then, the focus shifts to the two dimensions of fractions within the government and the ruling party that the prime minister must face -- factions in the ruling party and sectionalism in the government. To overcome his legal limitation and these political constraints, the prime minister must rely on informal sources of power to effectively utilize legal authority. The second part of this paper introduces various informal sources of power, and presents four leadership styles. Which leadership style a prime minister adapts is dependent on what informal sources of power are available to him and how he utilizes them. The third part will be three case studies to show how four different prime ministers -- Suzuki Zenko, Nakasone Yasuhiro, Takeshita Noboru and Hashimoto Ryutaro -- utilized or failed to utilize their sources of power in pursuing administrative and tax reforms, showing their effectiveness and ineffectiveness as a leader. The conclusive part will introduce four different leadership styles of the prime minister.

Although academic literature on the role of the bureaucracy and the ruling party is abundant, the prime minister's function in policymaking has been largely neglected until recently. The first systematic study on the prime minister by Kenji Hayao argues that the leadership of the prime minister is crippled by the selection process of the LDP presidency, by intra- and inter-party politics, by the sub-government, and by the small size of the prime minister's support staff. Hayao uses Nakasone's educational reform effort as well as his tax reform proposal as case studies, with both efforts ending in failure. Focusing on the ineffectual aspects of the prime minister's power, Hayao successfully illustrates the constraints that can block the prime minister in the exercise of leadership.[2] Although Hayao also argues that the prime minister can have an important impact on policy, he fails to offer examples.[3]

---

[1] Karel G. van Wolferen, *The Enigma of Japanese Power* (New York: Alfred A. Knopf, 1989).

[2] Kenji Hayao, "The Japanese Prime Minister and Public Policy" (Ph.D. dissertation, the University of Michigan, 1990). See also Kenji Hayao, *The Japanese Prime Minister and Public Policy* (Pittsburgh: University of Pittsburgh Press, 1993).

[3] Ibid., especially chapter 8, 238-57.

In contrast, this study presents both successful and unsuccessful case studies to prove the author's thesis: The prime minister plays a crucial role in the policymaking process by utilizing a combinations of various sources of power to exercise leadership. This study identifies the sources of power available to Japanese prime ministers -- some from legal authorities and others from informal sources. Is the institution of the prime minister weak, or do political constraints block the prime minister from achieving policy goals? An examination of each source of power enables a determination of the limitations the prime minister faces and the resources that are at his disposal to be an effective national leader. Three case studies provide examples of how different prime ministers have failed or have succeeded in applying their political resources.

LEGAL AUTHORITY

The executive power of the Japanese prime minister is not precisely defined by the Constitution. It states that executive power is vested in the cabinet (Article 65) and that the prime minister represents the cabinet (Article 72). Article 2 of the Cabinet Law, as well as Article 6 of the Constitution, defines the prime minister as head of the cabinet. This status is supported by his constitutional authority to appoint and dismiss cabinet members (Article 68), and his authority to protect cabinet members from legal actions during their tenure (Article 75).

However, his role as a representative and head of the cabinet is ambiguous. For example, Article 72, which defines the job of the prime minister, reads: "The Prime Minister, representing the Cabinet, submits bills, reports on general national affairs and foreign relations to the Diet and exercises control and supervision over various administrative branches." The wording created a debate over whether the prime minister represents the cabinet only when he submits bills or when he conducts all the duties described in the article. This is an important question. If "representing the cabinet" applies only to the submission of bills, the prime minister would have the authority to exercise control and supervision over the executive branch independent from the cabinet. This was indeed the intent of Article 64 in the original English language draft proposed by the American Occupation authorities.[4]

Article 66 of the current Constitution, however, implies limitations to the prime minister's authorities by referring to the cabinet's responsibilities: "The Cabinet, in the exercise of executive power, shall be collectively responsible to the Diet." The Cabinet Law more clearly limits the prime minister's executive power. First, Article 5 defines his role as a cabinet representative when he "reports on general national affairs and foreign relations" to the Diet as well as when he submits bills. Second, according to Article 3, the authority and responsibility of executive power is divided among cabinet members. This provides direct authority over administrative operations to relevant ministers, not the

---

4 Article 64 of the American draft reads, "The Prime Minister introduces bills on behalf of the Cabinet, reports to the Diet on general affairs of State and the status of foreign relations, and exercises control and supervision over the several executive departments and agencies."

prime minister. The prime minister legally holds direct authority only over the agencies under the Prime Minister's Office, such as the Defense Agency and the National Land Agency. Over most administrative branches, he has only indirect authority. As Gotoda Masaharu states: "The prime minister has no legal authority to control or supervise each minister. Ministers do not receive individual directions from the prime minister unless his direction meets certain conditions."[5]

The prime minister can block administrative operations with the authority given by Article 8 of the Cabinet Law, but the final decision on operations is decided in cabinet meetings. Furthermore, even his indirect authority is limited. Article 6 of the Cabinet Law does not allow him to hold executive power independent from decisions made in the cabinet. Thus, he can control or supervise the executive branch only to the extent that he is authorized to do so by the cabinet meeting. In other words, to influence administrative operations, the prime minister theoretically must go through the cabinet, which requires unanimous consent to approve any cabinet decision. The prime minister's control over the cabinet, therefore, determines his influence over the government.

Due to these legal constraints, there had been a strong call for measures to strengthen the power of the prime minister. This became one of the three major themes in administrative reform efforts under the Hashimoto Ryutaro government. Several proposals were made to strengthen the prime minister. The prime minister would have a clear legal base to initiate policy and hold executive power in emergency cases based on prior agreements of the cabinet. The newly created Cabinet Office would be a powerful assistance organ for the national leader by acting as a coordinator of different interests of various ministries. Despite these institutional changes, however, the fact remains that the prime minister still must face political constraints.

INTRA-PARTY FACTIONALISM INTER-AGENCY SECTIONALISM

Although the prime minister has constitutional authority to appoint and dismiss cabinet members, the political reality is that he does not have a free hand in forming his cabinet. The long-time ruling Liberal Democratic Party was a coalition of several different groups with different political goals. To become prime minister, a candidate had to first form a coalition of factions that would support him, and then maintain that support to be an effective leader. The assurance of appoints of cabinet members from each of the inner groups of the government party was the condition necessary to gain support from the entire party organization.

Powerful prime ministers have enjoyed relative freedom over appointments, but even they have not been able to totally ignore the wishes of the other factions. Ignoring the factional balance can create a severe split within the party. If this happens, the prime minister no longer has support from a majority in the Diet, which can lead to a vote of

5 Gotoda Masaharu, *Seiji towa Nanika* (Tokyo: Kodansha, 1988), p. 90.

no-confidence forcing him out of office. The appointment of cabinet members is a tool whereby the prime minister can hold the party together to pursue his policies.

Among the legal authorities of the prime minister, the appointment and dismissal authority is the only one given to him independent of a unanimous vote in the cabinet. Cabinet members, although formally appointed by the prime minister, maintain strong loyalty to their faction leaders and often have acted as representatives of their groups to the administration.[6] This factionalism has weakened the appointive power of the prime minister and his leadership in the cabinet.

According to a sociology scholar, Nakane Chie, factions within political parties are the product of the characteristics of a Japanese society which puts more emphasis on vertical relations, such as leader-follower and superior-junior relations, than on horizontal relations among colleagues. In Nakane's view, Japanese communities are usually organized in a pyramid- shape hierarchy of ranks which consists of many very personal, man-to-man relations between superiors and juniors, the basis of human relations in Japan. Japanese leaders, therefore, are directly supported by sub-leaders who themselves have their own followers.[7]

Formal, institutional group organizations are often eroded and subsumed by the unity of sub-groups with the traditional values of human relations. Nakane's description of the way the Japanese organize themselves fits perfectly with the structure of Japanese political parties with a formal party leader and members grouped into factions. Prime Minister Ohira Masayoshi once said: "When there are three politicians, there will be at least two factions." The new single-seat electoral system for the lower house and the injection of public funds weakened some functions of LDP factions, leading to their reorganization. As far as this cultural heritage remains, however, factionalism within Japanese political parties is likely to remain in one way or another.

In addition to factionalism within the government party, the prime minister must deal with another kind of fraction within the government -- inter-agency rivalry. Each section of the bureaucracy has its own interest and client industry that it must protect.

Although the prime minister is the central figure in the government, he cannot micro-manage the many different issues he must deal with due to time constraints and other limitations. Because of his central role in the larger political scene, the majority of his day-to-day administrative actions are handled by ministries and government agencies. The indirectly elected prime minister and his cabinet hold all the executive power, nonetheless the non-elected civil servants in the bureaucracy play an influential role in policymaking in Japanese politics.[8]

---

6 Arguments for this function of LDP factions, see Haruhiro Fukui, "Japan: Factionalism in a Dominant Party System," in *Faction Politics: Political Parties and Factionalism in Comparative Perspective,* eds. Frank P. Belloni and Dennis C. Beller (Santa Barbara: ABC-Clio Inc., 1978), pp. 65-66.

7 Chie Nakane, *Human Relations in Japan: Summary Translation of* "Tate Shakai no Ningen Kankei" (Tokyo: Ministry of Foreign Affairs, 1972), pp. 57-84.

8 The classic study on this view is *Tsuji Kiyoaki, Shinban Nihon Kanryosei no Kenkyu* (Tokyo: Tokyo Daigaku Shuppan-kai, 1969).

Throughout their careers, elite bureaucrats learn to design, draft, and implement legislation on issues under in the jurisdiction of their ministries. Their major interest is to protect their ministry's interests and expand its authority: they tend to put their ministerial interest over national interest. In the postwar era, individual ministries have created their jurisdiction and become empowered themselves through various laws. The Ministry of International Trade and Industry, for example, worked to have a multitude of functions assigned to it by 109 separate laws in the late 1970s.

Knowledge of the complicated network of laws is a great asset to the elite bureaucrats who can cite various legal restrictions to block policy initiatives of other political actors. Politicians do not have as deep of knowledge and are at a disadvantage. Sectionalism backed by expertise often becomes a major obstacle for the prime minister and his cabinet in initiating major policies.

Although ministries are technically subordinate to the cabinet, bureaucrats are responsible only to their ministers. Because Japan's postwar ruling party has reshuffled the cabinet almost once a year, an individual serving as minister generally has little time to accumulate the experience and knowledge necessary to become influential in actual decision making within his ministry. The Japanese system has allowed even incompetent ruling party members to be appointed as cabinet members, and this has weakened the influence of the minister vis-a-vis civil servants over the long run. Given this lack of experience and expertise, many ministers have had to completely rely on the civil servants in their ministry. All their official statements in the Diet are prepared in advance by career bureaucrats. When ministers cannot answer the questions of other Diet members, the high-level bureaucratic officials answer them on behalf of the minister. This is quite different from the situation in the British Parliament where no non-elected government officials can attend a session.

Although the minister holds appointive authority, the appointments of the vice minister as well as other positions are almost always decided within the bureaucracy, with the minister rubber-stamping the decision. During his short tenure, the minister more often than not represents the interest of the ministry vis-a-vis the cabinet and the ruling party. As minister, an elected legislator has an excellent opportunity to build personal relations with the bureaucracy and related industries. Unlike in France, in Japan the minister does not have elite bureaucrats who serve as his private advisers and watchdogs. In order to gain trust and administrative assistance from elite bureaucrats, the minister is expected to be loyal to his ministry, which makes it difficult for the prime minister to coordinate conflicting interests in the cabinet.

Career bureaucrats spend their entire careers in a single ministry and resist policy changes that negatively affect their clients. LDP zoku members, who increased their power in the issue-specific policymaking process in the 1970s and the 1980s, often allied with the related ministries to protect their client industries. In return for such protection, the client industries provided them with financial and other assistance. Such sectionalism has continued to strengthen since the 1970s and has been an issue facing each prime minister. According to a former assistant to the prime minister, the leadership of the prime minister depends on his will and ability to "crush the walls of [such sectionalism] . . . . Otherwise, they can do nothing during their tenure."[9]

Recent prime ministers have faced these two types of fractions: intraparty factionalism and issue-specific sectionalism as illustrated visually in Figures 1 and 2. Between the establishment of the LDP in 1955 and the early 1970s, when the influence of the LDP *zoku* members was limited, the prime minister faced two separate fractions (Figure 1): sectionalism among civil servants within the government, and intraparty factionalism based on political ambitions within the ruling party. The prime minister controlled the party by placing his faction member at the post of secretary general.

Figure 1   The Conceptual frame work of the prime minister

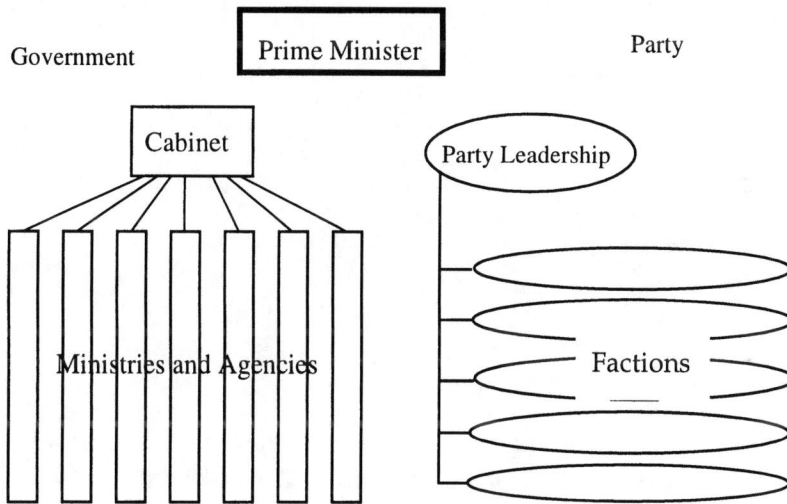

Since the mid 1970s, two major changes have occurred in this political structure that affected the prime minister's relations with these two fractions. First, because the LDP secretary general no longer belonged to the prime minister's faction, the prime minister's control over day-to-day party affairs weakened. Second, the issue-specific *zoku* groups were formed among the factions within the LDP. The *zoku* groups often acted as allies of their client agencies that shared the same policy interests. As a result, the prime minister had to face issue-specific sectionalism from within the ruling party and from within the government.

---

9 Raisuke Miyawaki, "Difference in the Governing Style between Nakasone and Takeshita," paper presented at the Johns Hopkins University's School of Advanced International Studies, December 3, 1992.

Figure 2.   The Framework with strong Zoku

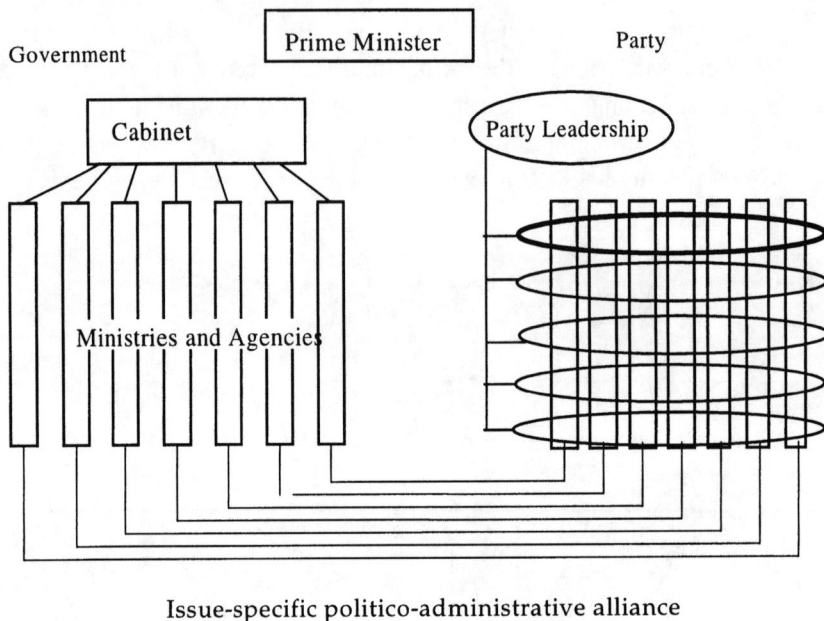

Issue-specific politico-administrative alliance

The non-LDP coalition government under the leadership of Hosokawa Morihiro in 1993-94 faced a situation similar to that which confronted the LDP between 1955 and the early 1970s. While most *zoku* members did not have the same degree of influence, issue-specific sectionalism still existed among civil servants within the executive branch. Instead of intraparty factionalism, Hosokawa faced partisanship among the coalition parties. Because political ideas and ideologies vary among the parties, the coalition government may prove more fragile in terms of unity and face even stronger fractions among their members than the LDP-led government faced.

Under the Murayama Tomiichi Administration, however, *zoku* members began to regain their influence over policy decision making, and established almost the same degree of influence after the LDP recaptured a majority in the lower house in September 1997.[10] While *zoku* member regained their influence, LDP factions lost control over their members. The new electoral rules, including single-seat districts for the lower house and the provision of public money for political funds, gave extra political leverages to the party leadership, especially the secretary general, who controls the funds and the

---

10 For the changes of decision-making process under the administrations of Hosokawa, Murayama and Hashimoto, see Tomohito Shinoda, "Japan's Decision Making Under the Coalition Governments: 1993-98," *Asian Survey*, July 1998.

candidacy selection. Instead of the traditional factional conflicts, conflicts between the mainstream (or pro-leadership) group and the anti-mainstream group were more frequently observed under the administrations of Hashimoto Ryutaro and Obuchi Keizo.

Prime ministers who successfully contained the fractions within the ruling party and the government were effective leaders, while those who lost control over the party and the government and allowed the fractions to stop their policies were ineffective.

INFORMAL SOURCES OF POWER

Executive power is vested in the cabinet and not in the prime minister. The legal authority vested in the post of the prime ministership is limited. The prime minister's effectiveness in pursuing his policies, therefore, depends in good measure on various informal sources of power. His leadership style is determined by the political resources available to him and by how he utilizes them. Informal sources can be divided in two major categories: resources as a political insider or "internal sources;" and support from outside political circles or "external sources."

INTERNAL SOURCES

1) PARTY LEADERSHIP

Among the most important "internal" political resources under the LDP government was the prime minister's status as leader of the ruling party. Obviously, a prime minister with a strong support base within the party has a strong administration. LDP factions would form a coalition that made up more than a majority of the LDP Diet members to choose the president -- thus the prime minister -- because no faction was large enough to single-handedly appoint their leader. If the prime minister's faction formed a majority within the coalition, he was able to take the initiative in deciding policies. If unity in the coalition was strong, the prime minister held considerable leverage over the policymaking process within the party. Prime Ministers Sato Eisaku, Tanaka Kakuei, and Takeshita Noboru enjoyed their status as leaders of the largest LDP factions. The size of their factions and the unity of their inter-factional coalitions were important sources of power for these national leaders.

The size of his faction and the unity of the coalition became more important over the past two decades because the prime minister's control over the party has weakened. From the mid 1950s to the end of the Tanaka Administration in 1974, prime ministers usually appointed one of their faction members as LDP secretary general, the number-two party post that handles the day-to-day party affairs. Since 1974, in an attempt to avoid too much concentration of power, the party has divided the presidency and the post of secretary general between two factions. The prime minister had to delegate most of the authority over party affairs to a senior LDP member of a different faction. With his weaker direct control over the party, keeping the party unity became a prime minister's primary concern.

2) CONTROL OVER THE BUREAUCRACY

While support from within the ruling party helps the prime minister exercise his leadership, staff support from the bureaucracy is essential for him to execute any policy decision. Diet members and the cabinet, who have a very limited number of personal staffers, have long relied on the bureaucracy for drafting bills, supervising the implementation of policies, and interpreting existing laws for administrative operations. As discussed earlier, the prime minister does not have direct authority over the bureaucracy, and bureaucrats tend to protect their sectional interests. Opposition from the bureaucracy often becomes a major obstacle in the prime minister's pursuit of his policies.

Powerful prime ministers have found a way to reach and then effectively control the bureaucracy. Prime Minister Tanaka Kakuei built extensive personal connections with many bureaucrats in various agencies, which he utilized to pursue his policies. Prime Minister Takeshita Noboru, who served as the finance minister for four consecutive terms under the Nakasone Yasuhiro administration, used his personal ties with finance ministry officials in his efforts to introduce a new consumption.

3) TIES WITH THE OPPOSITION PARTIES

Relations with the opposition parties can be a determining factor in the enactment of the prime minister's policies. Japan's legislative process with limited time often works against the ruling party. The short duration of Diet sessions, the two-house system and the committee system mean that filibuster and time-consuming measures by the opposition parties can be effective. The prime minister's ability to persuade the opposition parties is often crucial in legislative actions. Prime Ministers Tanaka Kakuei and Takeshita Noboru, for example, were famous for their strong ties with the opposition parties and effective use of them.

EXTERNAL SOURCES

4) PUBLIC SUPPORT

Informal sources of power are not limited to political circles. "External" support is also important. Public support, for example, plays an increasingly important role in Japanese politics. Although popularity alone cannot bring a politician to the post of the prime minister, it can significantly affect his leadership within the party and the cabinet. High popularity, for example, helped Prime Minister Nakasone pursue administrative reforms in 1982-86 and maintain his administration for five years, the third longest term for a postwar prime minister. Hosokawa Morihiro was also helped by high popularity to achieve the politically difficult electoral reform in 1993. Low popularity, on the other hand, was a factor in forcing Prime Ministers Yoshida Shigeru, Kishi Nobusuke, Tanaka Kakuei, Uno Sosuke, and Takeshita Noboru out of office.

Because public support plays an important role, many prime ministers have emphasized public relations activities. In the television age, a major part of public image is formulated by the appearance and eloquence on the air. Prime Minister Miki Takeo, Nakasone Yasuhiro and Kaifu Toshiki used their eloquence to their advantage. At the same time, however, the prime minister's high visibility can work against him. The most extreme example of this is Yoshida Shigeru, who called an opposition party member an "idiot," which forced the prime minister to dissolve the lower house.

5) SUPPORT FROM BUSINESS AND THE U.S.

Support from the business community and the United States often plays an important role in helping the prime minister maintain stability in his administration. Their disapproval may lead to his resignation. Yoshida Shigeru, Hatoyama Ichiro, Tanaka Kakuei, and Miki Takeo left office soon after the business community requested their resignations. Suzuki Zenko's poor handling of relations with the United States led to the anti-Suzuki movement within the party, which resulted in his resignation. Prime Ministers Nakasone Yasuhiro and Kaifu Toshiki had friendly relations with American presidents, which contributed their popularity at home.

In short, these informal sources of power, both internal and external, help the prime minister exercise his institutional power to pursue his policies. His effectiveness as a national leader, therefore, depends on the kinds of informal sources of power he as an individual can muster and his personal ability to utilize them. These sources are not consistent with each administration but vary depending on the political climate, the issues at hand, and the individual who is the prime minister. The following case studies will demonstrate how the prime ministers utilized or failed to utilize their sources of power in pursuing major reforms.

(CASE STUDY 1) SUZUKI AND NAKASONE ON ADMINISTRATIVE REFORM

In the 1980s, fiscal reconstruction was the primary policy goal in Japanese politics. The Suzuki Zenko (1980-82) and Nakasone Yasuhiro (1982-87) Administrations tried to cut government spending through administrative reform. Administrative reform was, in a way, a typical prime ministerial issue. The issue was so vast that it incorporated almost all the administrative agencies, requiring the prime minister's involvement for policy coordination and advancement to achieve success.

When Suzuki entered office in July 1980, more than one-third of the national budget for Fiscal Year 1980 depended on national bonds. The failure of his predecessor, Ohira Masayoshi, to introduce a new indirect tax left Suzuki with no other option but to introduce spending cuts for fiscal reconstruction. Suzuki, who succeeded the premiership and the leadership of Ohira's faction, committed himself to Ohira's political goal of reducing the deficit. "Financial reconstruction without tax increase" became his administration's political slogan on which he publicly stated that he would stake his political life as prime minister. Suzuki later pledged "no deficit-financing bonds in FY 1985."

However, Suzuki was not interested in how spending was cut, and choosing to remain closer to the sidelines, he delegated much of the decision making to Nakasone Yasuhiro, whom he had appointed as director general of the Administrative Management Agency (AMA). Suzuki had no idea how seriously Nakasone would take the reform challenge and found himself surrounded by aggressive movements.[11] Nakasone asserted himself. He formed the Second Ad Hoc Commission for Administrative Reform (the Commission hereafter), and named a prominent business leader, Doko Toshio, head of the Commission. This appointment assured support from the business community in the activities of the Commission.

The first proposal from the Commission was presented to the prime minister in July 1981, just four months after its inception. The proposal contained recommendations such as the so-called "zero ceiling" or freezing the spending of each ministry, a reduction of subsidies and personnel as well as a significant decrease in spending on welfare and public works programs. The Suzuki Cabinet accepted this proposal and approved a cabinet decision to cut 10 percent from subsidies across the board in the FY 1982 budget outline.

This across-the-board freeze (and later reduction) approach for all administrative agencies was described as the "starve-out" strategy by an opposition party leader. This strategy was effective, particularly when combined with the Commission's principle of making "feasible and practical" proposals, and of involving the bureaucracy in policymaking. The Commission and its secretariat kept in close contact with the individual ministries and their patron LDP *zoku* members in order to make their proposals feasible and practical before they were made public. With a ceiling on total spending for the individual ministries, LDP members and the ministries had to expose the subsidies and administrative operations that were the most wasteful among their programs. By the time the actual proposal was announced, a basic agreement had been reached between the Commission and the ministry, creating a situation in which neither individual ministries nor the LDP could refuse the agreement.[12]

By the fall of 1981, the Commission had organized four expert committees, one of which was in charge of restructuring public corporations. Prime Minister Suzuki privately and publicly expressed his determination to privatize three public corporations whose operations were considered inefficient: the Japan Telegraph and Telephone Public Corporation, the Japan Tobacco and Salt Public Corporation, and the Japan National Railways (JNR). The privatization of the national railways, with 400,000 employees and

---

11 Yanagisawa Hakuo, Akaji Zaisei no Junen to Yonin no Sori tachi (Tokyo: Nihon Seisansei honbu, 1985), p. 56.
12 See Gotoda Masaharu, Naikaku Kanbo Chokan (Tokyo: Kodansha, 1989), p. 74.

an accumulated debt of 13 trillion yen, was considered politically the most difficult task the Commission would undertake because of its strong union. JNR union members were a large part of the General Council of Trade Unions of Japan, or *Sohyo*, the electoral base of the Japan Socialist Party.

Reform of the JNR would involve great political risk for and require commitment of the prime minister. At a private meeting with the expert committee chairman Kato Hiroshi, Suzuki affirmed that he would definitely support the reform proposals for of all three public corporations.[13] As AMA Director General, Nakasone spent considerable energy on privatizing the JNR. He formed the so-called Shadow Commission to discuss the JNR issue and other reform issues.[14] The Commission Chairman Doko also devoted special attention to the reform of the JNR, because this was the most visible issue and likely to become a symbol of the entire administrative reform effort.[15]

Public support particularly for reform of the Japan National Railways grew as the Commission movement progressed. Adding to the fuel, one of the Commission's expert members, a journalist, wrote an article in an influential opinion magazine on the inefficiencies of the railways.[16] The public, already dissatisfied with JNR's continuous fare increases and the low quality of its service, reacted strongly to this article, putting increased pressure on the JNR and forcing them to conduct an internal survey of their own operations. The results of the survey, announced in an April 1982 report, even surprised the JNR president about how bad JNR operations were. This created additional leverage for the Commission's efforts.

While administrative reform attracted public support, Prime Minister Suzuki suffered a setback in his efforts to reduce the government deficit. Despite his determination, Suzuki could not break from the traditional style of Japanese politics and did not intervene in the process of setting the government-guaranteed producer's price of rice within the LDP, a form of subsidy to rice farmers. Suzuki emphasized the importance of party harmony. Intervention in such a politically sensitive issue might have created disharmony within the party. Suzuki was unwilling to cause disharmony by standing up to agricultural interests and their patron LDP *zoku* members. As a result, the government decided to increase the rice price by 1.1 percent, against the Commission's recommendation to freeze the price to which Suzuki had earlier committed.

Seeing that Suzuki broke his own pledge to follow the Commission, Chairman Doko was very disappointed and expressed his desire to resign from the chairmanship. Although the increase was small in size, it violated the Commission's principle of an across-the-board budget ceiling which equally burdened all the ministries. Many thought that this exceptional step would trigger other interest groups' demand and lead to the collapse of the entire administrative reform effort, catalyzed by Suzuki's unwillingness to stand up for the hard-line measures to tackle the rice price, one of the symbolic major deficit items.

---

13 Kato Hiroshi and Sando Yoichi, Doko san to tomo ni (Tokyo: Keizai Oraisha, 1983), p. 124.
14 Nakasone Yasuhiro, Seiji to Jinsei (Tokyo: Kodansha, 1992), 304.
15 See Kato and Sando, Doko san to tomo ni, pp. 84-86.
16 Yayama Taro, "Kokutetsu Roshi Kokuzoku-ron," Bungei Shunju (April 1982), pp. 92-112.

Economic conditions of the nation provided additional difficulty for Suzuki. The economic recession lasted longer than had been expected and handed the Japanese government a 6-trillion yen revenue shortage in FY 1982. This dismantled Suzuki's already fairly unrealistic pledge of "no deficit-financing bonds in FY 1985." Meanwhile, Suzuki's mishandling of relations with the United States triggered an anti-Suzuki movement within the LDP, led by former prime minister Kishi Nobusuke and other members of the Fukuda Takeo faction. Suzuki was passive in striving to maintain intraparty support for his administration, leaving him powerless to outlive the criticism. Unable to maintain party harmony, Suzuki resigned as prime minister in the midst of administrative reform efforts.

Throughout his term, Suzuki, though verbally expressing commitment to reform efforts, did not actively participate in the progress. In the end, beaten by the challenge, he withdrew. Had Suzuki been willing to take bold steps, such as intervening in the rice price setting and combating the anti-Suzuki movement, the manner in which he left office could have been remarkably different.

Figure 3. Suzuki and Administrative Reform

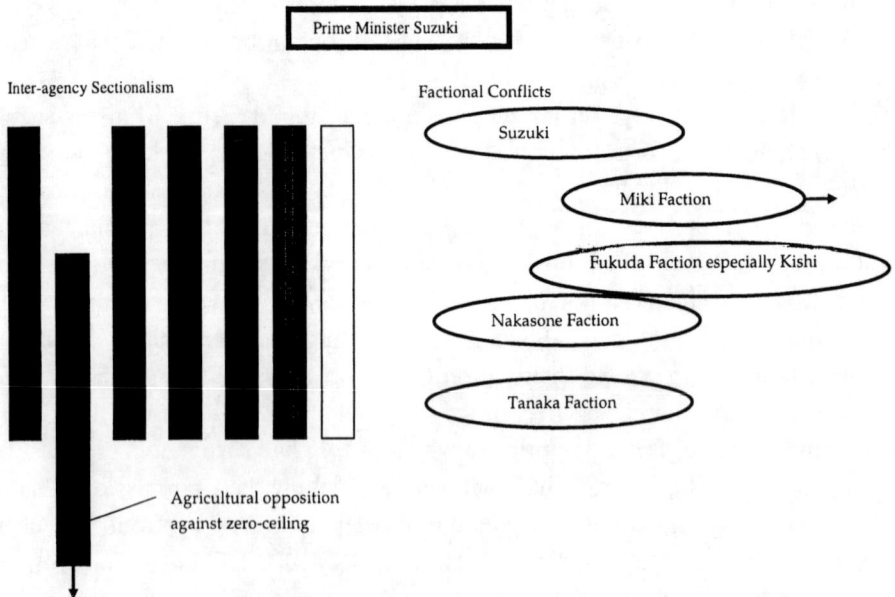

Nakasone, who succeeded Suzuki, had already been personally involved in the efforts of administrative reform. He knew the details of the issue before he became prime minister and kept himself deeply involved, and enthusiastically sought public support for his policy. Advisory councils for Nakasone were tools to identify problems and to gain public support to deal with issues, which included freezing spending levels and privatizing public corporations.

After the Commission was closed, Nakasone quickly moved to persuade Doko to chair a new commission that would oversee the implementation of administrative efforts. Nakasone was fully aware of the importance of this business leader as a symbol of reform. Under the leadership of Doko, administrative reform had become a national movement supported by the people, thus muting any criticisms from the opposition parties. With Doko's second appoint that support could be fostered.

In August 1983, Doko's commission submitted a proposal to schedule legislation on administrative reforms. Prime Minister Nakasone then asked the Cabinet Secretariat and individual ministries to make a schedule for its implementation. Chief Cabinet Secretary Gotoda looks back:

> In the schedule, everything was written: what operation would be completed by when. This needed to be legislated, and that would be announced as a government order. [Mr. Nakasone] had the LDP authorize [such schedules], and created a situation in which the government and the party together had to act quickly. He was very tactful.[17]

By having the schedule authorized, Nakasone successfully made its implementation a matter of fact in his political agenda.

Nakasone's handling of administrative reform brought him an increase in public support in Spring 1984. According to a Yomiuri Shinbun survey, 49.2 percent of the people polled supported the Nakasone Cabinet, up 12 percent from Fall 1982. Riding the tide of growing public support, Prime Minister Nakasone extended the ordinary Diet session for 77 days in an attempt to pass legislation to privatize the public corporations. Nakasone was well aware of the power of public opinion. He once compared administrative reform effort to a glider, and said, "as long as the winds of public mass media support continue to blow, it can fly. If the wind of support diminishes, the glider will stall and crash."

Nakasone successfully contained sectionalism by maintaining the "starve-out" strategy. Because every agency was "starved out," no single agency could complain of hunger. This strategy forced government agencies to come up with their own feasible solution. To assist the government agencies in finding feasible solutions, Prime Minister Nakasone appointed, and had the help of Chief Cabinet Secretary Gotoda Masaharu, a former bureaucrat who knew the limitations of the bureaucracy well.

Further, the politically difficult privatization of the Japan National Railways, which was under the jurisdiction of the Transportation Ministry, was conducted after the privatization of the two other public corporations, the Japan Tobacco and Salt Public Corporation under the Finance Ministry and the Nippon Telegraph and Telephone Public Corporation. The railways thus could not maintain an anti-privatization position.

Because the government deficit was recognized as a serious problem, LDP members could not oppose the general direction that the administrative reform effort was heading.

17 Gotoda, *Naikaku Kanbo Chokan*, p. 74.

Because all the agencies suffered, their patron LDP members could not complain, and thus there was no serious disagreement among various *zoku* groups. Nakasone assertively recruited the support of an inter-factional group of senior LDP members who used to work for the prewar Home Ministry. They shared Nakasone's view on administrative reform and organized to support the effort. This helped bind different factions within the LDP and maintain party unity.

Nakasone was also helped by timing. The Western industrialized nations were suffering from large governments that discouraged the vitality of the private sector. The Reagan Administration cut taxes in an attempt to create a smaller government. The Japanese people were fully aware of the need to cut the budget deficit, and administrative reforms to cut the wasteful spending in the public sector were a popular solution. Nakasone took the necessary actions to ensure they understood the issues to secure their support.

In short, Prime Minister Suzuki Zenko could not succeed in his administrative reform attempt because his involvement was indirect and passive and because he avoided political confrontation within the ruling party. Prime Minister Nakasone Yasuhiro, on the other hand, achieved administrative reform by effectively using different sources of power without causing a serious division with public opinion, disharmony among LDP factions, or conflicts of interests among various government agencies and their patron LDP *zoku* members.

Figure 4.   Nakasone and Administrative Reform

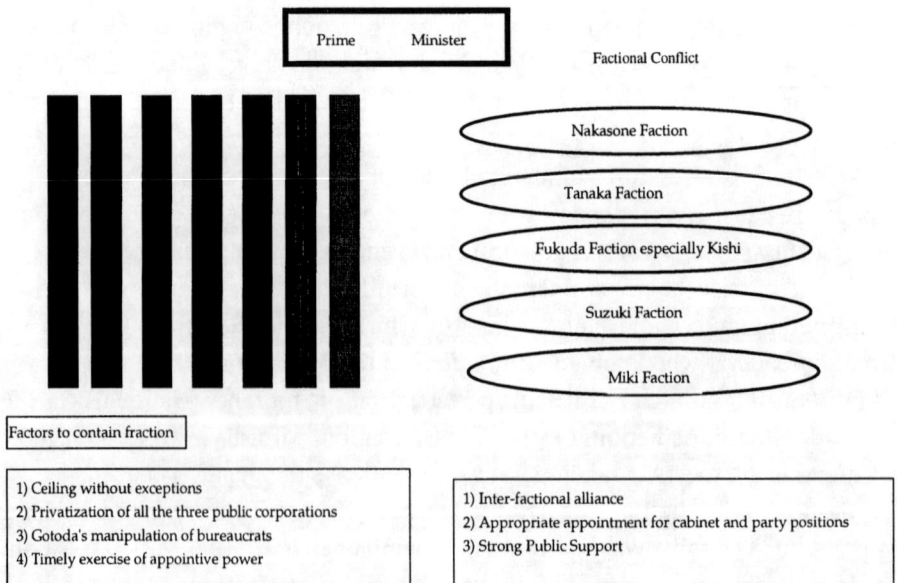

Prime   Minister

Factional Conflict

Nakasone Faction

Tanaka Faction

Fukuda Faction especially Kishi

Suzuki Faction

Miki Faction

Factors to contain fraction

1) Ceiling without exceptions
2) Privatization of all the three public corporations
3) Gotoda's manipulation of bureaucrats
4) Timely exercise of appointive power

1) Inter-factional alliance
2) Appropriate appointment for cabinet and party positions
3) Strong Public Support

(CASE STUDY 2) NAKASONE AND TAKESHITA ON TAX REFORM

When Nakasone was re-elected LDP president in October 1984, he wanted to present another major issue after administrative reform to tackle during his second two-year term. The need for a tax reform had been pointed out by a group of tax experts in the Government Tax Commission.

As the economy expanded, however, it became obvious that the tax system was out of date and creating many distortions. First, salaried workers in Japan complained that they suffered a disproportional tax burden. The second distortion was that commodity and consumption taxes violated the principle of fairness and equality. The tax base for the commodity tax was limited to 85 items, a result of aggressive lobbying for tax exemption status by the relevant industries. Furthermore, tax reform was expected to contribute to the internationalization of the tax system. With business transactions becoming increasing international, continued heavy reliance on individual and corporate income taxes was an ineffective policy. In the eyes of tax experts, Japan needed to change the ratio of direct and indirect taxes by introducing a new indirect tax, as many Western countries had done.

Tax reform would affect various economic activities in the nation. Although the introduction of a new tax itself is under the jurisdiction of the Ministry of Finance, the overall tax reform efforts involved most of the government agencies and various groups of LDP *zoku* members. The reform process would require the deep commitment of the prime minister.

Prime Minister Nakasone, who had successfully orchestrated administrative reform, was not a tax expert, and the tax policymaking process was complicated, involving the Government Tax Commission, the Liberal Democratic Party's Tax Commission, and the Ministry of Finance. He was not able to handle the technical matters. By appointing 10 of his close advisers to the Government Tax Commission, Nakasone tried to influence the tax policy process. However, these ten advisers themselves did not have the necessary expertise on tax issues, so their influence was very limited. The tax experts on the Commission dominated the deliberations.

Nakasone stated that his administration would not introduce a large-scale indirect tax, reflecting his preference for a manufacturers' sales tax. His statement was taken as a campaign pledge for the 1986 double election, and many LDP candidates echoed the prime minister in their own campaigns to win their seat. This became a major constraint on Nakasone's efforts to reform the tax system, as he could not smoothly retract the statement after so much had been made of it.

Nakasone's lack of expertise in tax issues was evident in his preference for manufacturers' sales tax over a value-added tax (VAT). His choice was opposed by tax experts in the government, by the LDP, and by the business community -- camps he needed as allies to achieve his goals. Support was thus lacking. Against his preference, the prime minister had to choose a VAT with an invoice system, and named the new tax *uriage zei* or sales tax.

Nakasone, knowing he was in his final year as prime minister, felt that he did not need to maintain public support. He was willing to sacrifice his popularity to see through a difficult policy agenda. When he veered from the position, the public and the media, as well as interest groups, felt that the prime minister had lied to them, and they strongly expressed their objections to any tax reform under Nakasone -- trust was gone. Nakasone underestimated the public response. This was ironic because he had relied on public support for the successful conclusion of administrative reform.

The public and the media felt that the government was attempting to introduce a drastic change in the tax system without discussing the issue thoroughly. For many, tax reform became a hot debate only in December 1986, and it took just two months after this to introduce the tax reform bills in the Diet. Senior LDP members admitted that the proceedings on tax reform were hasty and that this haste and an inadequate explanation of the issue to the public were among the causes of its failure.[18] The lack of effort to persuade the public and industries accelerated the anti-sales tax movement. The opposition of interest groups such as retailers and textile industries mobilized both LDP and opposition party members to oppose the tax reform.

Ironically, the election victory in 1986, which introduced many new LDP members, hurt Nakasone's tax reform effort by weakening party unity. Junior LDP members, elected for the first time in the 1986 election pledging that no large-scale indirect tax would come out of an LDP administration, found themselves needing to campaign against the indirect tax in order to sustain the support base of these interest groups for their re-election.

In attempt to ease criticism, Nakasone introduced tax exemptions on seven categories of item. In his view, an indirect tax with exemptions would not be a "large-scale" indirect tax. The introduction of exemptions, however, further weakened party disharmony. A fierce battle took place in the LDP Tax Commission among interest groups and their patron *zoku* LDP members who were trying to win tax exemption status. Subsequently, 26 categories were added to the original seven. In the final proposal, 41 categories received tax exemptions. These tax exemptions helped legitimize Nakasone's claim that his sales tax proposal was not large-scale. But they created new distortions and inequalities -- the very characteristics that the government had intended to eliminate with the introduction of the new tax.

The indirect tax created dissatisfaction among tax experts who had wanted a fairer, more equal tax system, as well as industries that did not receive tax-exemption status for their products and services. Among the most vocal industries was the textile industry. According to a MOF official, its representatives argued that among the three basics in life -- clothing, food, and housing -- clothing was the only one to be taxed. They decided to vigorously oppose the sales tax., further weakening support for the VAT.

Junior members and LDP *zoku* members were against Nakasone's tax reform. The LDP's defeat in local elections in spring 1987 further accelerated the anti-sales tax

---

18 Watanabe Michio, who was later to succeed the leadership position of the Nakasone faction, interview by Fukuda Yukihiro, in Fukuda Yukihiro, *Zeisei Kaikaku e no Ayumi* (Tokyo: Zeimu Keiri Kyokai, 1988), p. 634.

sentiment in the LDP as politicians heard the voice of electorate. Even so, the sales tax bills were introduced in the Diet. There Nakasone found that the opposition parties had teamed up against his tax reform, and were backed by strong public and media support. The opposition parties used a traditional filibuster in the Japanese Diet for the first time in 12 years, "cow-walking" (walking extremely slowly during their voting) to use up the already limited deliberation time allocated to the lower house for voting on the budget proposal. This and the opposition from within its own party made it impossible for the LDP to force the bills through the Diet.

Figure 5   Nakasone on Tax Reform

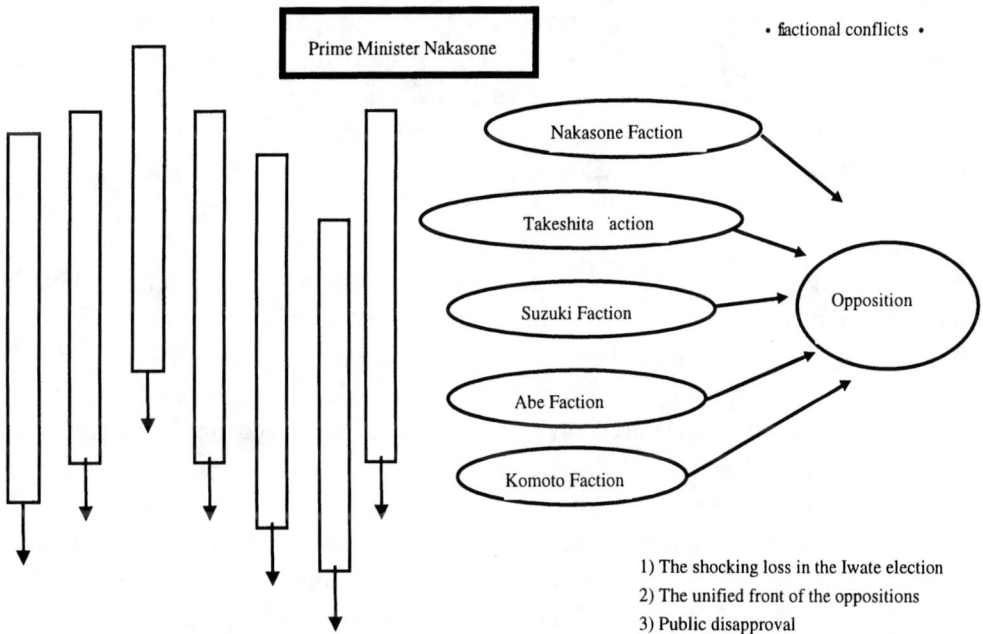

Prime Minister Nakasone

• factional conflicts •

Nakasone Faction

Takeshita action

Suzuki Faction

Opposition

Abe Faction

Komoto Faction

1) The shocking loss in the Iwate election
2) The unified front of the oppositions
3) Public disapproval

Sectoral interests demanding
tax exemption status

As Nakasone's term expired as LDP president and therefore as prime minister, the task of finishing the tax reform was handed down to his successor. Three LDP leaders -- Takeshita Noboru, Miyazawa Kiichi and Abe Shintaro -- declared their candidacy for the LDP presidency each agreeing to pursue the tax reform issue. The three candidates preferred that the next prime minister be selected through negotiations among themselves, but they could not come to any agreement. The three delegated the authority to decide who would be his successor to the prime minister. Nakasone's pick was Takeshita who had played an instrumental role as LDP secretary general in the attempt to introduce the sales tax.

Prime Minister Takeshita learned many lessons from the failed sales tax legislation attempt. He chose to introduce a value-added tax, with a "no-exemption" principle so that there would be no winners or losers resulting from the tax reform. This avoided a possible split among industry representatives within the LDP.

Takeshita enjoyed the benefits of being the leader of the largest faction in the LDP. Once Takeshita decided on the no-exemption principle, senior members of his faction actively sought party consensus by persuading members of the other LDP factions to support the new tax plan. The Takeshita faction boasted the largest number of *zoku* members within the party. They played an important role in pushing for tax reform by persuading other *zoku* members, client industries, and related ministries to support the reform efforts. This worked to suppress the opposition.

Knowing that the lack of an explanation to the public from Nakasone was one of the major causes of his sales tax failure, Takeshita tried to develop the issue through "open discussions." His administration organized public hearings nationwide, and the prime minister went on a speaking tour to explain the need for tax reform. These efforts had positive results in that government officials were informed of the problems and complaints of tax payers in different industries. Reflecting these opinions, Takeshita's consumption tax was formulated to include a tax exemption for small businesses with annual sales of less than 30 million yen. This effectively exempted 90 percent of farmers and many retailers who constituted an important LDP voter base. The MOF and MITI provided subsidies and some compensation to each industrial sector without breaking the no-exemption principle. Interest groups and their patron LDP *zoku* members no longer had a strong reason to oppose the tax reform.

Takeshita also picked a new consumption tax with an account-bookkeeping system, instead of Nakasone's sales tax with an invoice system. An account-bookkeeping system would lessen the administrative costs and would not force small businesses to present the details of every business transaction. Once Takeshita decided on the account-bookkeeping system and the no-exemption principle, it was not difficult for the LDP Tax Commission to reach its final decision. The commission's Deputy Chairman Murayama Tatsuo recalls: "The fact that the members of the largest faction made the decisions was one of the main factors for its successful introduction. When they decided on the account-bookkeeping system and the no-exemption principle, it was difficult for other LDP factions to oppose it."[19]

Prime Minister Takeshita also effectively used LDP Tax Commission Chairman Yamanaka Sadanori. Yamanaka, who boasted about his power and autocracy, took most of the responsibility for the political decisions made in the policy formation of the tax reform bills. Yamanaka, for example, decided that the consumption tax rate should be three percent instead of the proposed five percent rate in Nakasone's sales tax. With this rate, tax reform became a net tax cut. Economic conditions allowed Yamanaka to refuse the MOF's request to raise the rate. The bubble economy created more tax revenue than had been expected. This allowed the consumption tax rate to be set at three percent without causing a serious revenue shortage.

---

19 Murayama Tatsuo, member of House of Representative and former finance minister, interview by author, Tokyo, August 10, 1992.

After the tax reform bills were introduced in the Diet, Takeshita's strategy to get them through was tactful. He chose an extraordinary Diet session as the forum for the tax deliberations, a session in which the LDP had two opportunities to extend the duration of the Diet. Prime Minister Takeshita used as a negotiating tool his authority to dissolve the lower house and call an election. The opposition parties, the *Komeito* and the Democratic Socialist Party, whose members were involved in scandals, could not risk a general election in which they would suffer a loss. Although they did not vote for the tax reform bills, they agreed to participate in the Diet floor sessions on the condition that they could amend the bills. This allowed the LDP to legitimately pass the bills in the Diet.

In short, Prime Minister Takeshita Noboru successfully introduced a controversial tax reform by persuading his faction, his party, various industries and their client LDP *zoku* members, the public, and, to some degree, the opposition parties to support his bills. Takeshita's skill in building a consensus within the party and orchestrating reform efforts was crucial to the successful introduction of the consumption tax.

Figire 6.   Takeshita on Tax Reform

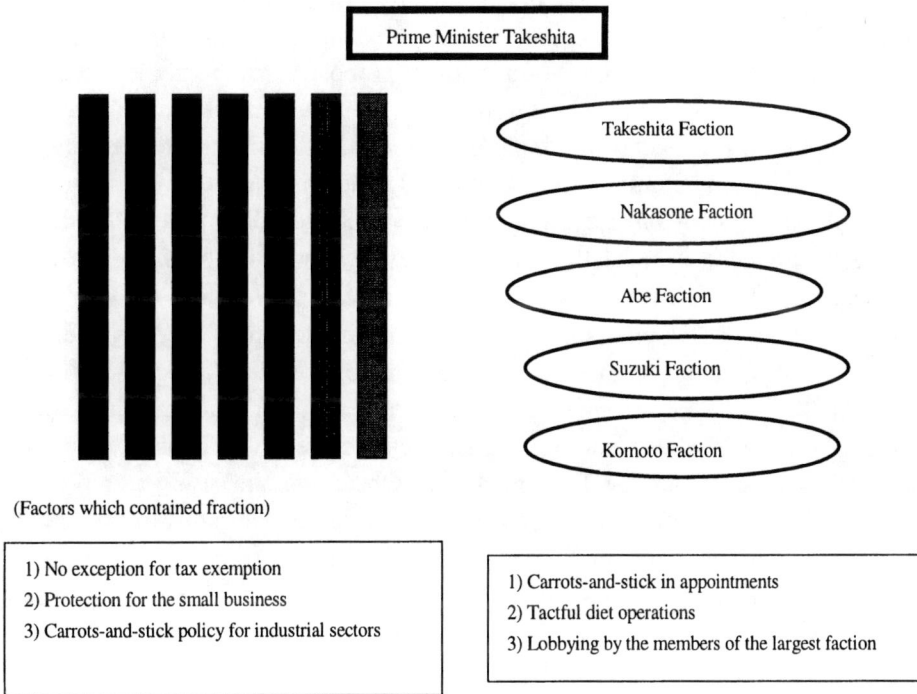

Prime Minister Takeshita

Takeshita Faction

Nakasone Faction

Abe Faction

Suzuki Faction

Komoto Faction

(Factors which contained fraction)

1) No exception for tax exemption
2) Protection for the small business
3) Carrots-and-stick policy for industrial sectors

1) Carrots-and-stick in appointments
2) Tactful diet operations
3) Lobbying by the members of the largest faction

(CASE STUDY 3) HASHIMOTO ON ADMINISTRATIVE REFORM

The need for administrative reform reemerged under the Hashimoto Ryutaro administration. This time, the focus was shifted to reform of the national bureaucracy largely due to the *jusen* problem which involved seven housing loan companies that had gone bankrupt. The *jusen* crisis sparked heated debate about the need to reform the MOF and divide its functions among independent agencies. Critics argued that the MOF's authority was too strong, and that its use of fiscal authority for the financial market distorted the government policy, creating problems such as the crisis of housing loan companies. The need for bureaucratic reform also emerged when a suit over the transfusion of HIV-tainted blood was filed. The Ministry of Health and Welfare was blamed for failing to take appropriate measures when an American authority issued a world-wide alert that all blood should be heated to kill HIV. Public distrust against the national bureaucracy was stronger than ever under the Hashimoto's leadership.

Adding to the fire was MOF's *jusen* liquidation scheme that would require the use of taxpayer's money to pay off the incurred debts. The public protest peaked when the Diet released documents, against MOF's opposition, that contained the top 100 borrowers of housing loans. The information revealed that corporate borrowers were responsible for more than 95 per cent of the non-performing loans, and that many of the borrowers had loans with more than one housing loan company. The MOF had been aware of these practices and the size of the bad loans, but took no action to correct the problems.

The opposition New Frontier Party adamantly criticized the use of public funds to bail out the *jusen*. Its members began a sit-in, blocking entry to the budget committee room to protest the ruling coalition's budget proposal that contained such a plan. Although the public as a whole was critical of the government plan, more and more people expressed their concern for Japan's economy as the sit-in extended into its third week. The Economic Planning Agency expressed concerns that a delay in approval of the budget could slow down Japan's economic recovery. According to a poll more than 70 percent of respondents wanted the politicians to pay more attention to prosperity and economic issues.[20] The sit-in ended with a compromise agreement between the ruling coalition and the NFP, which assured time for a sufficient debate over the budget bills in the Diet. The Hashimoto government managed to resolve the politically difficult *jusen* problem, but the public continued to expect the prime minister to reform the bureaucracy.

In the summer of 1996, entering the last year of the lower house's four-year term, election pressure grew among Diet members. Observing the rising popularity of his cabinet in September 1996, Hashimoto dissolved the lower house to call the first election under the new electoral law which introduced single-seat districts.[21] During the election campaign, virtually all the political parties, including the LDP, pledged to carry out administrative reform, reflecting public distrust against government agencies. In the October 20 general election, the LDP gained 239 seats, up from 211, in the 500-seat lower house. While the result was generally seen as a victory, the LDP still came up short and was not able to form a majority.

One month after the general election, Prime Minister Hashimoto Ryutaro inaugurated the Council on Administrative Reform. Fifteen members were appointed: three politicians, three business leaders, six scholars, two media representatives and one labor

---

[20] *Nihon Keizai Shinbun*, 12 March 1996.

leader. The legal base of the Council was not as strong as Nakasone's Commission which had been established with legislation. Hashimoto felt the immediate need to get going on administrative reform efforts, and did not go through the process of obtaining legislative approval. Even the ruling LDP did not officially approve of the establishment and membership of the Council, which left room for the ruling party members to freely attack its recommendations. In order to suppress potential opposition, Hashimoto appointed himself chairman of the Council, thus forcing his government to act on the recommendations of the Council.

A week later, Prime Minister Hashimoto called the first meeting of the Council. He asked the members for recommendations for three issues: "what functions the state should fulfill in the 21st century;" "how the government should be restructured to perform these functions better;" and "how best to strengthen the Cabinet's functions." As an example, he introduced the so-called "Hashimoto vision." In his vision, the government's policy areas were divided into four goal-driven themes - 1) the nation's survival, 2) the expansion of national wealth, 3) national welfare, and 4) education and culture. Hashimoto also proposed that the number of government agencies be reduced from the current 22 to ten in accordance with his campaign pledge to half their number. On the following day, Hashimoto stated in his policy speech before the Diet that "Although resistance and difficulties are inevitable, I am fully committed to the cause of administrative reform (direct translation -- I will put it through even by burning my own body)." As the public saw Hashimoto's determination, his popularity rate in a Kyodo News poll rose to 58.3 per cent up from 43.4 per cent at the beginning of his term.[22]

As the deliberation of the Council proceeded, some government agencies, especially the MOF, felt threatened. When Hashimoto categorized the two major functions of the MOF into two different categories of policy areas (fiscal policy to nation's survival and monetary policy into the expansion of national wealth) for example, MOF officials felt that might mean the ministry would be divided. They tried to manipulate the direction of deliberations by changing information materials that the secretariat provided for use in the Council. When Hashimoto found that the secretariat officials from the bureaucracy changed his categorization, he decided to ask members themselves of the Council to provide information materials. As a result, the Council proceeding became more independent of bureaucratic influence.

As Hashimoto's leadership in his administrative reform efforts was seen as being quite strong, his popularity rate hit the highest of 59.2 per cent.[23] In September 1997, the Council presented an interim report that included rather drastic plans to streamline the bureaucracy. The plan called for strengthening the Cabinet, privatizing postal saving and insurance services, dividing the politically powerful Ministry of Construction, and decreasing the number of government agencies from 22 to 13, including a newly created, powerful support organ for the prime minister, the Cabinet office. If these plans were

---

[21] According to a Kyodo News poll of September 28-29, 1996, for example, the approval rate for the Hashimoto Cabinet rose to 52.3 per cent from 47.0 per cent on July 13-14.

[22] A poll taken by Kyodo News Service on December 7-8, 1996.

[23] A poll taken by Kyodo News Service on July 12-13, 1997.

realized, Hashimoto's reform could be, at least as significant as Nakasone's administrative reform in the 1980's which privatized the national railways. When presenting the Council's interim report to the representatives of the three coalition parties, the LDP, the Socialist Democratic Party (SDP) and *Sakigake*, Hashimoto had to bow and ask them to "respect the proposal as much as possible."

The Council, already weak without legal backing, met with trouble when Hashimoto's popularity declined over the appointment of Sato Koko in a cabinet reshuffle. Sato's appointment was a political gift to the conservative wing of the LDP led by former prime minister Nakasone. The LDP was split into wings: one which supported the existing coalition with the Socialists and *Sakigake,* and the other which called for a conservative coalition with the New Frontier Party (NFP). Hashimoto without strong power base within his own party was running the government on this delicate balance between the two wings. Reappointing the leaders of the pro-coalition group into LDP leadership positions, such as Secretary General Kato Koichi, Hashimoto needed to offer some form of appeasement to win the support of the conservatives. Hashimoto was in effect forced by Nakasone to appoint Sato head of the Management and Coordination Agency, a key position for Hashimoto's top priority issue of administrative reform.

Sensitive to public opinion, Hashimoto was first hesitant to appoint Sato who had a criminal record stemming back to the highly publicized Lockheed scandal which involved with the selection of airplanes for a major Japanese airline. LDP Secretary General Kato revealed Hashimoto's agony, stating in a television discussion program, "Until the final moment, the prime minister was torn between Mr. Nakasone's pressure and public opinion." The public reaction was much stronger than Hashimoto expected. According to a Kyodo News poll, 74 percent of the respondents said that they were against Sato's appointment. Hashimoto's popularity rating dropped dramatically from 60 per cent to 28 per cent.[24] After a week of turmoil, Sato "voluntarily" resigned. At a press council Hashimoto bowed deeply and expressed his apology to the public that he "did not consider public opinion enough."

As Hashimoto's popularity eroded, LDP's *zoku* members, or policy tribes, took the opportunity to attack the prime minister's administrative reform. They started arguing that there was no need to respect the recommendations of the Council which had no legislative approval. LDP members who were seeking to maintain voter support in the postal industry, for example, adamantly opposed the idea of privatizing the postal saving and insurance services. Special Post Offices, which make up 80 percent of Japan's 24,600 postal outlets, serve as a solid support base for many LDP members in election times. Hashimoto's privatization plan and the absorption of the telecommunication function into the proposed Industry Ministry would effectively dissolve the Ministry of Post and Telecommunication (MPT), an unpopular move among those offices.

Other *zoku* members also joined the movement against Hashimoto's reform plan. The powerful construction *zoku* members, for example, publicly opposed the plan to divide the function of the Ministry of Construction (MOC) into two newly created ministries. Against their campaign pledges for administrative reform, LDP members swarmed to

---

24 *Tokyo Shinbun,* September 17, 1997.

attack Hashimoto's reform plan in order to protect special interests, an old habit the ruling party had developed under the one-party dominance system.

The mass media was supporting the privatization of postal saving and insurance services which the Council proposed in the interim report. These services provided large financial resource for quasi-governmental organizations which had been criticized by many economists and the public for their inefficient investments. The postal saving service attracted as much as 35 per cent of individual savings by offering a higher interest rate made possible by the injection of tax money.[25] Many economists argued that this created a large-scale distortion of Japan's financial market.

The public, however, did not feel this market distortion and was satisfied with postal saving services. According to an *Asahi Shinbun* survey, 54 per cent of those polled were against the privatization of these services.[26] The poll showed that people who lived in less populated area with no commercial banks desperately needed the services, and that those who lived in urban areas did not have particular dissatisfaction with them. This was completely different from the national railway situation under Nakasone's administrative reform in which the dissatisfied, angered customers formed a strong political support base for privatization.

In December 1997 after a series of political negotiations, the Council's final report was introduced. While Hashimoto managed to keep the framework of 13 agencies and the plan to strengthen cabinet's function, he had to yield in several areas. The privatization plan of postal services was abandoned. The services would be continued under the Postal Service Agency for five years, and would later be run by a newly created government-run corporation. All the functions of the Construction Ministry would be continued under a new Ministry of National Land and Transportation. In the report, an agreement was not reached on the separation of the fiscal and financial functions of the MOF between the LDP and *Sakigake* which strongly supported a total separation. But later, a political compromise was reached. According to the compromise, the MOF would keep its influence over financial policies by maintaining its authority over financial crises.

It is important to note that the interim report of the Council created winners and losers among the government agencies. The ministries, like the MPT which faced a possible dissolution, desperately sought political support for its survival. The postal *zoku* LDP members openly attacked Hashimoto's reform plan, feeling that the MPT alone was chosen to be sacrificed to demonstrate his reform efforts. This was different from Nakasone's administrative reform which forced all the government agencies to feel the same pain.

For his administrative reform, Hashimoto desperately needed public support. But before the reforms could be approved he lost it and his reform effort came up short. Public support became important especially after the breakup of the long predominant LDP in 1993. No one faction in the ruling party is a dominant power on the political scene, and the prime minister's power base within the ruling party is subsequently weakened. With a weaker power base, a prime minister must attract considerable public

---

25 The total postal saving amounted 225 trillion yen at the end of 1996.
26 A poll taken by *Asahi Shinbun* on September 7-8, 1997, *Asahi Shinbun*, 10 September, 1997.

and media support. But Hashimoto lost it by making a fatal mistake in the cabinet reshuffling in an attempt to politically compensate the conservative wing of the LDP. This tilted the power balance between his party and himself. Hashimoto's leadership was seen as weak, and LDP members felt free to destroy his reform plan for which the prime minister had promised to stake his political life.

Figure 7. Hashimoto on Administrative Reform

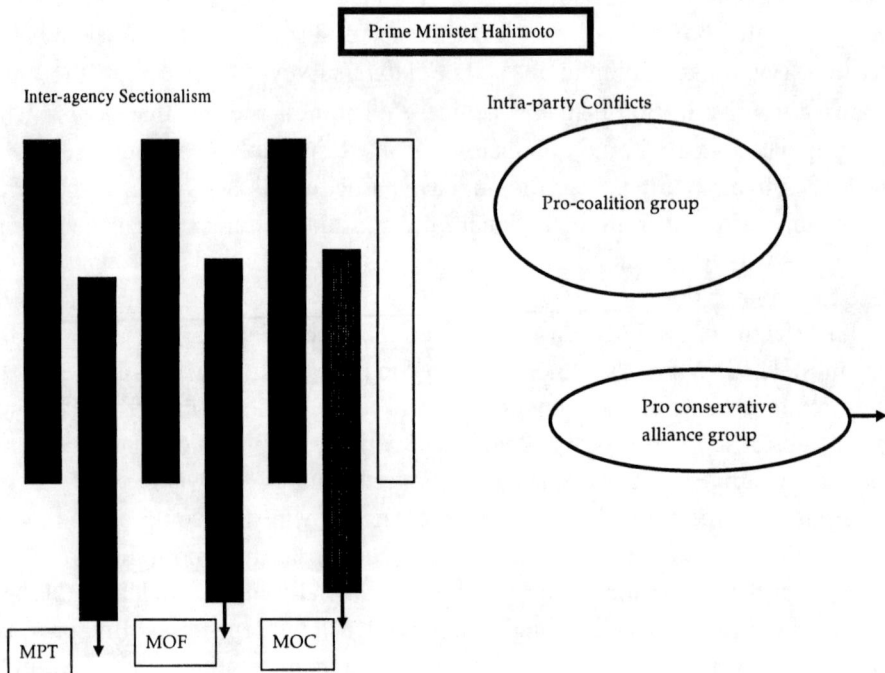

CONCLUSION

Is the Japanese prime minister effective as a national leader? This study centers on this question. The leadership of the prime minister is indeed limited. Why? The conventional answer is that political constraints limit his vast legal authority, leaving his role in the policy process relatively passive and unimportant. This study, however, provides a different answer. Even though the legal authority of the prime minister is very limited, he has at his disposal various sources of power with which he can play an imperative role in policymaking and be an effective leader. Because prime ministers must rely on informal sources of power to effectively utilize institutional sources of power, their effectiveness varies depending on their background, experience, political skills, and personality.

The case studies in this study show that when the variations of sources of power are grouped, four different leadership styles emerge: The Political Insider, the Grandstander, the Kamikaze Fighter, and the Peace Lover. The political insider is a leader with abundant internal sources of power who enjoys stable support within the ruling party and close ties with the bureaucracy and the opposition parties. The other three leadership styles lack internal sources. The Grandstander directly seeks external support from the public and the media for his policy goals to supplement his lack of internal sources of power. The Kamikaze Fighter tries to achieve an unpopular policy by sacrificing his political leadership role. The Peace Lover is an indecisive leader who fails to achieve a controversial policy goal because he tries to please all the actors.

THE POLITICAL INSIDER

Of the four prime ministers observed in the case studies, Takeshita Noboru exemplifies the typical "political insider." In his tax reform attempts of 1988, he vigorously took advantage of his status as leader of the largest LDP faction. His stable power base within the party stemmed from his successful formation of a strong majority coalition within the party with two other factions. His faction also boasted the largest number of LDP *zoku* members, who were effective in their specific policy fields. For example, once Takeshita decided on the no-exemption principle for his consumption tax, senior members of the Takeshita faction played an important role in achieving party consensus by persuading other *zoku* members, their client industries, and the related ministries to support the tax reform efforts. Takeshita's status as a faction leader helped contain both sectionalism and factionalism.

Further, Takeshita had strong control over the bureaucracy. Takeshita, who was taught by Prime Minister Sato Eisaku to establish personal ties with individual bureaucrats, had a personal network in the Ministry of Finance where he had been a minister for four consecutive terms under the Nakasone Administration. Takeshita successfully mobilized the entire ministry and even drew cooperation from the Ministry of International Trade and Industry in the process of introducing a consumption tax. Takeshita, in short, had abundant political resources to avoid fractions.

In recent LDP history, Sato Eisaku and Tanaka Kakuei are prime ministers who effectively used their resources as political insiders. Both were the leaders of the largest LDP faction. At the same time, Sato and Tanaka had strong ties with bureaucrats. It is interesting that all three prime ministers who enjoyed stable support from within the party -- Sato, Tanaka, and Takeshita -- could not maintain external support, and left office.

THE GRANDSTANDER

A prime minister with less internal support must be a "grandstander" to seek external support from the public and the media. Prime Minister Nakasone Yasuhiro, whose faction was the second smallest of the five LDP factions, was well aware of the importance of public support. With limited inner-party and bureaucratic support, Nakasone enthusiastically sought public support for his policies. He openly expressed his desire to become a "top-down president-like leader" in the bottom-up oriented Japanese society. In his attempt to do so, he became the first prime minister who extensively used his advisory councils. Advisory councils for Nakasone were tools to identify current problems and to gain public support to deal with issues. One of Nakasone's advisors recalls: "Nakasone faced the electorate directly with a showy performance. He made every effort to steer Japan in new directions as the leader of the electorate."[27]

Public support has been essential to prime ministers who faced internal conflict within the ruling party. For example, Yoshida Shigeru's image as a charismatic leader and hard negotiator with the American Occupation authority attracted public support and allowed him to become an effective leader in reconstructing the Japanese economy and concluding the 1951 San Francisco Peace Treaty. Ikeda Hayato was another prime minister who effectively took advantage of public support to achieve the "income doubling plan." Yoshida and Ikeda as well as Nakasone had a clear political vision and directly sought public support to suppress potentially volatile opposition within the ruling party and the opposition parties.

THE KAMIKAZE FIGHTER

In his last year as prime minister, Nakasone Yasuhiro became less sensitive to public reaction and turned into a "kamikaze fighter," one who sacrifices public support and his political career to pursue a politically unpopular policy -- in Nakasone's case, tax reform. His statement that his administration would not introduce a large-scale indirect tax was taken as his campaign pledge for the 1986 double election, and this statement became a major constraint on Nakasone's efforts to reform the tax system. The public and the media as well as interest groups felt that he had lied to them, and they strongly objected to the tax reform proposal. Especially for younger LDP Diet members, adhering to the campaign pledge against the new tax was vital to sustain their support base for reelection. Since it was his last year as prime minister, Nakasone was willing to sacrifice his popularity to see through a difficult policy agenda. His peers in the LDP, however, did not want sacrifice their political career, and chose to kill Nakasone's tax proposal.

In short, for a prime minister with limited internal political resources, failure to attract external support can be detrimental to his fight against fractions within the government and the ruling party. When Hatoyama Ichiro tried to normalize relations with the Soviet Union, for example, he met strong opposition from LDP members and business leaders. To suppress the opposition within the party, Hatoyama promised he would resign so that the bilateral relation could be restored. Also, Kishi Nobusuke had to

---

27 Raisuke Miyawaki, "Difference in the Governing Style between Nakasone and Takeshita," unpublished paper presented at the Johns Hopkins University's Paul Nitze School of Advanced International Studies, December 3, 1992, p. 3.

resign as he promised he would after the revision of the U.S.-Japan Security Treaty passed the Diet. Prime ministers with less internal political resources, like Hatoyama, Kishi and Nakasone, are more likely to invite fierce inter-factional struggles without receiving strong external support. They often voluntarily step down from the prime minister role as a trade off for votes on their respective agenda.

PEACE LOVER

While kamikaze fighters sacrifice their post for a policy goal, others are not willing to take chances. These are the "peace lovers." Suzuki Zenko, who was known for his emphasis on party harmony, was a typical peace lover. After the fierce inter-factional conflicts in the 1970s, especially between the factions of Tanaka Kakuei and Fukuda Takeo, the party wanted a party president who had a wider support base within the party in order to avoid serious conflicts. Suzuki knew exactly why he was chosen for the post and repeatedly emphasized his role in keeping party harmony.

Emphasizing party harmony as the top priority, however, is no way to handle politically difficult tasks like administrative reform, which the Suzuki Administration initiated. Suzuki was unwilling to take the necessary risk to achieve administrative reform because he thought that such a risk would invite discord within the ruling party. For example, the prime minister's advisory council recommended an across-the-board freeze on government spending, including the subsidy for rice prices. Suzuki, however, was unwilling to stand up to agricultural interests and their patron *zoku* members. As a result, the rice price increased two years in a row. This decision not only disappointed the Commission officials but also damaged the momentum for reform efforts to cut governmental spending. The public, the media and business leaders criticized Suzuki, and political pressure began to mount against him. Suzuki believed that if he remained as prime minister, he would create party disharmony, so he decided to resign in the midst of administrative reform efforts.

Prime ministers, like Suzuki, lacked a sense of risk-taking and strong determination, and they failed to achieve their policy goals. Both Kaifu Toshiki and Miyazawa Kiichi lacked of determination allowed the political reform plans killed in the Diet. Miyazawa's leadership failure even brought an end to the LDP's 38-year reign.

CLASSIFYING HASHIMOTO

The three prime ministers appearing in the first two case studies are classified into the four leadership styles: Takeshita Noboru as the political insider; Nakasone Yasuhiro in his administrative reform as the grandstander; Nakasone in his tax reform as the kamikaze fighter; and Suzuki Zenko as the peace lover. Which of the four styles can Hashimoto Ryutaro be classified as?

Hashimoto was elected LDP president in September 1996 not because of his power base within the party but because of his popularity among the public. Hashimoto was often described as the lone wolf. He had very few enthusiastic followers within the party, even in the Obuchi faction to which he belonged. While Hashimoto had expertise in some policy areas and many admirers in the bureaucracy, his ties with the opposition parties were limited. Therefore, it probably is not appropriate to classify him as a political insider.

With the limited internal sources of power, Hashimoto actively sought public support. After Hashimoto managed to pass the politically difficult *jusen* bills, he was rewarded by the public when the LDP gained more seats in the October 1996 lower house election. Without losing the momentum from the election victory, he formed the Council on Administrative Reform, and named himself chairman. In his policy speech, he expressed his commitment to the reform efforts. As the public saw Hashimoto's determination, his approval rate rose strengthening his control over the government and the party.

During the first two years, Hashimoto showed direction, and his policies moved forward backed by public support. Over a revision of the land-lease law for American bases in Okinawa in spring 1997, Hashimoto successfully acquired the support from the opposition New Frontier Party when the government failed to make an agreement with the Social Democratic Party. In September 1997, Hashimoto won his second term as LDP president without a contest. At his political peak, Hashimoto's Council introduced an interim report which contained many difficult reorganization proposals to streamline the national government agencies. At this point, he could be classified as "grandstander," taking advantage of public support to supplement his weak power base inside of the political circle.

Everything fell apart after the cabinet reshuffling of September 1997. Hashimoto appointed to the cabinet Sato Koko, a man with a criminal record for taking a bribe. This appointment was made in order to win the support of the conservatives for the success of the administrative reforms on which he staked his political life, as a kamikaze fighter would. He decided to sacrifice public support in order to gain an internal support. At this point, Hashimoto was no longer a grandstander.

The public reaction was much stronger than Hashimoto expected. His popularity rating dropped dramatically. As Hashimoto's popularity eroded, LDP's *zoku* members took the opportunity to attack the prime minister's administrative reform. After his failure to maintain public support, the prime minister became more like a "peace lover," as he scrambled to keep political support for his reform efforts. Although Hashimoto managed to maintain the framework of 13 ministries, many political compromises were made. The final report for Hashimoto's administrative reform was a major setback from the interim report.

With limited legal authority, the prime minister must depend on informal sources of power to shape his leadership style and to determine the effectiveness of his effort. The political insider employs his abundant power within the ruling party, the bureaucracy, and the opposition parties to influence policy. Having less internal sources, the grandstander relies on his ability to attract considerable support from the public and the media. The kamikaze fighter sacrifices his political career. The peace lover tries to avoid serious confrontations at all costs.

Of the four leadership styles, the political insider is least likely to emerge in the near future. Because of the breakup of the long predominant LDP, no one faction or party is a dominant power on the political scene. With fewer than ever internal political resources to command, a prime minister must attract considerable public and media support to effectively maintain a fractious coalition government in achieving his policies. A popular prime minister can achieve his goal in the grandstander fashion. A leader who does not possess outside support may choose to sacrifice his political career as a kamikaze fighter, or he may decide to sacrifice his policy objective and strive to accomplish little as a peace lover.

In today's situation, a prime minister can be effective by exercising will and attracting public support for his policies. Personal contacts within the government remain vital, and kamikaze fighter tactics can be effective. But the grandstander employing public education and attracting media support, and with a clear vision statement seems to be the best bet for an effective administration.

Chapter 2

VIETNAM'S TRANSITION TO A MARKET ECONOMY

RAYMOND J. AHEARN

SUMMARY

As Vietnam's *doi moi* economic reform program enters its 10th year, a political struggle within the ruling Communist Party continues to take place over the pace and scope of the reforms. Reformers in the party are pushing for a further increase in the role of the private sector in economic activity, while conservatives want the state to continue to play the dominant role in Vietnam's development. The eighth National Party Congress, scheduled for June 1996, could clarify which group has the upper hand. The outcome of this leadership struggle could have important implications for Vietnam's full integration into the world trading system as well as for U.S.-Vietnamese economic relations.

BACKGROUND

Vietnam's reform program, known as *doi moi* or economic renovation, began in 1986 in response to deteriorating internal and external conditions. At home, the economy was in desperate straits, afflicted by hyper-inflation and widespread food shortages. Abroad, the Soviet Union, its most loyal ally, was cutting back on its large foreign aid program.

In these circumstances, Vietnam's leaders adopted pragmatic, albeit partial, reforms to regain economic growth. The main stated objective was to replace a centrally planned economy, dominated by state-run enterprises, with a "regulated market economy." The internal contradiction of a controlled free market is indicative of divided views within the Vietnamese Communist Party leadership over how much reliance should be placed on the private sector.

At the heart of the reforms adopted in the late 1980s were measures that eliminated price controls on most key goods, established land use rights for farmers, clarified the legal status of private businesses, and tightened government spending. As part of the latter attempt, efforts were made to limit subsidies to state-owned enterprises (SOEs) by providing them greater autonomy in production, investment, and pricing decisions. The authorities also moved to open the economy to foreign trade and investment and to attract foreign assistance.

DOI MOI RESULTS TO DATE

Vietnam's economy has prospered since the reforms commenced in 1986. After years of negative growth, economic activity increased on average by 3.9% from 1986-1990 and by 7.6% from 1991-1993. The economy grew by 8.8% in 1994, and by 9.8% in 1995. Another year of 9-10% growth is forecast for 1996 -- rates of growth that have led to much media speculation that Vietnam is primed to become the next Asian tiger.[1]

Vietnam, however, remains a very poor country with a per capita income level around $230 at nominal exchange rates.[2] An estimated 36 million people (about half the population) live below the poverty line, and the country is basically at the level of development where Thailand was 30 years ago. Nevertheless, the living standards of most Vietnamese have improved dramatically in the last 10 years and most Vietnamese reportedly feel that the government is moving the country forward.[3]

In terms of specific sectors, the agricultural reforms, which were aimed at transforming the state-run collective farms into private, family-based production units, have been most successful to date. Over the last decade, Vietnam has overcome its dependency on food imports to regain its historical position as a net food exporter. Rice production has led the way. Vietnam is currently the world's third largest rice exporter, after Thailand and the United States. In addition, more family-based farms, which now account for over 90% of total production, are growing exportable cash crops such as coffee, corn, rubber, sugarcane, and cashew nuts. The extension of long-term leases for farmers to till the land is widely credited with creating incentives for farmers to make the requisite capital investments in the land.

In addition to family-based farm units, small and medium size enterprises (SMEs) have proliferated as government policy towards private enterprise has become more tolerant. An estimated 25,000 SMEs now dominate service industries such as real estate, restaurants, transportation, and tourism, and account for a growing proportion of light manufacturing, mostly in consumer goods. Some statistics suggest that SMEs, which are capitalized at an average of only $17,000, account for 40% of industrial output, and employ two-thirds of the labor force.[4] While official government data can be unreliable, these firms appear to be the most dynamic sector of Vietnam's economy despite important handicaps.

Gaining access to capital is the most critical handicap SMEs face. To obtain capital from banks, these firms (particularly those that have no connection to the overseas Vietnamese or Chinese communities) must put up hard assets for collateral that are worth twice the value of the loan. Even then, they can borrow only short-

---

[1] World Bank data.

[2] Because much of the economy does not involve cash transactions, real incomes are considerably higher.

[3] Bulman, Robin. "Vietnam Remains Poor Despite A Wealth of Progress Made," *Journal of Commerce*, March 21, 1995, p 3.

[4] Comer, Bruce. "SMEs -- Vietnam's Engine for Growth", *The Vietnam Business Journal*, Vol. 2, Nov-Dec. 1994, pp. 20-23.

term -- less than one year -- and at relatively high rates. While the country has attracted several billions of dollars in foreign aid and investment, very little has reached Vietnam's small companies in terms of joint ventures.[5]

Despite progress in closing down some 6,000, mostly small and town-based SOEs since *Doi Moi* commenced, Vietnam still operates an estimated 6,500 SOEs. The largest SOEs dominate strategic sectors of the economy such as banking, construction, energy, telecommunications, steel, and chemicals.[6] Altogether, the SOEs reportedly still account for 75% of Vietnam's assets, obtain about 65% of the bank credit, and employ a third of the labor force, but they account for only 40% of the country's GDP and do little for new job creation.[7]

To improve the efficiency of the SOEs, the government is trying to put together several dozen conglomerates, known as general corporations, in industries such as steel, coal, power, and textiles. Patterned after the South Korean model of huge conglomerates or *chaebol*, the government hopes that combining several SOEs in the same field will allow them to compete more effectively internationally while at the same time retaining control over their activities.[8]

So far the government has resisted outright efforts at privatization, but it has established a pilot "equitization program" in which it has sought to issue shares for 21 small state firms. The hope is to raise money, while retaining majority control. So far the program has had little success, but the government is set to list 200 companies for equitization this year.

Regarding external economic relations, Vietnam's reforms have opened up the country further to foreign trade and investment. Combined with inflows of capital, expanding trade ties with countries in the region have helped Vietnam weather its drastic reduction in commercial ties with the former communist countries of the Soviet bloc. As trade with the former Soviet Bloc countries dropped from 80% of Vietnam's total trade in the 1980s to under 10% today, trade with other Asian countries -- led by Japan and Singapore -- has more than taken its place.

Since a liberal foreign investment law was passed in 1987, Vietnam has attracted close to $19 billion in foreign commitments covering nearly 1,500 projects. Asian countries -- Taiwan, Hong Kong, Japan, Singapore, South Korea, and Malaysia -- account for nearly 70% of the investment commitments or approvals. While approximately 80% of the projects have been started, most in the form of joint ventures with wholly or partly-owned state enterprises, only 30% of the capital has been disbursed. Bureaucratic delays in getting licenses, a murky legal status on land-use rights, pervasive corruption throughout the bureaucracy, a poor infrastructure, and lack of managerial skills are among the explanations frequently cited for the gap between project approvals and actual disbursement of capital.

---

[5] Ibid., p. 21.

[6] Schwarz, Adam. "The Way We Were: Breaking Up Is Hard To Do for Vietnamese State Firms, *Far Eastern Economic Review*, March 2, 1995, p. 58.

[7] Schwarz, Adam. "Economic Monitor: Vietnam", *Far Eastern Economic Review*, April 25, 1996, p. 52; and Chamber of Commerce and Industry of Vietnam.

[8] Schwarz, Adam. "Steps in the Dark", *Far Eastern Economic Review*, October, 26, 1995, p. 52.

DEBATE OVER ECONOMIC POLICY

Although the Vietnamese Communist Party has relinquished some of its control over the economy as part of the *doi moi* reform process, it still exercises near absolute political power. Decisions are made collectively and behind closed doors. Opposition to the Communist Party rule, in the streets or in the press, is not tolerated. Political and religious dissidents are jailed or otherwise repressed. While a new party constitution promulgated in 1992 makes it possible that the party could become more representative of different interest groups in the future, key decisions are made by a handful of party officials.[9]

Vietnam today, however, is not the highly regimented, centralized, and doctrinaire Communist state that it was a few decades ago. People may not have political freedom, but the *Doi Moi* process has weakened the position of the party, particularly in economic and social affairs. In these areas, the Vietnamese people appear to have considerable personal freedom. Provincial and local officials also have considerable power, and often act contrary to decrees issued from Hanoi. Top party leaders are most often described as pragmatists who are focused on two overriding objectives: bringing economic prosperity to Vietnam and maintaining the party's monopoly on political power. The pace and scope of the economic reforms, however, is a matter of serious divide among Vietnam's ruling elite.

Two camps are now locked in debate running up to the eighth Vietnamese Party Congress, scheduled for this June. One group of so-called "reformers" advocates more active policy reforms that support development of a stronger private sector, the contraction of the largely inefficient state sector, and the country's economic integration into the world economy. A second group of "conservatives" worry that an increase in the pace of economic reforms could have negative consequences for Vietnamese society, including the potential to undermine the party's monopoly on power through an increase in societal demands for political reforms.

The reformers, led by Vo Van Kiet, the prime minister and party's third ranking official, judge that the economy is at a critical crossroads. They believe that if the economy is to keep growing at current rates over the next five years, around $40 billion of investment capital will have to be raised from both domestic and foreign sources. To raise half of the capital domestically, a major transfer of resources out of the state sector into the private sector would be necessary. Mobilizing foreign capital will require that investors and aid donors be convinced that the reform process is moving forward with a restructuring of the legal, financial, and administrative foundation of a market economy.

Conservatives, led by President Le Duc Anh, tend to be more wary of opening the country to foreign influences as well as any rapid rush towards economic reform. Their immediate concerns are focused on the side-effects of economic reform, particularly on the widening income gap between the mostly peasant population of the countryside -- who tend to be strong supporters of the Communist Party -- and

---

[9] Goodman, Allan E. "Vietnam in 1995: It Was a Very Good Year," *The Washington Quarterly*, Spring 1996, pp. 137-150.

the population of the cities, and on an erosion of "moral values." Their longer-run concerns are fixated on deflecting threats to their monolithic authority and control.

To deal with the income gap, many conservatives advocate higher taxes, more restrictive land-use laws, more centralized control of businesses, and a reduction of the autonomy with which local People's Councils can authorize joint ventures. All these steps arguably go against the main direction of the *doi moi* reform process and would have a dampening effect on foreign direct investment.[10]

Conservatives are also opposed to any fundamental restructuring of the SOEs. As the economy has experienced rapid growth without any radical restructuring of the state enterprises, conservatives believe that Vietnam's economic development can be state-led. In addition, the possible displacement of hundreds of thousands of war veterans (a key party support group) employed by SOEs is a more important consideration to this group than the growth-impeding aspects of SOEs.

In the run-up to the Communist Party congress, a draft report issued by the party has been widely interpreted as bolstering the position of the conservatives. While the report does not call for the reversal of economic reforms already put into place, it argues that the state sector should play the leading role in the country's industrialization process, with a goal of increasing the state sector's contribution to GDP from around the 40% level today to 60% by 2020. The report also urges that resources should also be concentrated on developing the state sector in key ares such as the financial system, insurance, trade and other service industries.[11]

A campaign against "social evils," launched in February, 1996 has also been widely reported in the press as an indication of growing conservative influence. This campaign, which has included attempts to limit prostitution, corruption, and the use of only foreign names in advertising, has unsettled many foreign investors and may be contributing to a drop in foreign investment approvals.[12]

It is, however, uncertain whether the conservatives are gaining the upper hand. In the prelude to previous party congresses, similar signs of conservative rumblings have surfaced, only to be followed by a return to the status quo after the party congress. In addition, some signs point to a possible growing ascendancy of the reformer camp. These include the dismissal in April, 1996 of conservative Politburo member Nguyen Haa Phan, and a commitment by the party to bring "younger" members into the Centralized Committee.

POLICY IMPLICATIONS

In assessing the leadership conflict, most analysts believe that the political consensus in favor of *Doi Moi* is unlikely to be reversed. As the legitimacy of the Communist Party depends on rising living standards induced by rapid economic growth, few analysts believe that ideology will prevail over this imperative.

---

[10] Goodman, Allan E. p. 145.

[11] Chua, Reginald. "Vietnam Sets Lofty Goals for Economy While Maintaining State's Primary Role," *New York Times*, April 10, 1996, p. A8.

[12] Grant, Jeremy. "Investment in Vietnam Drops," *Financial Times*, May 6, 1996, p. 7.

A number of external forces also make it likely that the rhetoric of Vietnam's leadership will continue to be socialist while its practice continues to be increasingly capitalist. For example, Vietnam's membership in the Association of South East Asian Nations (ASEAN) and its application to become a member of the World Trade Organization (WTO) are strong forces for keeping the country moving in the direction of a more market-oriented economy. For Vietnam, membership in both groupings will help it gain wider access to markets and increase its acceptability to international investors. In addition, preconditions for loans established by the World Bank, and the Asian Development Bank provide strong pressures for continuing the reform process.

Continuing divisions among the top leadership, however, are likely to ensure that the pace of Vietnam's transition towards a market economy will not be smooth. A likely scenario, barring a crisis, is for a continuation of the two-steps forward and one-step back routine where the state sector will continue to play a large role and where small entrepreneurs will continue to operate somewhat handicapped.

Despite the considerable progress made over the past decade, Vietnam's transition towards a market-oriented economy has a long way to go. In this context, Vietnam's leadership struggle could affect the movement towards normalization of commercial relations with the United States.[13]

Currently, a number of statutory provisions preclude Vietnam from being eligible for preferences such as most-favored-nation (MFN) treatment, Export-Import Bank trade financing, and Overseas Private Investment Corporation (OPIC) insurance guarantees for private investment. To become eligible for the restoration of these economic benefits, Vietnam would have to make a number of fundamental reforms in the areas affecting SOEs; emigration; labor policies; government control over trade and investment flows and Vietnam's legal system. In addition, human rights and press freedom could be important considerations as well.

The Clinton Administration recently provided the Vietnamese authorities with a framework paper detailing a list of steps Vietnam would have to take in order to enter into a trade agreement with the United States -- a necessary action before Vietnam could be granted MFN treatment. Many of the steps involve a reduction of the Vietnamese government's still heavy control over trade and investment flows as well as improvements in its legal system.

How fast Vietnam may undertake these reforms, many of which are required as well for admission to the WTO, could be affected by the policy and ideological struggle being waged among Vietnam's top leadership. The outcome of the party congress, thus, will be monitored closely by the U.S. government and private sector.

---

[13] For a full discussion, see *Vietnam-U.S. Relations: The Debate Over Normalization*, CRS Issue Brief 93081, Updated May 1, 1996 [By Robert G. Sutter].

Chapter 3

EAST ASIA AND THE PACIFIC

ROBERT SUTTER

Introduction

This report examines selected congressional perceptions on salient issues and their short term outlook concerning U.S. policy in East Asia and the Pacific. It does so in the context of a brief assessment of congressional and other U.S. debate over U.S. policies in the region since the end of the cold war. In addition to published sources cited in footnotes, the report is based on interviews conducted during September and October 1998 with 25 congressional staff who deal directly with issues involving U.S. policy toward East Asia and the Pacific. Those consulted included staff from foreign policy, defense, and economic policy committees, as well as staff from the personal offices of Members with a special interest in the region. Roughly half those interviewed were Republicans, half Democrats; roughly half worked for the Senate, and half worked for the House. In order to insure that the staff members would be as frank as possible in giving their personal views on policy issues, those interviewed were assured that their remarks would not be personally attributed.

A survey of this nature cannot provide a definitive assessment of congressional views on regional issues. For instance, as is noted below, since the interviews focused on staff who deal directly with issues involving U.S. policy toward East Asia and the Pacific, they generally did not proportionately capture those in Congress who favor retrenchment or oppose U.S. involvement in East Asia and the Pacific. They and the Members they work for presumably would not normally seek congressional assignments focused on the region.

The study does provide an overview of selected congressional attitudes that may assist Members and staff interested in comparing their views on regional issues with those of their colleagues; it also provides an overview of congressional thinking behind often competing policy positions adopted on salient regional issues facing the newly elected 106[6h] Congress.

For those readers already familiar with background on the post cold war U.S. policy debate on issues involving East Asia and the Pacific, please turn directly to the section "Congressional Views at the End of the 105th Congress" on page 7.

Background: Post-Cold War Debate Over U.S. Policy in East Asia and the Pacific

There has been a fairly widespread perception in the United States of a lack of clear direction in U.S. policy toward East Asia and the Pacific since the end of the cold war. Some have argued that perhaps a more experienced foreign policy leader, with a clearer vision of Asia/Pacific policy and a greater election mandate than the 43 percent of the popular vote gained by Mr. Clinton in 1992 would have been more decisive in formulating policy toward the region. On the one hand, it is argued that such a President could have set a course of action and stuck to it -- thereby avoiding the repeated tugs-of-war among competing interests. On the other hand, since the end of the cold war, Americans have been deeply divided over foreign policy, and contending policy perspectives cannot easily be bridged to develop coherent policy toward this region or other important areas.[1] For example, President Bush was a seasoned and attentive foreign and defense policy player; he notably had a clear view of China policy and stuck with it, but he found his policy assailed from various sides after the 1989 Tiananmen crackdown in the more fluid and pluralistic U.S. foreign policy debates after the cold war.

Because security issues and opposition to Communist expansion no longer dominate U.S. foreign policy, economic interests, democratization abroad, and human rights have greater prominence in policymaking. Various pressure groups and other institutions interested in these and other subjects also have enhanced influence in policy making. Such fluidity and competition among priorities has more often than not been the norm in American foreign policy. Presidents Woodrow Wilson and Franklin Roosevelt both set forth comprehensive concepts of a well-integrated U.S. foreign policy, but neither framework lasted long. The requirements of the cold war were much more effective in establishing rigor and order in U.S. foreign policy priorities, but that era is over.

The post-cold war period has seen substantial changes in the way foreign policy is made in the United States. In general, there has been a shift away from the leadership of the foreign policy elite in the past and toward greater pluralism. This pluralism increases the opportunity for input by non-governmental or lobby groups with an interest in foreign policy, and it increases the importance of Congress. For example, it is characterized by:[2]

- A much greater range of agencies within the executive branch involved in foreign policy, with the rise of the economic agencies (Commerce, Treasury, and U.S. Trade Representative (USTR) of particular importance.

- A seeming reallocation of power within government, away from the executive branch and toward the Congress.

---

[1] See discussion in, among others, Ross, Robert, (ed). *After the Cold War*, Armonk, NY, M.E. Sharpe, 1998, pp.

[2] This is taken from Harding, Harry, *Public Engagement In American Foreign Policy*, The American Assembly, Columbia University, February 23-25, 1995, pp. 8-9.

- Much greater participation by non-governmental organizations and lobby groups that attempt to shape foreign policy to conform with their interests.

- Much less consensus within Congress, and within the broader public, over foreign policy.

There is consensus, however, that foreign policy should not be expensive. The fate of the international affairs budget in the U.S. Congress in 1995 and 1996 indicates that Americans want foreign policy both to cost less and to give more domestic benefit. Unfortunately, Americans do not agree on how to accomplish this. Few Americans are aware that foreign policy spending accounts for less than one percent of the federal budget. There appear to be at least three different tendencies or schools of thought regarding post-cold war U.S. foreign policy. These approaches are not necessarily exclusive. In particular, a U.S. leader may demonstrate aspects of one tendency at some times and aspects of another at other times. An understanding of what these schools stand for suggests the difficulty of gauging the direction of U.S. policy toward East Asia and the Pacific, or other key areas of international concern.[3]

One prominent school stresses a relative decline in U.S. ability to affect decisions of many governments in the cacophony of conflicts that has emerged since 1990 and reduced U.S. ability to protect its interests. It calls for the United States to work harder to preserve its important interests while adjusting to its limited resources and influence. Advocates of this position expect continued international instability and limited U.S. ability to respond. They observe that there is no international framework to shape policy, that U.S. policy must use a complex mix of international, regional, and bilateral efforts to achieve policy goals, and that security, economic, and cultural-political issues will compete for priority in policymaking. They argue that with relative homeland safety in this uncertain environment, pressing domestic problems will take precedence over U.S. attention to international affairs and restrict the financial resources available for foreign policy, defense, and international security. They also believe that policy making will remain difficult because the executive branch may well remain in control of one political party and the Congress in control of the other party.

This school, seen reflected in the commentary of leaders like George Bush, Henry Kissinger, and others, argues that these circumstances require the United States to work closely with traditional allies and associates. Regarding East Asia and the Pacific, they argue that it is inconsistent with U.S. goals not to preserve longstanding good relations with Japan and with friends and allies in Asia whose security policies and political-cultural orientations complement U.S. interests. In policy toward other regional powers -- Russia, China, and India, they note that all three are preoccupied with internal political-development crises and do not appear to want regional instability. All seek closer economic and political relations with the West and with the advancing economies of the region. Washington would be well advised, they say, to work closely with these governments wherever there are common interests. In considering U.S. assets available to influence regional trends, they call on the United

---

[3] For an analysis, see among others, Ross, Robert, *op. cit.*, pp. 74-77.

States to go slow in reducing its regional military presence. The economic savings of cutbacks would be small; the political costs could be high insofar as most countries in Asia encourage the United States to remain active in the region to offset the power of Japan and/or China.

A second school of thought argues for major cutbacks in U.S. international involvement, including military involvement, and a renewed focus on solving such domestic problems as crime, drug use, economic competitiveness and educational standards, homelessness, poverty, decaying cities, and transportation infrastructure. Variations of this view are seen in the writings of Patrick Buchanan and other well-known commentators, and in the political statements of Ross Perot. Often called an "America First" or "Neo-isolationist" school, they argue that the United States has become overextended in world affairs and has been taken advantage of in the current world security-economic system. They call for sweeping cuts in spending for international activities, favoring a U.S. pullback from foreign bases and major cuts in foreign assistance and foreign technical/information programs. They are skeptical of the utility of international financial institutions and the United Nations, and of international efforts to promote free trade through the World Trade Organization (WTO). They advocate termination of international economic talks that help to perpetuate a liberal world trading system that in practice increases U.S. economic dependence and injures some American workers and industries. Some favor trade measures that are seen as protectionist by U.S. trading partners.

A third position argues that U.S. policy needs to promote more actively U.S. interests in international political, military, and economic affairs, and use U.S. influence to pressure countries that do not conform to the norms of an appropriate world order. Proponents, along with others, also see a growing convergence of domestic interests on foreign policy and vice versa. They see the United States unable to solve domestic problems on narcotics, crime, and the environment, for example, without addressing these issues in a global context. Supporters of this position want the United States to maintain military forces with world-wide capabilities, to lead strongly in world affairs utilizing economic instruments when advantageous, and to minimize compromises and accommodations.

This school of thought has been present in American politics throughout this century. But for several reasons it is stronger today than at any time since the 1960s. During the Reagan Administration, after a prolonged period of introspection and doubt following the Vietnam War, oil shocks, and the Iran hostage crisis, the American public became much more optimistic about the future of the United States. This trend was reinforced by the end of the cold war, a victory for the U.S.-backed system of collective security and for U.S. political and economic values. The outcome of the 1991 Persian Gulf War with Iraq further inspired confidence in U.S. military doctrine, equipment, and performance and in America's international leadership ability.

Those who support this view acknowledge that America faces serious economic challenges, but they are optimistic that the United States can succeed in a competitive world economy. They also insist that the United States is better positioned than any other country to exert leadership in the realm of ideas and values, political concepts, life-style, popular culture, and international organizations. They perceive a global power vacuum, caused notably by the collapse of the Soviet empire, which allows the United States to exert influence. They are not deterred by warnings of over extension of limited military and economic resources, resistance to U.S. intervention into the affairs of others, and future relative decline of U.S. government economic, military, and other resources. They argue that Russia, China, and India will remain preoccupied with domestic problems. They acknowledge that Japan and Western Europe are economically powerful but also that they are uncertain how to use their new power and that they lack American cultural attractiveness and influence.[4]

In recent years, advocates of this third tendency have been most vocal in pressing for strong policy in support of democracy and human rights. They have argued for a more active U.S. foreign policy, which has led some targeted countries to view U.S. policy as interference in their internal affairs. Advocates have opposed economic or trading policies of other countries seen as inequitable or predatory. They have pressed for strong policy against proliferation of weapons of mass destruction. Members of this school also argue variously for sanctions against countries that practice coercive birth control, seriously pollute the environment, harbor terrorists, and promote the drug trade. They believe the United States should be more assertive in promoting humanitarian relief and in recognizing the legitimacy of people's right to self-determination.

Specific Policy Disputes and Agreements

Against the background of sharply competing views and much greater pluralism in the making of U.S. foreign policy, it was not surprising that there were frequent disputes over U.S. policy on sensitive East Asian and Pacific issues, and that those disputes often pitted congressional critics against Administration policy makers. Sometimes the disputes led to sharp turns in policy. In 1994, President Clinton--facing growing criticism from U.S. businesses and their congressional supporters-- reversed policy on linking China's trading status with its human rights record; in 1995, the President shifted policy and agreed to allow Taiwan's President to visit the United States--a move urged on him by resolutions backed by all but one Member of Congress.

Clinton Administration China policy was particularly prone to be influenced by a continuing tug-of-war among competing U.S. interests reflected in the Congress.[5] Congressional critics, backed by sympathetic U.S. groups, notably used the occasion of the President's annual waiver of the Jackson-Vanik provision on China's most-favored-nation (MFN), known after 1998 as "normal trade relations," status. They debated a broad range of U.S. concerns regarding Chinese government human rights practices and policies, trade issues, flagrant patent and copyright violations, weapons

---

[4] American proponents of this view often are focused on specific issues like human rights, trade policy, proliferation of weapons of mass destruction, or others. One articulation of this school is seen in the work by Joseph Nye entitled *Bound To Lead*, Harvard University Press, 1992.

[5] For background, see *China-U.S. Relations*, by Kerry Dumbaugh, CRS Issue Brief 98018, and *China: Interest Groups and Recent U.S. Policy*, by Robert Sutter and Peter Mitchner, CRS Report 97-48.

proliferation concerns, and the Chinese authorities' approach to salient domestic and foreign policy issues including Taiwan, Tibet, and China's increasing military modernization.[6]   Allegations of illegal Chinese government contributions to U.S. political campaigns, and allegations of illegal U.S. transfers of missile technology to China were focal points of heated congressional criticism in 1996-1997 and 1997-1998, respectively. The lobbying of strong U.S. business interests desiring a bigger stake in the China market helped to assure that normal trade relations continued despite strong congressional criticism.   Notably, it was widely believed in Congress and the Administration that ending MFN was too extreme, as it would hurt U.S. consumers and traders along with U.S. enterprises engaged in China trade.

There was active congressional criticism of the Administration's handling of the danger posed by North Korea's efforts to develop nuclear weapons and ballistic missile delivery systems.[7] The Clinton Administration reached an agreement on October 21, 1994 with North Korea, establishing the so-called agreed framework, designed to check Pyongyang's suspected nuclear weapons program in return for U.S. supplied fuel oil and two nuclear power reactors to be funded by South Korea and Japan. Many in Congress criticized the accord and were reluctant to supply funds for the fuel oil, but each year the Congress backed, sometimes grudgingly, the Administration's request for funds for the oil.

Prolonged U.S. economic growth and falling unemployment in the 1990s helped to mute congressional criticism of U.S. trade policies, which did not make much of a dent in the widening U.S. trade deficits with several trading partners in the region, especially Japan and China.[8] Active U.S. trade diplomacy and threats of targeted sanctions met with widespread congressional support and helped to head off possible congressional initiatives including legislation to protect U.S. industries or other economic interests adversely affected by East Asian competition.   The Asian economic crisis of 1997-1998 came as a surprise to both the Administration and Congress. Many in Congress were skeptical of the utility of U.S.-backed International-al Monetary Fund (IMF) rescue packages for ailing East Asian economies, and criticized the Clinton Administration's requests for added U.S. funding for the Fund.[9]

Many in Congress also placed strong emphasis on U.S. values, especially political values associated with democracy and human rights. They applauded when Clinton Administration officials stood firm in the face of authoritarianism and

---

[6] Presidential candidate Clinton had strongly supported these congressional debates in 1992, but gradually reversed his policy until he decided in 1994 to delink the annual waiver from China's human rights and other policy practices and behavior.

[7] See, *North Korea's Nuclear Weapons Program*, by Larry Niksch, CRS Issue Brief 91141.

[8] See, *China-U.S. Trade Issues*, by Wayne Morrison, CRS Issue Brief 91121, and *Japan-U.S. Trade*, CRS Info Pack IP201J.

[9] See, *The Asian Financial crisis, the IMF, and Japan*, by Dick Nanto, CRS Report 98-434, and *The Asian Financial Crisis*, by Richard Cronin, CRS Report 98-74.

oppression, as in the case of Burma; but they urged a stronger Administration stance in dealing with repression in East Timor, Cambodia, and other areas.[10]

Areas of General Agreement. Despite the many issues in dispute, there was majority support in the Congress for several major features of Clinton Administration policy in the region during the 1990s:

- The U.S. market remained open to East Asian and Pacific exports, despite the growing U.S. trade deficit.

- There was broad support in the Congress for the Administration's determination to maintain a strong military presence involving about 100,000 U.S. troops in the western Pacific.

- Despite strong criticism from some Members, Congress generally went along with Clinton Administration efforts gradually to lower the priority given to U.S. values of democracy and human rights in the conduct of U.S. policy toward China and some other East Asian countries.[11]

Congressional Views at the End of the 105th Congress

Congressional staff members consulted for this study differed sharply on appropriate U.S. policy approaches on many sensitive regional issues. But the interviews reflected several areas of broad agreement on features of Administration and congressional decision making, and general priorities for U.S. policy attention.

Clinton Administration Leadership

Many strong congressional backers of Clinton Administration policies agreed with the views of congressional critics that the Administration's policies in the region did not reflect well thought out or coherent approaches to East Asia and the Pacific. To some, the Administration appeared to divide recent policy responsibility among key Administration actors, with the White House leading on China policy, Treasury leading on the Asian economic crisis and policy toward Japan, and the State and Defense Departments engaging in a seeming tug-of-war over policy toward North Korea. To others, Clinton Administration attention to issues seemed to be reactive or episodic.

One example cited was President Clinton's attitude toward the Asia Pacific Economic Cooperation (APEC) forum. At first, the President appeared to be pushing hard to initiate a summit of regional leaders at the APEC annual meeting in Seattle in 1993, but he allegedly lost interest in the process in subsequent years. A strong

---

[10] See, *Burma-U.S. Relations,* by Larry Niksch, CRS Report 96-3;, *Indonesia-U.S. Relations,* by Larry Niksch, CRS Report 97-186; and *Cambodia,* by Robert Sutter, CRS Issue Brief 98036.

[11] These points were confirmed with congressional staff interviewed in October 1998.

congressional supporter of the President's engagement policy toward China was dismayed by what he saw as a lack of follow through by the Administration leadership after the Washington and Beijing summits of 1997 and 1998. He was particularly interested in pursuing opportunities to ease U.S.-China economic and trade difficulties, judging that after the summits the time was right to press China on market opening and other trade issues. He speculated that President Clinton had appeared to be more interested in using China summitry to distract attention from his legal problems at home than in providing the implementing actions needed to bring concrete benefit for American trading and other interests.

Meanwhile, congressional supporters of the Administration's efforts to sustain most favored nation tariff treatment, known since 1998 as "normal trade relations," for Chinese imports were critical of a "lackadaisical" Administration approach toward defending the trade status in annual congressional debates on the issue. More often than not, they felt they were left to their own devices, without strong Administration leadership, to defend the Chinese trade privileges.

Several congressional supporters of Clinton Administration policies in the region argued that the above criticisms were unfair or not very important. In their view, the bottom line in judging Administration policy were the results for U.S. interests. They viewed these generally positively, noting continued U.S. prosperity, strong U.S. power and influence in the region, and prevailing regional conditions of peace and stability advantageous for the United States.

Strict coherence in U.S. policy and consistent, high-level Administration attention to regional policy issues were unwarranted in their view. The problems of the region tended to be diverse and episodic; the Clinton Administration was seen logically to be following this pattern. Moreover, beset by many policy issues at home and abroad, high-level U.S. leaders could not be expected to give consistent priority to East Asia and the Pacific.

Several in this group added that congressional complaints about the absence of coherence and consistency in U.S. strategy toward the region were typical complaints by those out of power to discredit those in power. In reality, they argued, the United States had not had a coherent strategy toward East Asia since the cold war period of the so-called "Nixon doctrine" saw a major realignment of U.S. military forces in the region. Since then, they judged, U.S. policy has been more episodic and reactive.

The Role of Congress

In considering the appropriate role of Congress in U.S. policy toward the region, all those consulted agreed that the key to effective U.S. foreign policy was effective leadership by the executive branch; Congress played a vital role but could not be expected to lead in policy formation.

Even the harshest congressional critics of Clinton Administration policy maintained that the U.S. constitutional division of powers gave primacy to the President in the conduct of foreign affairs. Many congressional staff added the view that Congress is not good at making foreign policy: its structure is too diverse to provide coherent leadership; and its tools in foreign policy focus on legislative injunctions, sanctions, funding decisions, and appointment decisions that are often too rigid and difficult to adjust to changing international circumstances.

A few congressional staff consulted for this study were sharply critical of the role Congress has played in U.S. policy toward East Asia and the Pacific. One staff member, who strongly disagreed with congressional critics of the U.S. engagement policy toward China, viewed congressional criticism of China as based largely on ignorance. Others pointed to what they saw as a decline in Congress' role in foreign affairs as a result of a perceived failure to pass foreign affairs and foreign assistance authorizing legislation, that in past decades had been used to influence the direction of U.S. foreign policy.[12] In contrast, several staff members maintained, the congressional committees dealing with trade issues--including legislation important to Administration interests--were seen to exert powerful influence on U.S. foreign policy and were reportedly sought out by Clinton Administration leaders for consultations and compromises.

While conceding leadership to the executive branch, many congressional staff consulted for this study supported an active congressional role in making U.S. policy toward the region. As one observer put it, the Administration needs to be the "author" of policy, but Congress plays a key role as "editor." A prevailing view was that there were numerous perceived shortcomings in Administration policy that needed to be adjusted, corrected or stopped through rigorous congressional oversight, and if needed, legislative steps.

Congressional activism in U.S. policy toward the region had several sources, according to congressional staff. Many advised that since Congress sensed weaknesses in Administration policy, or a need to make up for seeming Administration inattention to salient questions, it intervened with steps designed to strengthen U.S. policy in sensitive areas. And when congressional Members pointedly disagreed with the thrust of Administration policy, they tried to use levers at hand to push the policy in a direction more acceptable to them.

Several congressional staff members, both those supporting and critical of Administration policy, claimed that partisanship played an important role in congressional criticism or support of Administration policy. They had the impression that congressional-Administration relations were strongly colored by partisan considerations at the end of the 105th Congress, and that policy toward East Asia and the Pacific was affected by this trend.

Several other congressional staff members denied significant influence of partisanship on policy toward the region. In contrast to those who saw partisanship behind often sharp congressional criticism of the Clinton Administration's China policy, for example, some advised that congressional criticism of Administration policy on China and other issues was broadly and demonstrably bi-partisan. Others judged that critics of Administration policies on China, North Korea, IMF funding and

---

[12] The Appropriations Committees have been seen to step into this situation and used the "power of the purse" to "influence policy (see discussion of North Korea on Page 13).

the Asian economic crisis, and other issues had ample justification without considering partisan concerns.

Competing Congressional Approaches on East Asian Issues

Congressional staff consulted for this study tended to agree that there was a major split in Congress between two approaches to East Asian issues. On one side were congressional observers who emphasized the importance of U.S. engagement, especially economic engagement, with East Asian countries as the prime means to secure U.S. interests in regional prosperity and peace. These observers tended to judge that in the post cold war environment, with no overriding security threat to U.S. interests in the region, economic exchange provided the best way to promote greater openness and transparency, not only in economic areas, but over time in political and security areas as well. In these circumstances, according to this view, U.S. economic interests benefit, but so do U.S. interests in promoting greater social and political pluralism, greater international interdependence, and conformity to acceptable norms of behavior.

On the other side were congressional observers who judged that relying on economic engagement would not meet U.S. policy objectives. In their view, such engagement must be done in tandem with vigorous U.S. political and security measures designed to secure changes in those areas sought by the United States. These observers cited perceived trends in Indonesia and China to argue that relying on economic engagement cannot be expected to result in political and security outcomes desired by the United States. The United States "should not economically strengthen corrupt or authoritarian systems." They urged Congress to use rhetoric, sanctions, and other means to press East Asian governments to conform to political and security standards supported by the United States.

A third important congressional approach to regional issues was duly noted by those consulted for the study, even though they did not personally subscribe to it. This view echos the sentiment of the "America First" school of thought seen in the political rhetoric of Ross Perot and like-minded politicians. It favors greater U.S. disengagement from what it sees as counterproductive and draining involvements in East Asia and other areas. Thus, they tend to favor U.S. military pull back from the region, reduction of U.S. commitments through the United Nations, International Financial Institutions and other means to deal with problems in the region and elsewhere, and avoiding international trading arrangements which they feel do not benefit U.S. working people.[13] Because the sample of congressional staff consulted for this study was focused on those with particular interest and involvement in U.S. policy toward East Asia and the Pacific, it presumably failed to proportionately include congressional observers who view involvement in these issues as counterproductive to U.S. interests.

Senate "Centrism". The split in congressional opinion between those relying largely on economic engagement to foster U.S. interests in East Asia and the Pacific,

---

[13] Leading proponents of this view regarding East Asia include Ted Galen Carpenter of the Cato Institute, Washington, D.C.

and those who stress the need for continued strong political and security pressure along with economic engagement, was seen as greater in the House than in the Senate by several congressional staff interviewed for this study. These congressional observers also tended to see wider divides on these policy approaches in the House International Relations Committee than in the Senate Foreign Relations Committee. The reasons for this perceived difference were seen as the following:

- Senators with "centrist" positions on sensitive policy issues in East Asia and the Pacific (e.g. China policy) have been able to use their power to "hold" legislation they disapprove of until compromises are reached that meet their concerns. House Members have no such power. One House Republican staffer with moderate views who tended to be supportive of administration China policy maintained that to force compromise over what he viewed as extreme legislation on China required intervention by House leadership-- something that could not be done on a routine basis.[14]

- Senators tend to represent constituencies larger than most House districts; this reportedly prompts them to have a "broader" policy perspective, less focused on particular issues that might be seen pushing U.S. policy in one direction or another.

- Elected only every six years, Senators are said to be able to adopt a more detached view of U.S. policy concerns in East Asia and the Pacific, less swayed by the constituency interests and concerns that are seen as capable of driving House Members to push U.S. policy in particular directions.

Priority Issues

Issues in U.S. policy toward Northeast Asia had priority over issues in Southeast Asia, according to congressional staff consulted for this study. The confrontation with North Korea was often cited as the most dangerous flashpoint, having the potential to quickly draw the United States into a land war in Asia. U.S. relations with China were widely seen as posing the most important long-term strategic challenge for U.S. interests. In this context, Taiwan-mainland China relations were viewed as an important point of tension--one with the potential to involve the United States in a military confrontation with China.

---

[14] In this regard, a Senate staff member emphasized a perspective on the ongoing U.S. congressional debate on China that was also echoed by some others. He viewed the congressional coalition against the Administration's China policy as led by elements of the political right and the political left, who under other circumstances appeared to have little in common. Thus, in the ranks of congressional critics of the Administration's China policy were seen religious conservatives concerned about Chinese practices on abortions and treatment of independent Christian worship; Members with strong pro-labor leanings, along with right-populists sympathetic to Patrick Buchanan and Ross Perot who have common ground in their concern about loss of U.S. jobs overseas; liberal leaning Members concerned with human rights abuses in Tibet and the suppression of dissent in China; and Members concerned with China's rising military power as a possible security danger to U.S. interests. Allied against this coalition, in the view of this staff member, are Members of the generally pro-business wings of both parties, who tend to favor continued trade and investment with China.

The region-wide Asian economic crisis and frustrations in U.S.-Japan economic relations headed the list of priority issues for several congressional staff. They had little confidence in Clinton Administration or other expert assessments of the crisis, which were seen as having proven largely wrong or behind the trend in viewing the crisis. They judged that the size and scope of the Japanese economy made it a linchpin of future economic stability in Asia and a major ingredient in the continued health of the U.S. economy.[15]

A few congressional staff consulted for this study gave prime emphasis to the perceived movements in Southeast Asia, notably Malaysia and, to a degree, Hong Kong, away from reliance on free-market economic policy and toward more government management in economic processes. They saw these steps as contrary to U.S. interests in fostering free and open economic markets. The crisis in Indonesia loomed as a big problem for some in Congress, who saw political as well as economic and social uncertainty there posing not only a significant economic challenge but also a crisis in the Southeast Asian regional order. Indonesia has been a bulwark of the Association of Southeast Asian Nations (ASEAN) and its region wide security body, the ASEAN Regional Forum (ARF)--both of which are key organs for U.S. interaction with Southeast Asia.

Several congressional observers judged that burgeoning U.S. trade deficits with Japan, China, Taiwan, Korea, and others in East Asia would seriously exacerbate U.S. relations in the region in 1999, even though they had received only limited attention in 1998. Only a few of those interviewed gave high priority to issues of human rights and democratic values in countries like Burma, Indonesia (especially East Timor), Cambodia, and Vietnam. The issue of full accounting of U.S. prisoners of war/missing in action (POW/MIA) from the Vietnam war was rarely mentioned. No significant issues were raised regarding U.S. policy toward Australia, New Zealand, and the Pacific Island states. When queried, staffers judged that U.S. relations with its Australian ally were seen as excellent, and previously strained relations with New Zealand were improving. Congressional initiatives in policy regarding the Pacific island countries were seen to come mainly from Members from the region or with a special interest in the region.

Specific Issues

North Korea. A crisis in U.S. policy toward North Korea represented the most important Asian issue at the end of the 105th Congress, according to many staff consulted for this study. Media reports in August 1998 said that North Korea was constructing what appeared to be a major underground facility for manufacturing nuclear weapons. North Korea on August 31,1998 launched a nuclear-capable ballistic missile over Japan. Congress reacted strongly. At first it voted to cut off or severely condition funding for U.S. obligations under the 1994 agreed framework; and later agreed to compromise language in the omnibus funding bill (H.R. 4328, signed

---

[15] By contrast, bilateral security issues with Japan were rarely mentioned. One staff member highlighted problems for U.S. bases in Okinawa. For background, see *Japan-U.S. Relations*, CRS Issue Brief 97004.

into law on October 21, 1998, P.L. 105-277) approving staged funding allocations amid several U.S. presidential certifications.

In interviews conducted while the Clinton Administration and congressional critics were working out the compromise language in H.R. 4328, some congressional staff members made clear their intent to use congressional control of the funding for U.S. obligations under the agreed framework as a means to prompt a toughening of Administration policy toward North Korea. A few judged that the United States should set more firm conditions in interactions with North Korea; and if North Korea continued provocations and otherwise failed to meet those conditions, the United States should be prepared to "walk away" from the agreed framework and other negotiations with the North, until such time as the North was prepared to negotiate again in what these congressional observers hoped would be the basis of a "new strategic bargain" in U.S.-North Korean relations. These staff members judged that North Korea would return to negotiations in part because it needed food aid and wanted the United States to lift U.S. economic and diplomatic embargos against the North. To deal with the potentially more dangerous situation on the Korean peninsula that might result from terminating the U.S.-North Korean agreed framework, the congressional staff urged greater U.S. and allied military preparedness, including development of theater missile defense, as effective means to deter North Korean adventurism.

A larger number of congressional staff consulted for this study were not prepared to abandon the agreed framework.[16] The situation on the Korean peninsula was seen as too dangerous, and North Korea too heavily armed and capable of unpredictable actions. In their view, there was no viable current alternative to the agreed framework, even with its perceived shortcomings. Some congressional staff said that the Clinton Administration policy had been successful in that North Korea was weaker and more isolated than in the past; and the danger of conflict seemed much less than in 1994 when the agreed framework was signed.

This larger group of congressional staff generally favored closer Administration interaction with Congress to come up with ways to toughen U.S. policy without seriously upsetting the stability of the peninsula. In general, they sought to avoid the appearance of U.S. accommodation and acquiescence to North Korean provocations, while evading any hard-to-control reactions from North Korea.

Asian Economic Crisis. This broad ranging problem was seen by several interviewed staff as beginning to have an important impact on the U.S. economy, and therefore it was said to warrant greater attention in Congress. Concerns focused notably on U.S. relations with Japan, Indonesia, Malaysia and the IMF.

Concerning *Japan*, there was agreement among those who raised this issue that the Japanese economy represented a key to regional economic revival; there was also

---

[16] About half of those interviewed discussed North Korean issues in some detail. Three of them were inclined to "walk away" from the agreed framework if North Korea did not change recent provocative policies and actions. The rest were not prepared to abandon the agreed framework.

agreement that economic conditions in Japan would not improve soon. Some interviewed staff warned against what they saw as the hard public line, taken notably by the U.S. Treasury Department and supported by President Clinton, that pressed the Japanese government to adopt sweeping economic reforms. Sensitive to Japanese political and social constraints and perceived rising anti-U.S. sentiment in Japan, these staff warned against possible counterproductive reactions in Japan if the United States appeared to be pushing the Japanese government "into a corner." They favored a more carefully orchestrated and balanced U.S. approach, including Congress as well as the Administration working in close interaction with Japanese officials and opinion leaders in ways designed to persuade the Japanese to make needed economic reforms. They added that the United States should be prepared to adjust its demands and goals where they appear unrealistic or counterproductive. They also favored giving more emphasis to areas of U.S.-Japanese common ground.

Other interviewed congressional staff saw little alternative to the current U.S. Administration's hard line toward Japan. Such outside pressure was seen as needed to prompt change by entrenched Japanese government decision makers. It also served as a warning to others in Asia who might be tempted to follow narrowly self-serving or merchantilist policies involving large increases of exports to the U.S. market as they try to shake off the effects of the Asian economic crisis. The hard public line also provided political protection against U.S. domestic critics who claim that the U.S. government was not doing enough to protect U.S. economic interests in the face of seemingly unfair Japanese and other Asian trading practices.

On *Indonesia,* interviewed congressional staff were focused as much on the political and security implications as on the severe economic decline. Indonesia's economy was not seen as of critical importance to the United States economy. But Indonesia's large size and strategic location meant that economic and political instability there would have important repercussions throughout Southeast Asia. Many congressional staff saw the Clinton Administration-backed IMF rescue efforts in Indonesia as flawed, though some said they had no viable alternative to offer. Congress was seen as willing to increase humanitarian aid to the many millions of Indonesians falling below the poverty line.[17] Some congressional observers also favored using the currently fluid political situation to push for tangible progress toward greater democracy and for autonomy (some sought independence) for East Timor and other disputed regions; others argued for caution in pushing too hard for such changes in what all agreed was a delicate political situation that could eventuate in fragmentation of Indonesia.

Malaysia's reassertion of state guidance in economic development, coincident with the arrest and beating of leading pro-free market political leader Anwar Ibrahim, was seen as an ominous sign by several staff. They viewed with concern a possible broader backlash in the region against U.S.- and *IMF-* backed free market prescriptions for the Asian economic maladies. In this context, some noted the Hong Kong government's unusual intervention into the Hong Kong stock market; others pointed to Chinese government backtracking on efforts to reform state-owned-enterprises.

---

[17] Seventy million dollars in such aid was approved in the Omnibus Appropriations Bill H.R. 4328 that passed Congress and was signed into law (PL 105-277) on October 21, 1998.

Against this backdrop, staff interviewed recommended continued strong U.S. support for free market initiatives in East Asia. They supported U.S. funding for the IMF, requested by the Clinton Administration, even though such funding was viewed as a necessary evil in the eyes of some; several were critical of IMF practices and argued for strict conditions on IMF funds in order to prevent continuation of what they saw as inefficient economic arrangements among IMF recipients in East Asia, or use of IMF funding as de facto subsidies for East Asian enterprises competing with U.S. companies. In the view of some staff, U.S. free-market economic engagement with Asia would have been boosted by the congressional passage of so-called fast track legislation--allowing for expedited congressional consideration of trade agreements negotiated by the Administration. Some staff also argued for greater U.S. economic assistance for distressed Asian populations, greater U.S. diplomatic and congressional exchanges--including those involving congressional travel abroad--with concerned Asian leaders, and continued funding and support for Radio Free Asia and other programs to publicize and support U.S. economic and other values in the region.

China. Although many congressional staff interviewed saw U.S.-China relations as a key issue determining U.S. interests in East Asian peace and stability, there were few issues of immediate concern to them at the end of the 105th Congress. For some, the summit meetings of 1997 and 1998 had not been followed by significant initiatives by either the Chinese or U.S. Administrations that would possibly change or upset the equilibrium in U.S.-China relations and thereby prompt renewed debate in Congress. For others, there remained wide ranging differences with Clinton Administration policies regarding China over human rights, trade, weapons proliferation, Tibet, Taiwan, and other issues, but the time did not appear appropriate to attack these issues in late 1998. A few expected these issues to be featured in 1999 in congressional debate and in the context of increasing Republican and Democratic competition for the presidential nomination.

An exception to this modest level of congressional concern over China policy was voiced by several congressional staff members over Clinton Administration policy toward Taiwan. Even some supporters of the Administration's engagement policy toward China judged that the President's statement in Shanghai on June 30, 1998 stating publicly the "three no's" (no U.S. support for one China, one Taiwan, Taiwan independence, or Taiwan representation in international organizations where statehood is required) represented unwarranted acquiescence to PRC pressure at the expense of U.S. interests in relations with Taiwan.[18] Citing congressional resolutions in support of continued close U.S. relations with Taiwan that passed the Congress in the aftermath of the President's trip to China, the staff members indicated that they and their Members remained on guard against further perceived Administration accommodation of Beijing's demands at the expense of Taiwan and U.S.-Taiwan relations.[19]

---

[18] For background, see *Taiwan*, by Robert Sutter, CRS Issue Brief 98034.

[19] In a related development, one staffer noted a view said to be held by some in the Administration that the Clinton Administration would endeavor in 1999 to use more active U.S. government support for Taiwan's entry into the World Trade Organization WTO) as

(continued...)

More broadly, congressional staff interviewed divided sharply over U.S. policy toward China. On one side, a few judged that Congress played a negative role in U.S.-China relations; they were particularly frustrated with the annual congressional debates pegged to consideration of China's trade status. One warned that the United States could not allow relations with China to deteriorate for the sake of particular U.S. concerns over human rights, Taiwan, trade or other issues; he saw potentially disastrous consequences flowing from U.S.-Chinese confrontation over these issues. On the other side were several strong congressional critics of Administration policy. Some resented Administration efforts to describe the U.S. debate as between advocates of "engagement" versus advocates of "isolation." What they sought was a toughening of Clinton Administration engagement that would allow for adequate protection of legitimate U.S. interests in relations with an increasingly muscular and still Communist China. They favored strong U.S. pressure on human rights and other areas of dispute in U.S.-China relations that could affect the nature of China's 21st century. Some also advocated a strengthening of U.S. relations with Japan, employing theater missile defense systems there and in Taiwan, and other steps they felt would buttress U.S. resolve in the face of perceived PRC assertiveness and pressure.

---

[19](...continued)
leverage to pressure PRC leaders to come to terms on WTO entry that would be acceptable to the United States. Taiwan has already reached agreements with most of its WTO trading partners, but is blocked on account of Beijing's insistence that it must enter the WTO before Taiwan. In part to urge the Clinton Administration to be more supportive of Taiwan's WTO entry despite Beijing's position, the 105th Congress passed legislation (P.L.105-277) that included a provision urging Taiwan's WTO entry. For background, see *Taiwan*, CRS Issue Brief 98034.

Chapter 4

Taiwan's Economic Policy-Making in the Democratic Transition*

Gerald A. McBeath
University of Alaska at Fairbanks

Abstract

For over two decades, Taiwan was praised for its high growth rates and political stability. Then, in the final days of the Chiang Ching-kuo administration, Taiwan began to democratize. The first step in that process was the chartering of the Democratic Progressive Party (DPP) in 1986 and the second major step was the formation of the New Party (DP) from the *non-mainstream* faction of the ruling Kuomintang (KMT) in 1993. By the end of 1997, opposition party officials led most of the city and country governments in Taiwan, and opposition to the KMT challenges the majority in Taiwan's Legislative Yuan.

This article asks whether Taiwan's democratization has affected the formation and implementation of economic policies. It considers monetary, fiscal, regulatory, and industrial policy-making. For each policy area, we note changes in policy-making participants, in the adoption of policy instruments and operations of policy processes, and in policy outcomes. All policy types show some impact of the process of democratization; most affected, however, have been fiscal and regulatory policy-making.

The article is based on the author's field research in Taiwan during the spring semester, 1996, and in May-June 1997. Data sources include government publications, newspaper files, articles and books on Taiwan's economic policy-making, and personal interviews with Taiwan's economic policy-makers.

* This essay was presented first at the Conference "Taiwan: State and Society in Transition," sponsored by the Center for East Asian and Pacific Studies, University of Illinois at Urbana-Champaign, in September 1997. I thank Dr. Peter Schran of the University of Illinois for his insightful critique of an earlier version of this article. I am indebted to the Chiang Ching-kuo Foundation for International Scholarly Exchange, which funded the research in Taiwan on which the article is based.

INTRODUCTION

This article asks how policy-making in Taiwan has been affected by democratization; it focuses on policies at the intersection of the polity and economy. We begin by reviewing the characteristics of the policy-making process and the policy objectives during the first four decades of Kuomintang (KMT) rule. Then we summarize the changes, both domestic and international, which began to affect initiation and implementation of policy.

POLICY-MAKING CHARACTERISTICS

Taiwan's policy-making system up to the late 1980s was highly centralized, specialized, and closed. The system was authoritarian, and a very small elite operated it. Most estimates place the size of that power elite at around a dozen individuals.[1] The president headed the elite, joined by the premier, and several experienced cabinet ministers (usually from the Ministry of Economic Affairs (MOEA), Ministry of Finance (MOF), defense, and foreign affairs). All were members of the KMT's central standing committee. On occasion, in some policy areas, a private businessman would participate. In no cases were legislators or other opinion leaders included within the elite. Because Taiwan has had only three presidents of long and stable tenure over the last five decades (Chiang Kai-shek, Chiang Ching-kuo, and Lee Teng-hui), it has been relatively easy to trace the movements in and out of this small elite.

Centralized control was established through collective decision-making bodies at the pinnacle of party and state power: the KMT's central standing committee, which met on Wednesday, and the Executive Yuan Council (or cabinet), which met the following day. The president chaired the KMT committee and indirectly influenced the deliberations of the cabinet.

The policy-making system also was highly specialized. Each function had a separate office, with an elaborate system of monitoring its responsibility. Recruitment to specialized agencies and bureaus of the state was through competitive national examinations. The specialized bureaucracy gained a reputation for energy and technological competence; to work in a national government office increasingly brought pride and respect and was the first employment choice of university graduates.

To avoid the bureaucratic rigidity that narrow specialization breeds, policy coordinating organizations developed. The cabinet secretariat organized proposals for legislative and regulatory changes, and it formalized working groups of cognate agencies. The Council for Economic Planning and Development (CEPD), essentially a consultant for the cabinet, spearheaded coordination work with ministries and agencies and exercised overall planning responsibilities for new policy initiatives. Within ministries,

---

[1] See, for example, Robert Wade's discussion of the economic policy elite in *Governing the Market* (Princeton, NJ: Princeton University Press, 1990), 195.

coordination offices were formed, such as the Industrial Development Bureau (IDB), the primary agency implementing industrial policy within MOEA.

The policy-making system during this period was also closed. Elites held decisional meetings out of public view. They did not admit outsiders or attempt to expand the small number who could participate in policy-making.

POLICY OBJECTIVES

Policy-makers sought three interrelated objectives: security, stability, and growth. Protecting itself from what was thought to be an imminent invasion from the mainland occupied the most attention and resources during the regime's early years in Taiwan. Then, leaders needed to address diplomatic shocks after the People's Republic of China assumed China's seat in the UN and Japan and the United States derecognized the Republic of China on Taiwan.

Stability, especially of the domestic economy, interacted with security. Avoiding the radical consumer price swings that had disrupted the mainland market and the first years of KMT control on Taiwan became a central economic goal. Also, leaders used the power and resources of the state to avoid high unemployment rates, another economic goal.

Growth policies initially were designed to enable security and stability. Economic growth became a free-standing objective of leaders in the 1960s. The focus on equality as reflected in the regime's slogan "growth with equity" was added, almost as an afterthought, when Taiwan's high economic development rate caught the fancy of observers. The negative externalities of high economic growth, such as pollution, did not emerge as policy concerns until the era of democratization.

PRESSURES FOR CHANGE

Some international forces helped liberalize Taiwan's policy-making system. For example, the United States encouraged the development of Taiwan's technocratic elite, and, during the 1970s and 1980s, US human rights organizations put heavy pressure on Taiwan's leaders to democratize.

However, most pressures to change the policy-making system arose from inside it. The elite itself was divided with respect to the extent and pace of reform, but Chiang Ching-kuo staked out a clear position, initiating the era of democratization by allowing political opposition to form legitimately. The regime's opponents then criticized the objectives of the elite, particularly its definition of Taiwan's security threat. They, in combination with grassroots organizers and newly formed groups, launched large-scale social movements that placed new issues onto the national agenda.

Before political liberalization actually began, seven social movements had formed: the consumers movement (1980), the local anti-pollution protest movement (1980), a natural conservation movement (1982), the women's movement (1982), an aboriginal human rights movement (1983), the students' movement (1986), and protests by the New Testament Church (1986). In 1987, the year that the political liberalization drive formally began, an additional seven movements organized to expand rights and provide greater protection for laborers, farmers, teachers, the handicapped and disadvantaged, veterans, victims of human rights violations, and mainlanders who sought to visit their relatives in China.[2] New social movements gained momentum, including, by the late 1980s, opposition to nuclear plant construction and, by the mid-1990s, support of gay/lesbian rights.

These movements seriously crowded the policy space, and they changed the participants, processes, and outcomes of public policy. We look at four areas of economic policy-making—monetary policy, fiscal policy, both economic and social regulation, and industrial policy—to see what, if any impact, the democratization era has had.

MONETARY POLICY

Monetary policy refers to the actions taken by governments to attempt to regulate the money supply for the purpose of economic stabilization—reducing inflation, spurring employment, or both.[3]

PARTICIPANTS

The Central Bank of China (CBC) is Taiwan's highest monetary policy- making and implementing agency. As a decision-making body, the CBC is composed of three parts. A board of directors sets overall parameters for monetary policy. In 1998, the board had 14 members, all of whom were nominated by the cabinet and appointed by the president. Two ministers (from MOF and MOEA) sit as ex officio directors. Directors serve five-year, renewable terms. Although the majority of board members are government officials, the board includes at least one member each from the agricultural, business, and banking communities. (The CBC board has more government officials than the American Federal Reserve. It is unlike Japan's central bank, which is tightly intertwined with large corporations.) The board meets four times annually and is chaired by the governor. A second, less important part of the CBC is its board of supervisors, a body of five, with the director-general of Budget, Accounting, and Statistics sitting as an ex-officio member.[4] Their primary function is to audit the CBC's accounts.

---

[2] Hsin-huang Michael Hsiao, "The Labor Movement in Taiwan," in Denis Fred Simon and Michael Y. M. Kau, *Taiwan: Beyond the Economic Miracle* (Armonk, NY: M. E. Sharpe, 1992), 153-54.

[3] This and the following two sections extend the argument of chapter 6, "Policy-making in a Democratic Era," in the author's *Wealth and Freedom: Taiwan's New Political Economy* (Aldershot, UK: Ashgate, 1998).

[4] "The Central Bank of China," *Central Banking*, vol. VII, no. 4 (1997), 3.

The most powerful figure at the CBC is the governor, who influences the passage of policy by the board of directors, executes board decisions, and oversees bank operations. The governor is appointed by the president on the recommendation of the cabinet for a renewable, five-year term. Unlike the premier and cabinet ministers, however, the governor cannot be removed from office by the president before the expiration of his term. Invariably, the governor is drawn from the banking community; the 1998 governor, Sheu Yuan-dong, worked previously in the Bank of Taiwan.

Until late 1979, the CBC fell under the jurisdiction of the office of the president and ranked higher than MOF. Revisions in its organic law moved it to the Executive Yuan but did not change its independent role in monetary policy. The CBC has a close relationship with the MOF, which is now a parallel cabinet institution. In the division of responsibilities, the MOF administers and supervises all financial institutions while the CBC implements monetary and foreign exchange policy as well as foreign exchange management. The CBC cooperates with the MOF in the examination of financial institutions.[5]

In a process that compromises the independence of the CBC somewhat (while enlarging participation in monetary policy-making), the governor appears twice yearly at the Legislative Yuan to respond to interpolations on the current economic situation and monetary policy; once a year, the governor attends the Legislative Yuan to answer questions on the CBC budget. In 1997, the CBC sought to revise its organic law again, to give it greater independence as a separate legal entity with full control over its budget.[6] Although bank officials worry that special interests could take advantage of the CBC's budgetary dependence, there is little evidence that legislators have attempted to do so.

MONETARY POLICY INSTRUMENTS AND PROCESSES

The Central Bank of China Act stipulates that the CBC follow four objectives: promote financial stability, guide sound banking operations, maintain the stability of the internal and external value of the currency, and foster economic development. Its chief function is stabilizing the market, and it uses five different policy instruments to accomplish this objective: open market operations, rediscount and temporary accommodation facilities, reserve requirements, policies related to accepting or releasing re-deposits of financial institutions, and selective credit controls.

The most important and flexible policy instrument available to the CBC is open market operations—the buying and selling of securities. The CBC can influence the amount of reserves and the level of inter-bank call-loan market interest rates through

---

[5] Central Bank of China, *The Central Bank of China: Purposes and Functions (1961-1991)* (Taipei: 1996), 11; see also *The Financial System in the R.O.C* and *The Financial Market Integration in Chinese Taipei* (Taipei: Ministry of Finance, Bureau of Monetary Affairs, 1996).

[6] Personal interview with Ty Lin, Assistant Director-General, Central Bank of China, May 27, 1997.

open market operations. This is a relatively new instrument for the CBC because Taiwan historically has not had a large and active debt securities market allowing the CBC to move a high volume of securities. Before 1988, the government usually had a budget surplus, and there were few issues of government bonds and treasury bills. Moreover, after 1983, sustained trade surpluses created a surge of liquidity in Taiwan's financial markets. What the CBC did was issue negotiable certificates of deposit and savings bonds in its own name, which allowed it to absorb excess funds.[7] Now, when bank excess reserves are high, promoting inflation, the CBC can issue certificates of deposit to reduce market liquidity; when reserves are low, conversely, it can purchase the securities it issued previously.

Rediscount and temporary accommodation facilities are a less effective policy instrument of the CBC. Changes in the discount rate do not have large impacts on banks' costs because the CBC rarely opens the discount window.[8] In most cases, then, the bank uses this instrument either to signal its intentions or in combination with open market operations.

The third policy instrument is change in the reserve requirements of banks. Because small changes in reserve requirements may cause a ripple effect on the money supply and market interest rates, the CBC has been reluctant to use this tool. It has adjusted reserve requirements only when high or low excess reserves are projected to continue for a long period.[9] When used at all, this policy instrument also has been accompanied by open market operations.

The fourth policy instrument is unusual in central banking systems. The CBC can accept or release deposits of banks or the postal savings system, which affects the amount of money in reserves. The postal savings system has the largest amount of depositors' funds in Taiwan. (Assets in 1996 were US $81.39 billion.) Much of the security of this system lies in the fact that it may not make loans to individuals or enterprises from the general public's deposits. The CBC retains most of the postal savings system deposits, which account for about half of the bank's reserve money.

The final policy instrument is selective credit controls. The CBC used these to curb asset price inflation in the late 1980s. The rise in asset prices resulted primarily from Taiwan's rapid accumulation of huge trade surpluses; it was manifested in soaring stock and real estate prices. To dampen this inflation, the CBC imposed credit controls on bank loans secured against vacant lots and on bank loans to investment companies.[10]

The CBC's adoption of these policy instruments, like that of most nations' central banks, is clouded in secrecy. When directors meet, they do so behind closed doors. Responding to criticism about the excessive confidentiality of bank operations, the governor has begun calling a press conference after board meetings. In 1997, the CBC

[7] "The Central Bank of China," 1997, 17-18; see also Fa-Chin Liang, "Monetary Policy in Taiwan," in Joel D. Aberbach, David Dollar, and Kenneth L. Sokoloff, eds., *The Role of the State in Taiwan's Development* (Armonk, NY: M. E. Sharpe, 1994), 233-236.

[8] "The Central Bank of China," 1997, 18.

[9] "The Central Bank of China," 1997, 19.

[10] "The Central Bank of China," 1997, 21.

announced that it would attempt to increase the visibility of its policy-making process by disclosing, at least in summary form, the contents of all board discussions.[11] These actions came in direct response to democratization pressures.

Private influences on the CBC take several forms. Private industry representatives sit on the board. The bank also sends out estimates on the current economic and financial situation to important businessmen.[12] Too, in Taiwan's relatively small economy, everyone in business and finance observes movement in commodity prices, interest rates, and in the value of the NT dollar. In this sense, CBC decision-making occurs with a keen eye to adverse popular reactions. Before he was appointed deputy governor of the CBC, Shea Jia-dong (then director of the Institute of Economics at the Academia Sinica) commented that CBC policies were "more influenced by the cabinet and legislators in the late 1980s. As a result, promoting economic and export growth supplanted financial stability as the CBC's primary goal."[13]

The CBC plays important roles in foreign exchange management. Formerly, Taiwan had a fixed exchange rate system. With the establishment of the Taipei foreign exchange market in 1979, the bank implemented a flexible exchange rate system but still intervened in the market often. Then, when it attempted gradually to appreciate the NT dollar to deal with burgeoning trade surpluses after 1985, which led to speculative capital inflows, the CBC relaxed most of its foreign exchange controls. It followed this action by releasing controls on remittance of capital abroad, initiating a process of financial liberalization that continues.[14]

The CBC also is responsible for managing Taiwan's huge balance of payments surpluses, which reached a peak of US $100.4 billion in mid-1995 and which exceeds Taiwan's annual need for foreign exchange to meet import payments. It invests most of the reserves in government bonds issued by major industrialized countries. The remainder it has used to develop a foreign currency call-loan market in Taiwan, aid local enterprises in overseas investments, mergers, and acquisitions, and offer financial aid to other governments.[15]

OUTCOMES

The CBC takes credit for playing a "leading and significant role in conducting a monetary policy that is aimed at maintaining price and financial stability as its first priority objective".[16] This credit-claiming is based on highly favorable statistics. From

---

[11] "The Central Bank of China," 1997, 11.

[12] Personal interview with Ty Lin, May 27, 1997.

[13] Jia-dong Shea, "Taiwan: Development and Structural Change of its Financial System," in Hugh T. Patrick and Yung Chul Park, *The Financial Development of Japan, Korea, and Taiwan* (London: Oxford University Press, 1994), 226.

[14] "The Central Bank of China," 1997, 25-27.

[15] "The Central Bank of China," 1997, 28-30.

[16] "The Central Bank of China," 1997, 14.

1960 to 1996, real GDP rose an average of 8.64 percent a year, while per capita GDP increased from US $143 to US $12,872. With the exception of the two global oil crises in the 1970s, consumer prices over this period rose an average of only 3.3 percent per year.

Equally notable is the effective use of monetary policy in dealing with systemic shocks. Following the first oil crisis in 1973, consumer prices rose by 47.5 percent in 1974. The CBC took several measures to absorb excess liquidity; most importantly, it sharply increased interest rates on deposits. Observers credit the aggressive CBC actions for the drop in the inflation rate to 5.2 percent in 1975.

After the second major oil crisis that began in 1979 and lasted into 1980, inflation shot up again to 13.8 and 21.5 percent respectively. Again, the CBC raised interest rates on deposits, which corralled inflation rates to their post-war average. (Since 1980, the CBC has used interest rate regulation infrequently, relying instead on open market operations and other instruments.)

A shock comparable to the oil crises resulted from cross-strait tensions in July-August 1995 and March 1996. These spurred huge capital outflows, a depreciation of the NT dollar, and a decline in stock and real estate prices in Taiwan. The CBC intervened authoritatively to stabilize the NT dollar exchange rate (using about US $20 billion of its foreign exchange reserves).[17]

The heavy selling of US dollars to shore up the value of the NT, however, tightened monetary conditions already complicated by runs on a few local financial institutions. The CBC then lowered required reserve ratios on deposits four times; it released postal savings re-deposits and conducted open market purchases of securities. It also bailed out several overdrawn local banks. These measures stabilized monetary conditions within three or four months.

The CBC's money supply regulation was one factor easing Taiwan's adjustment to the Asian financial crisis, beginning in mid-1997. Taiwan's system responded better than that of any other East or Southeast Asian state save China, and economic growth rates continued to be high.[18]

Most observers credit the CBC for very cautious decision-making. They fault it with trading efficiency in banking operations for stability, but they also acknowledge its effective role in confronting systemic shocks and crises.

FISCAL POLICY-MAKING

Fiscal policy refers to the development and adoption of national budgets, incorporating decisions on government spending over the fiscal year (with respect to amounts and categories), taxation policies to generate revenue, and whether the budget is

---

[17] Personal interview with Mao-hsi Chang, Director, Treasury Department, Central Bank of China, May 15, 1996.

[18] *Economist*, "Taiwan: In Praise of Paranoia," November 7, 1998; see also, Shirley W.Y. Kuo and Christina Y. Liu, "Taiwan," in Ross H. McLeod and Ross Garnaut, *East Asia in Crisis: From Being a Miracle to Needing One?* (London: Routledge, 1998), 179-88.

balanced, produces a surplus or results in a deficit. We review participants in Taiwan's fiscal policy-making, the process and the outcomes, emphasizing spending policy.

PARTICIPANTS IN FISCAL POLICY-MAKING

A host of agencies, interests, and individuals are involved in Taiwan's fiscal policy-making. In the Executive Yuan, a specialized office, the Directorate-General of Budget, Accounting, and Statistics, takes the lead in budget preparation. Each of the ministries, commissions, and agencies of the central government has an interest in its own budget for the next fiscal year. The cabinet deliberates on the budget and receives input from the KMT's central standing committee, which will often adopt a resolution pertaining to the budget.

The Legislative Yuan allocates more time to budget deliberations than to any other topic. The legislature's budget committee is most extensively involved, but the other nine substantive committees, each of which oversees executive branch ministries and commissions, also hold deliberations. Print and electronic media cover budget deliberations on the floor of the Legislative Yuan.

Political parties inspect budget allocations and tax proposals carefully, and the DPP has a dedicated budget office. Economic interests, in particular business associations, monitor the budget process. Labor organizations may be involved too.

THE BUDGET PROCESS

In general, the budget process in Taiwan is incremental, allocating a slightly higher budget for the next fiscal year than for the current one. Different processes occur in the two branches of government, but constitutional restrictions give the executive greater influence over the outcome than the legislature.

The Directorate-General of Budget, Accounts, and Statistics starts out the budget process nearly a year before the next fiscal year begins and administers it throughout. Its forecasting team prepares a two-year forecast of government expenditures, revenues, income growth, and prices. The finance ministry prepares its own revenue estimates, and the budget office consults with it before submitting the overall package to the Council for Economic Planning and Development. The CEPD arrives at its own estimates of the outcomes of different budget scenarios. The product of these consultations is the primary guide used by ministries and agencies in formulating their budget requests.[19]

The budget office then gathers agency budget requests and distributes them to subcommittees of the cabinet, each of which is chaired by a minister without portfolio, as one means to increase the impartiality of the process. Subcommittees may revise budget requests, and subcommittee chairs reconcile differences in preparing a final version of the executive budget for cabinet review. The constitution requires the executive to submit its budget to the Legislative Yuan by March 31, where the process takes a different turn.

The legislature holds one or two general budget sessions, attended by the director general of Budget, Accounts, and Statistics and the finance minister before sending the budget to committees. The Legislative Yuan has one budget committee, which gives the executive budget package the greatest scrutiny. The committee, however, has quite a small staff (eight in 1998) and little cumulative expertise. The budget committee is one of the more powerful legislative committees; it has a full complement of members (18) and a partisan distribution weighted toward the KMT (10 of 18), "escorting" it through the legislative process. Because the majority supports the Executive Yuan's request, the opposition parties figure more prominently and critically in budget deliberations in committee.[20] Most organized has been the DPP, which has a party budget center and a list of cuts it annually proposes in government expenditures.

Any member of the Legislative Yuan may attend the budget committee meetings. Usually, ministers and directors make budget presentations and answer questions at the committee stage. Only committee members, however, can vote on whether to advance the budget to a second reading. During this time period, each of the other committees reviews budgets for agencies it oversees.

The constitution requires the Legislative Yuan to act on the budget by the 31st of May, the last day of the year's first session. The legislature rarely finishes its work before the end of May. When the budget reaches the floor, legislators who have filed budget amendments in committee may speak to them. This process occupies the legislature for two to three weeks and is widely attended. In 1996, because of the political situation concerning Premier Lien Chan, the legislature did not finish the budget for national enterprises on time. (Effectively, this is a second executive budget request, which is to be enacted by the end of June.)

The constitution also limits the legislature's fiscal powers as compared to the executive. The legislature may not increase the budget over the executive request. It can accept the executive's budget, reduce it in total, or reject it; it lacks the authority to make increases in preferred areas at the cost of those whose functions or performance it dislikes. An additional constitutional limitation on budgeting is the requirement that at least 15 percent of expenditures be allocated to education, science, and cultural programs. However, this constitutional restriction is observed infrequently; in the 1997 constitutional revisions, it was eliminated, much to the dismay of Taiwan's educators.

The budget process in the executive is more interactive and involves a wider range of interests than is evident in monetary policy. The Legislative Yuan provides even more opportunities for participation of partisan, ideological, and economic interests.

---

[19] See Chih-heng Yang, *The Structure of Fiscal Policy* (in Chinese) (Taipei: Institute for National Policy Research, 1991), 115-21; and Wade, 1990, 210.

[20] Personal interview with Yaw-hsing Lin, chair, Legislative Yuan budget committee, May 23, 1997.

BUDGET OUTCOMES

Over the period of democratization, Taiwan's fiscal policy has changed significantly in four ways: the composition of spending, increased expenditures over revenues, sources of revenue, and growth in size of the government.[21]

Table 1 compares expenditure categories in the central government budget over the ten-year period, FY 1985 through FY 1994:

Table 1. Changing Composition of Spending, FY 85-94

Expenditure Category	FY 1985	FY 1994
National Defense	38.2 percent	23.7 percent
General Administration	7.1 percent	9.2 percent
Education, Science, and Culture	11.5 percent	15.5 percent
Economic Development	18.5 percent	16.8 percent
Social Security	16.7 percent	20.9 percent
Debt Servicing	4.5 percent	10.4 percent
Other Expenditures	3.8 percent	3.6 percent

Source: Taxation and Tariff Commission, Ministry of Finance, *Government Finance of the Republic of China* (Taipei: 1995), 14.

Defense spending shows the greatest change over the ten-year period, declining from 38 to 24 percent of the budget. (The most precipitous decline in defense spending occurred earlier. In the 1950s and early 1960s, defense consumed about 75 percent of total central government expenditures, a far higher ratio than for any other country in Asia.) Defense spending increased by about 5 percent in the FY 97 budget, to respond to Chinese military exercises off Taiwan in late 1995 and early 1996. In the FY 1998 budget, the cabinet proposed a 3 percent increase (a smaller rate than for other budget categories; as a percentage of the total budget, defense slipped from 21.1 percent to 20.9 percent), primarily to purchase French and American warplanes to counter modernization of China's air force. The opposition DPP, which customarily seeks to cut the defense budget (but supported it after military exercises in 1996), found support to pare this request by US $140 million.

Economic development generally has been a stable expenditure. This includes public construction activity, which, under the six-year infrastructure development plan, expanded greatly and, along with social welfare spending, is a primary means of economic stabilization. Legislators find it hard to control the construction budget. Although estimates as to its size range to 30 percent of the overall budget, capital goods

---

[21] See Directorate-General of Budget, Accounts, and Statistics, "A Brief Introduction to the Central Government's Budget Act," and "Outline of the Fiscal Year 1998 Central Government Budget." (in Chinese) (Taipei: Executive Yuan, 1997).

spending is distributed throughout many budget categories.[22] Critics blame the growing size of the public construction budget for Taiwan's recent increase in corruption; both the size of projects and their management—from primary to secondary and to tertiary contractors—provide ample opportunities for kickbacks, payoffs, and waste.

An area of steady increase in expenditures is social security, which includes social insurance, social assistance, welfare services, national employment spending, housing and community expenditures, medical health, and also environmental protection spending.[23] In 1995, the legislature adopted a comprehensive national health insurance program accounting for more than 50 percent of the total social welfare budget. At a total cost of US $10 billion annually, the program extends benefits to the elderly, children, students, and housewives. Still, however, Taiwan's spending on social welfare is lower than most other industrialized nations but is likely to increase significantly, as the government plans to become the first Asian NIC to provide unemployment insurance.[24]

The third area of change is in debt servicing, which now takes one in ten dollars of government revenues. Until 1989 (FY 1990), Taiwan's budget typically registered a surplus every year. Since that time, there have been annual deficits. The largest increase came in FY 1992-94, as the government issued bonds to finance the Six-Year National Construction Program. The ratio of government debt to GDP jumped to 16.4 percent, but it has declined since then; in the most recent, FY 1998, budget, the deficit declined by 40 percent from the previous year, with the expectation of attaining balanced books by the year 2001.

Taiwan's external public debt is quite small relative to that of other industrial countries. The debt service ratio (the ratio of annual debt repayment to export earnings) is the generally accepted standard used by most countries to measure the repayment capability of the debtor country; a ratio below 20 percent is generally considered acceptable. Measured by this statistic, Taiwan fares well. Taiwan's debt service ratio has never exceeded 5 percent, and over the period from FY 1988 through FY 1994, it was less than 1 percent.[25]

The final area of change is in the size of government, which has increased greatly. In 1995, government expenditures consumed 31.5 percent of total GDP, which compared to an average of 23.1 percent in the 1970s. Moreover, a critical CEPD report in 1996 noted that the bureaucracy needed to be trimmed: salaries of government personnel took up 10 percent of GDP, about the same percentage as in Western developed nations but 4 percent higher than in Japan, Singapore, and Korea.[26] Given a high population density and relative ease of delivering services, the report concluded that a smaller government work force would allow cost reductions.

---

[22] Personal interview with Tien-tsai Hsu, independent legislator, May 21, 1997.

[23] Taxation and Tariff Commission, *Government Finance of the Republic of China* (Taipei: Ministry of Finance, 1995), 14.

[24] Peter Ching-yung Lee, "Social Welfare of Hong Kong, Singapore, and Taiwan," *American Journal of Chinese Studies*, vol. 3, no. 2 (October 1996), 229.

[25] Taxation and Tariff Commission, 1995, 18.

[26] *United Daily News*, June 29, 1996.

The sources of government revenue also have changed over the period of democratization. Economic liberalization—dropping tariff rates, reducing commodity taxes, and privatizing SOEs—has reduced customs duties and monopoly revenue as a share of revenue. Correspondingly, the shares of land tax,[27] value-added tax, and income tax have increased. The land tax is the most progressive of the three; overall, however, analysts do not find that the changing mix of government revenue has had much of an effect, either positive or negative, on income distribution.[28]

As the government plays a larger role in the economy through its expenditures, taxes have increased, but at a ratio corresponding to the rate of increase in state spending. Taiwan's tax burden (ratio of total tax revenues to GDP) remains among the lowest of the industrialized countries of the world. Its tax burden in 1992 was 19.1 percent. This compared to rates of 19.4 percent in Korea, 28.7 percent in the United States, 30.1 percent in Japan, 33.7 percent in Britain, 41.3 percent in Germany, and 42.4 percent in France.[29]

The Legislative Yuan plays a larger role in fiscal than in monetary policy, but it still operates at the margins. Although it focuses public attention on the budget, it does not change the bottom line more than 2 to 3 percent at most. Development of opposition to the government within this branch has led to heated criticism of defense spending and long-winded harangues on government waste, official corruption, and inefficiency. Opposition forces have increased the government's receptivity to spending more money on social welfare and to spurring economic recoveries. Nevertheless, even during the period of its weakest influence in the Legislative Yuan, the KMT was able to round up a majority in 1997 that supported all but $654 million of the Executive Yuan's US $46 billion budget request.

REGULATORY POLICY-MAKING

Monetary and fiscal policies can have either distributive or redistributive impacts. Distributive policies such as the government's provision of a public education system benefit everyone potentially. Policies that redistribute, however, rob Peter to pay Paul; they deliver benefits to certain groups or interests at the expense of others. For example, the development of the national health insurance system benefited lower income groups primarily and cost employers, who opposed it. Similarly, unabated inflationary price

---

[27] The land tax includes a land value tax (for property with assessed value, whether commercial, industrial, or residential), an agricultural land tax levied on farm land, and a land value increment tax levied on gains realized from the sale of land. See Taxation and Tariff Commission, *Guide to ROC Taxes 1995* (Taipei: Ministry of Finance, 1995), 104-120, for a description of the modernization of this traditional Chinese tax.

[28] Chi-wei Tseng and Wei-lin Mao, "Fiscal Policy and Economic Development in Taiwan," in Aberbach, Dollar, and Sokoloff, 1994, 269.

[29] Taxation and Tariff Commission, 1995, 32.

changes benefit asset holders at the expense of those on fixed incomes. In general terms, however, Taiwan's fiscal and monetary policies largely have had distributive effects.

Regulatory policies place controls, limitations, or restrictions on areas of economic and social life. They have a different nature from distributive and redistributive policies.

PARTICIPANTS IN REGULATORY POLICY-MAKING

The primary actors in regulatory policy-making are ministries and agencies of the Executive Yuan. Regulations are unlike laws in that they do not require the assent of the Legislative Yuan. Non-controversial regulations may be developed primarily by one department, bureau, or ministry. For regulations influencing more than one administrative unit, cabinet ministers or commissioners are involved, along with the secretariat of the Executive Yuan.

Economic and political liberalization, which require changes in laws, have opened this policy-making sphere to the Legislative Yuan and to scores of interest groups and associations.

CHARACTERISTICS OF REGULATORY POLITICS

Because government regulations curb freedom, it is not simple to put them into effect in a democratic society. The politics of the regulatory process are influenced by who wins and who loses from the effect of regulations and by whether the costs and benefits are broadly dispersed or narrowly concentrated.[30] The nature of the regulatory issue structures the opportunities for groups and mass publics to organize; it must be kept in mind when considering policy-making in Taiwan's democratic era.

James Q. Wilson distinguishes between four types of regulatory policy: majoritarian, interest group, client, and entrepreneurial. Majoritarian policies are those from which all benefit a little and all pay a little of the cost. One example is highway safety standards. There is no large incentive for any group to organize in support of such policies, and for them to be enacted, appeals need to be made to the broad majority.

Interest group politics, however, pit the economic interests of one group against those of another. Both costs and benefits are concentrated but accrue to different parties. Collective bargaining regulations are an example of interest group politics. Client politics also benefit one small group, but in their case everyone pays some of the cost, as in agricultural subsidies. Finally, entrepreneurial politics refer to issues where everyone would benefit a little (broad dispersion of benefits), but one group would pay most of the costs. To organize a majority supporting this legislation (an example of which is pollution control) often requires a political entrepreneur to overwhelm pitched opposition from business interests.

Although studies of the Legislative Yuan in Taiwan are in their infancy, we are fortunate to have one good study of the impact of economic interests in the regulatory process. This is our base for reviewing economic and social regulatory policy-making and de-regulation.

ECONOMIC REGULATION

During the first two decades of its rule on Taiwan, the KMT enacted controls over all areas of the economy. In addition to regulatory policies, however, the regime also owned vital economic interests outright. Possession of railroads, other transportation linkages, and the telephone, telegraph, and postal service gave the regime the ability to monitor the population's movements. Control over the banking and financial sector allowed the government to stabilize economic fluctuations, particularly inflation, capture scarce foreign exchange, and direct economic growth. Control over food processing, textile production, and trading in rice, salt, and oil completed the regime's monopoly over the basic necessities of life.

Typically, economic regulation involves either interest group politics or client politics. Hwang Shiow-duan describes one recent case concerning the land law that shows this process at work.[31] A section of the land law was revised in 1989 to require an occupational licensing examination for real estate agents; those without licenses had a transitional period of five years to attain one. At the expiration of the grace period, thousands of agents had not obtained licenses, and they petitioned the Legislative Yuan to loosen restrictions in the law. Those agents with licenses, however, objected, and they petitioned the legislature, too.

A joint meeting of the legislature's interior and judiciary committees evaluated the proposal and invited the rival groups to send representatives. A greater number of representatives of the unlicensed agents (who were more numerous than the licensed ones) attended the committee meetings; they lobbied furiously because they stood to lose their jobs if the restrictions were not relaxed. The licensed agents had fewer arguments on their side, as they would lose nothing if criteria were loosened.

Hwang reports that most legislators attending the meetings supported the unlicensed agents. Political parties took no stand because the issue had neither broad political nor ideological impacts, and legislators were on their own. They sided with the largest, noisiest, most intensely committed group.

Most of the public was unaware of this issue concerning the licensing of real estate agents, and they had at the best a marginal interest in it. This is typical of most interest group and client politics cases as well as of much economic regulatory policy-making.

---

[30] James Q. Wilson, "The Politics of Regulation," in James Q. Wilson, ed., *The Politics of Regulation* (New York: Basic Books, 1980), 357-394.

[31] Shiow-duan Hwang, "Interest Groups and Legislative Politics" (Paper presented at the International Conference on Political Development in Taiwan and Hong Kong, Center of Asian Studies, University of Hong Kong, February 8, 1996), 11-12.

Lobbying legislators (and bureaucrats) is critical to the favorable resolution of such issues; the economic interests of policy-makers themselves also bear strongly on the outcomes.

SOCIAL REGULATION

Attempts to correct social problems such as environmental pollution became national issues in Western states during the 1960s and 1970s. They changed the politics of these societies because the issues cut across the liberal/conservative fault lines of democratic party systems. Also, they brought new groups of people into politics who focused on single issues to the exclusion of traditional bread-and-butter concerns. Social regulation does have a substantial economic cost, and for that reason we consider it here.

Although deterioration in Taiwan's environment was clearly visible in the 1960s, an environmental protection movement did not form until the 1980s. The absence of opposition in the national legislature and strong KMT party control were major elements in retarding its development;[32] the Environmental Protection Agency (EPA) was not established until 1987.

The EPA drafted an environmental impact evaluation law and submitted it to the legislature in 1990. The proposed law would require public and private agencies to conduct environmental impact evaluations before construction of plants, housing, or golf courses. The issue was one of entrepreneurial politics, for everyone benefits marginally from evaluation of such impacts; however, it would cost businesses to conduct the evaluations, and possibly, developments would be delayed or canceled.

It took 15 months for the proposed law to reach the joint reviewing stage by three committees (interior, economics, and judiciary), which may indicate stalling by business-affiliated interests in the legislature. At committee review, only one business group representative, the Rebar conglomerate's Wang Ling-lin, opposed the proposal because it might retard economic development. Legislators in support of environmental protection dominated the process, and it quickly passed through the committee.[33] Once reaching the floor, however, it took nearly three years to complete the last two readings, again suggesting that the leadership opposed the legislation. They could not thwart an issue with broad popular appeal, but they could delay it.

Another entrepreneurial politics issue, that of opposition to expansion of nuclear power plants, reveals the tortured pace of some social legislation. Taiwan's fourth nuclear power project has been on the drawing board for over 15 years. Business leaders complain incessantly about the lack of sufficient power, and Taipower has sought the added capacity. Opposition to nuclear power plants developed in Taiwan after the TMI

---

[32] For a review of the movement in the 1980s, see Jack F. Williams and Ch'ang-yi Chang, "Paying the Price of Economic Development in Taiwan: Environmental Degradation," in Murray A. Rubinstein, ed., *The Other Taiwan: 1945 to the Present* (Armonk, NY: M. E. Sharpe, 1994), 237-56.

[33] Hwang, 1996, 15-16.

and Chernobyl meltdowns raised safety concerns. Also, Taiwan lacks adequate toxic waste disposal sites (prompting the government to negotiate with North Korea in 1997 for disposal of Taiwan's waste there). When the Executive Yuan requested budget approval for construction of the fourth project in 1996, the legislature responded to energetic anti-nuclear power protests by overturning the request. That same day, however, General Electric won the US $1.8 billion contract for the plant's two reactors. With this *fait accompli*, KMT leaders were able to assemble sufficient votes to revive the project.

In the area of environmental protection, a high visibility issue with majority support may overcome the opposition of development interests. The nuclear power plant protest shows that when those interests are supported by the executive, development can be delayed but not easily denied.

DE-REGULATION AND ECONOMIC LIBERALIZATION

Economic liberalization became popular in Taiwan from the mid- to late 1980s, continuing through the 1990s, and de-regulation of the economy has been a prominent topic. Some cases of de-regulation express majoritarian politics; most, however, represent interest group and client group politics. For example, major loosening of government controls on banking and finance pit established banking interests against newer interests such as credit unions, a clear illustration of interest group politics.

A number of de-regulation decisions were made by state technocrats who acted in anticipation of foreign pressures on Taiwan to liberalize its services sector. For example, financial capitalists who stood to benefit from liberalization of banking laws in 1989 did not press the government to revise the laws. The critical decisions were made by technocrats and government bureaucrats who shared a neo-classical economics perspective and an institutional relationship (through the economics department of National Taiwan University). Yet the design of banking law de-regulation—the requirement that new banks have assets of more than US $370.3 million—raised an insuperable market barrier for SMEs.[34]

A case of client politics is a recent statute encouraging private participation in transportation infrastructure projects. The issue arose in 1993 when the Executive Yuan froze construction of the high-speed railway through Taipei because of alarming budget deficits. The executive then requested legal authority from the Legislative Yuan to allow private participation so the project could proceed. It quickly drafted legislation and urged the legislature to adopt it.

Interests that would benefit from the new legal authority were the construction industry, those who had speculated on land near the railway line (large businesses), and local factions operating in areas adjacent to the line. These interests were able to compose

---

[34] Jenn-hwan Wang and Zong-rong Lee, "The State and Financial Capital: The Transformation of Taiwan's Banking Policy" (Paper presented at the American Sociological Association Conference, Miami Beach, FL, August 13, 1993).

a legislative coalition through log-rolling. Of the KMT members of the joint committee of transportation, interior, finance, and economics who participated in deliberations, most represented districts near the railway, were involved in construction-related enterprises, or were supported by local factions. They backed the legislation, which also bore the imprimatur of party support. Fewer DPP legislators had financial interests in the issue or represented districts near future railway stops. The DPP opposed the KMT on the issue, and it blamed the executive for a rushed process that produced bad legislation.[35] In this case, the clients were interconnected with the ruling party, with support in both the executive and legislature, and the legislation passed quickly.

Client politics also has figured prominently in the several cases of privatization over the 1990s. For example, communications workers employed in the Directorate-General of Telecommunications (DGT) vehemently protested the privatization of this government ministry, which occurred despite their protests in 1996. All other major privatization cases have brought about the organization and mobilization of opposing employee groups.[36]

The ability to discuss client and interest group politics in the context of Taiwan's regulatory regimes is the clearest indicator of democratic changes. Before the onset of democratization in 1986, the kinds of mobilization discussed above would not have been possible.

INDUSTRIAL POLICY-MAKING

Industrial policy refers to the use of state authority and power to guide the market. As Robert Wade explains it, the state promotes high levels of productive investment and assists in the transfer of new technologies to production; the state guides investment into areas that could not be developed without government sponsorship; and the state pushes industries into international competition.[37] Industrial policy's objective is to help industries grow faster or decline less disruptively "by affecting production and investment decisions of decentralized producers."[38] States with strong industrial policies are also corporate states; those without industrial policies are *laissez-faire*.

We review the participants in industrial policy-making in Taiwan, and then consider policy instruments and processes and policy outcomes.

---

[35] Hwang, 1996, 13-14.

[36] For a discussion of the politics of privatization in Taiwan, see the author's, "Taiwan Privatizes by Fits and Starts," *Asian Survey* (December 1997).

[37] Wade, 1990, 233.

[38] Johnson, 1982, 18.

PARTICIPANTS

Two agencies of the Executive Yuan play major roles in the formation and implementation of industrial policy. These are the Industrial Development Bureau (IDB) within MOEA and CEPD. The Legislative Yuan directs attention to industrial policy primarily through the budget process, as discussed above.

Unlike fiscal and monetary policy-making, industrial policy directly involves the business sector in Taiwan. Individual business persons, particularly significant capitalists such as Taiwan plastics king Wang Yung-ching, may be involved in national industrial policy decisions. Individual firms or corporations, and particularly conglomerates, usually figure in sectoral policies. Finally, business associations (industrial associations and chambers of commerce) and peak associations (such as the Chinese National Federation of Industries, the Chinese National Association of Industry and Commerce, and the General Chamber of Commerce, ROC) may participate actively in the formation and implementation of policies, and this involvement has grown over the period of democratization.[39]

POLICY INSTRUMENTS AND PROCESSES

The policy-making process in Taiwan's industrial development involves both large and small vehicles of change, both macroeconomic and sectoral economic policies. At the macroeconomic level, during the postwar period, Taiwan has undergone three primary and two adjustment phases of economic change. The state initiated and guided agricultural modernization in the 1950s. The government's land reform program was a clear attempt to reverse its failure to improve equality of land distribution while on the mainland. In Taiwan, opponents of land reform, the landlord establishment, were also potential opponents of KMT power. Land reform succeeded economically, giving incentives to the new owner-cultivators to increase agricultural production. It also succeeded politically, by removing the landed base of traditional local elites and creating a new class of cultivators whose increasing prosperity reminded them of their debt to the KMT. Agricultural modernization was primarily directed by the state; over time, it promised to increase the autonomy of farmers, but this was not obvious until the 1980s. Too, the government depended on the United States for the successful implementation of agricultural modernization.

The second stage of economic development was the policy of import substitution industrialization (ISI) in the 1950s. Although the state fell into this policy without conscious reflection of elites, the state directed implementation. State-owned enterprises (SOEs) were both agents and beneficiaries of ISI. The extensive pattern of controls during this period enhanced state power and seriously inhibited the private sector. In fact,

---

[39] For a more thorough discussion of business associations and their role in economic policy-making, see Gerald A. McBeath, "The Changing Role of Business Associations in Democratizing Taiwan," *Journal of Contemporary China,* Vol. 7, no. 4 (July 1998), 303-20.

the ISI period was one of the most intensely regulated eras in modern Taiwan history. The ISI strategy did not serve American economic interests in that US non-durable consumer goods exported to Taiwan declined; nevertheless, ISI launched Taiwan's industrialization, which was in the political and international interests of the United States. American economic and military aid to Taiwan played a critical role in economic stability and industrial development during this period, and the term "client state" can be used appropriately to describe it.

The third stage of Taiwan's economic development, export-oriented industrialization (EOI), launched a decade of double-digit growth, and is best explained through market forces. Small and medium enterprises (SMEs) aggressively expanded abroad, finding niches in the global marketplace because of labor-intensive production, and they fueled most of the surge of growth. Taiwan's linkage to the United States remained an important element, too, for American advisors urged Taiwan to liberalize, and the United States provided a very large market for Taiwan's goods. However, the state's influence over the process of export-led industrialization was unmistakable. Central policy-makers decided to liberalize by removing exchange and import controls. Government agencies created opportunities for the private sector and stimulated growth in export sectors. The term "developmental state" seems most appropriate for this stage in Taiwan's modern economic history.

The first structural adjustment of the 1970s and early 1980s in response to oil shocks, political shocks, and leadership succession showed the strong hand of the state again. State-owned enterprises were perhaps as vital to the economy in the mid-1970s as they had been in the early 1950s. Government spending on infrastructure projects and government support of industrial upgrading facilitated business expansion. The second structural adjustment of the late 1980s, continuing on through the present, continued this pattern. The causes of the second readjustment were different from the first. The new challenges included sharp appreciation of the NT dollar, wage increases, labor shortages, demands for environmental protection, and strong competition from other Asian NICs. Production facilities of SMEs moved offshore in search of lower cost labor and plant sites. In response, the focus of industrial policy has been to raise the level of technology of Taiwan's industries and to accelerate the development of new industries with higher value-added bases.

Decision-making on macroeconomic policy issues was highly centralized throughout this period. Although the MOEA and MOF frequently floated ideas, proposals, and plans, it was the central standing committee of the KMT that presided over the policy process, which was implemented by the cabinet and government ministries.

Sectoral policy-making shows more clearly the impact of the economic bureaucracy and also of the business sector. The two lead bureaucratic agencies are the IDB and CEPD, sometimes assisted by the cabinet secretariat. The secretariat staffs meetings of the cabinet. Its primary responsibility, however, is to coordinate the development of proposed laws and regulations for the Executive Yuan. The secretariat is divided into seven divisions, each of which works with a group of cognate ministries and commissions. For example, the fifth division covers MOEA, CEPD, the Council of Agriculture, and the Fair Trade Commission. Its director was placed in charge of developing responses to the outbreak of hoof-and-mouth disease in Taiwan's pig population in February 1997. She formed a task force of affected agencies to resolve such issues as environmental concerns over disposal of pig carcasses, thus restoring confidence in the industry and protecting pork prices.[40] When there is conflict between ministries, such as among MOEA, Interior, and EPA over the pace, cost, and environmental responsiveness of public construction projects, directors of divisions within the secretariat negotiate compromises for the cabinet to approve.

The CEPD is responsible for coordinating national economic planning and for setting economic priorities and targets. It conducts economic research and supervises major construction projects. In 1997, CEPD was in charge of some of the most important tasks of government administration in Taiwan: plans for the Asia-Pacific Regional Operations Center (APROC), legal revisions necessary for privatizing most remaining state-owned enterprises, and revisions to the national pension system.

The CEPD uses a planning process that is both bottom-up and top-down. It collects information from enterprise areas, groups, and industries, determining their needs. Then CEPD staff consolidate recommendations and prepare independent reports to the Executive Yuan, which are implemented by other agencies, such as the IDB. The more typical planning process used by the CEPD, however, is top-down; this is common in areas such as foreign trade where the government determines the policy direction. In such areas, the CEPD retains consulting companies to survey international trends. Some planning officials claim to make monthly visits to factories when developing overall economic policies, but such visits are in fact infrequent.[41]

Describing the changes in the operations of the CEPD since democratization, the director of the sectoral planning department commented: "Our method was more top-down in the past, for example the Ten Major Projects of the 1970s. Now, we are more democratic and our methods, both in politics and economics, are more bottom-up than before."[42] From the viewpoint of other parts of the economic bureaucracy, however, the CEPD in the present as well as in the past has been an hierarchical agency.

The IDB, on the other hand, operates in a bottom-up fashion, and it is both a planning and implementing agency. Established in 1970, the IDB is composed of seven divisions. The first four divisions focus on sectors of Taiwan's economy.[43] The fifth division

---

[40] Personal interview with Ho Mei-yueh, Director, Fifth Division, Secretariat, Executive Yuan, May 30, 1997.

[41] Of the 123 presidents, secretaries general, or other officers of industrial associations whom the author interviewed in his study of business associations, only four reported contacts with the CEPD. About half had been in touch with the IDB, however.

[42] Personal interview with Frank C. Hu, Director, Sectoral Planning Department, CEPD, April 6, 1996.

[43] Division I covers basic metals, the mechanical and transportation industries. Division II includes electrical and electronic engineering industries, instruments and industrial automation, and information and telecommunications. Division III includes petrochemical, special and general chemical industries. Division IV, the most diverse, covers textiles, food industry, consumer products and construction materials. For a breakdown of IDB responsibilities, see *Development of Industries in Taiwan, Republic of China* (Taipei: IDB, MOEA, 1995).

specializes in industrial land planning and development. The sixth division consolidates work of other divisions in the formation and implementation of Taiwan's industrial policies. The remaining, seventh, division supervises industrial associations and provides assistance in development of industrial and environmental security plans.

The general planning process of the IDB involves four elements: data collection, agency coordination, consultation with business groups and notification, and development of policy instruments to implement the plans. Each of these elements potentially involves individual firms, industrial associations, and peak associations.

The IDB uses four sources of information in the development of its plans. Bureaucrats will visit factories to develop an understanding of changes in a particular industry or send questionnaires to factories, and they will read trade publications, including annual reports of global corporations, such as Japanese companies. Second, the IDB requests information from industrial associations, which are important "bridges" to the individual factories and firms. However, Taiwan's industrial associations are uneven with respect to their capabilities and representativeness, and in the opinion of most of the two dozen IDB officials interviewed by the author in 1996 and 1997, they cannot be relied on for accurate industry-wide data.

The third and most reliable source of information for industrial planning purposes is government research institutes. The National Science Council funds academic research, some of which is directly relevant to industrial production, such as through the Science and Technology Information Center and the Center for High-performance Computing. In 1996, the MOEA allocated nearly one-half billion dollars to public and private non-profit research institutes for industrial applied research. Most funding went to the Industrial Technology Research Institute, with smaller amounts going to the Chungshan Institute of Science and Technology and the Institute for Information Industry.[44] It is from these research institutes that the IDB develops its estimates on emphases to develop. Finally, the IDB does make use of Taiwan's two largest economics research institutes, the Chung-Hua Institution for Economic Research and the Taiwan Institute of Economic Research.

The second element concerns sector-specific recommendations and five-year objectives for growth and change, produced by the first through the fourth divisions. Some of the divisions use product task forces in the development of plans. For example, in the second division there is a task force in electronics that brings together IDB, CEPD and other technocrats, scholars, representatives from research institutes and even companies and industrial associations. The IDB staff in electronics presents drafts to the task force, and based on their reactions will revise the plan.[45]

Once these plans are complete at the division level, the sixth division integrates them into an overall plan. It prepares a unified final report, in which it also considers the policy instruments needed to accomplish objectives—laws, incentives, and land acquisition

---

[44] *The Republic of China Yearbook 1997* (Taipei: Government Information Office, 1997), 312.

[45] Personal interview with Jong-chin Chen, Senior Engineer and Section Chief, IDB, MOEA, April 27, 1996.

issues (discussed in the fourth element below). IDB's final report is then reviewed by CEPD staff, who present another angle and may adjust the industrial plan slightly.[46]

The third element involves extensive consultation between IDB bureaucrats and the industrial sector. When developing the sectoral plans, attempts are made to present planning objectives that comprehend the entire industry, which may be difficult when there is tense intra-industry competition. Said the director of the first division, "We want a plan for all factories (producing automobiles). If all the factories are opposed to our plan, then the plan is wrong. We go for the majority . . . . (T)he business is in their hands."[47]

While IDB officials work with individual factories, many of which have questions or problems about the policy instruments used to advance industrial objectives, most of their consultations are with industrial associations. We indicated above that some industrial associations may be involved in task forces or other coordinating groups, working on specific industrial target areas. Industrial associations are also primary audiences for the first- and second-drafts of planning recommendations. The IDB holds meetings to explain plan developments and targets, and invites secretaries general and presidents of industrial associations to attend. It uses lists of members of industrial associations, and notifies factories directly. Describing the general tenor of the bureau's relationships with industrial associations, a senior engineer commented:

> The *Kung-hui* (industrial associations) are a bridge, and there should be a relationship of equals with them. We want to listen to their voice, as now we have an open society. We respect their voice, but some of the suggestions they propose we cannot accept. If we accepted all of their proposals, you could say that we are on an equal footing with them. But we have to look at whether their proposals are good for the industry as a whole, and not just for individual sectors of it.[48]

The final element of IDB planning involves the development of policy instruments, which occurs throughout the planning process and also involves extensive consultation with industrial associations and individual factories. In addition to recommending changes in legislation that would facilitate industrial growth, IDB manages nearly a dozen separate incentives. Incentives for automation include tax credits for the purchase of automated production technology and low-interest loans. Research and development (R&D) incentives include income tax credits, accelerated depreciation, matching grants, and professional consultation assistance. Incentives for purchasing new equipment include exemption from import duties. Personnel training is assisted with income tax credits. Income tax credits are also available for firms establishing international brands in Taiwan and those investing in "important" technology-based enterprises. Tax credits and low-interest loans are available for factories purchasing locally-produced environmental

---

[46] Personal interview with Chih-peng Huang, Director, 6th Division, IDB, MOEA, April 25, 1996.

[47] Personal interview with Cai-Bi Liang, Director, 1st Division, IDB, MOEA, March 28, 1996.

[48] Personal interview with Ming-ji Wu, Senior Engineer, IDB, MOEA, May 13, 1996.

protection equipment, for factories making expenditures on energy conservation technology, and for recycling operations. Finally, companies that merge to rationalize operations are entitled to exemptions from stamp and deed taxes.[49]

POLICY OUTCOMES

The outcomes of industrial policy are plans that emphasize specific sectors of the economy for development. For instance, in the 1990s, the government's growth strategy is posited on development of ten "emerging industries": communications, information, consumer electronics, semiconductors, precision machinery and automation, aerospace, advanced materials, specialty chemicals and pharmaceuticals, medical and health care, and pollution control and treatment. These industries were selected based on their significant market potential, linkage with other industries, high added value, and advanced technological level. Additionally, growth in them was regarded as particularly desirable because of their generally low-levels of pollution and limited dependence on energy supplies.[50]

The success or failure of Taiwan's industrial policy-making usually is determined by a comparison to its Confucian rivals in East Asia: Hong Kong, Singapore, Japan, and Korea. The state in Taiwan has been far more activist or interventionist than that in Hong Kong but less so than in Japan and Korea. This leads some critics to suggest that Taiwan has not been a corporate[51] state, and it lacks an industrial policy. For example, Kuo Cheng-tian argues that the state lacked autonomy from influential business interests and associations; that it could not direct the economy because it was insufficiently centralized and had a weak bureaucracy and planning agencies; and that leaders were more committed to military and political than economic development.[52] Gary Hamilton and Nicole Biggart acknowledge that Taiwan has a state planning system but believe the

---

[49] See *Guidelines for Investment Assistance and Factory Establishment Administration Measures for Manufacturing and Technical Service Industries* (in Chinese) (Taipei: Industrial Development Bureau, MOEA, 1995), 5-34.

[50] See *Strategies and Measures for the Development of the Top Ten Emerging Industries* (Taipei: Industrial Development Bureau, MOEA, 1994), 5-63.

[51] Corporatism is probably the most popular interpretation of Taiwan's development in the scholarly literature. Proponents of this approach picture the state as strong enough to formulate economic policy without becoming captive to rent-seeking groups. The state is actively involved in the market, able to influence the use of both public and private resources in accordance with a vision of how the industrial structure of the country should be evolving. The corporatist perspective does not ignore the development of new social forces but denies them autonomy. Although some industries may have led the state on occasion, overall, proponents of the strong state thesis argue, the government led the market and some industries at least some of the time. Identified with the corporatist perspective in studies of modern Taiwan's political economy are Robert Wade, Chalmers Johnson, Yun-han Chu, Alice Amsden, and Thomas Gold.

[52] Cheng-tian Kuo, *Global Competitiveness and Industrial Growth in Taiwan and the Philippines* (Pittsburgh, PA: University of Pittsburgh Press, 1995), 59.

government lacks an implementation procedure.[53] Gary Gereffi points to the potential that Taiwan had for economic direction through SOEs but remarks that ethnic cleavage made it difficult for the state to rely on unqualified support from the subordinate capitalist class to compete with the large, vertically integrated Japanese and South Korean conglomerates and general trading companies.[54]

Wade disagrees with these formulations of the state's role in the economy and finds that the state has been activist (through its SOEs and also through state research organizations, especially in new, high-technology sectors). Because of ethnic cleavage between mainlander bureaucrats, SOE managers and the Taiwanese business community, and also because of the absence of huge conglomerates like those in Japan and Korea, the state pressured the private sector indirectly, through import controls, domestic content requirements, entry restrictions, and tax incentives.[55] Throughout, actions of the government met defining tests of market guidance by:

> 1) redistributing agricultural land in the early postwar period; 2) controlling the financial system and making private financial capital subordinate to industrial capital; 3) maintaining stability in some of the main economic parameters that affect the viability of long-term investment, especially the exchange rate, the interests rate, and the general price level; 4) modulating the impact of foreign competition in the domestic economy and prioritizing the use of scarce foreign exchange; 5) promoting exports; 6) promoting technology acquisition from multinational companies and building a national technology system; and 7) assisting particular industries.[56]

However, Wade's argument does not test well in certain sectors, such as the automobile industry. In his comparison of Korea and Taiwan, Chu Yun-han finds that Korean economic officials created policy instruments and plans that affected the entire auto industry. In contrast, Taiwan's officials had much less influence on private firms because the state apparatus was poorly coordinated and lacked direct policy instruments and effective relationships with the private sector. He summarizes by noting that "the

---

[53] Gary C. Hamilton and Nicole Woolsey Biggart, "Market, Culture, and Authority," *American Journal of Sociology*, vol. 94 (1988), 52-94.

[54] Gary Gereffi, "Big Business and the State," in Gary Gereffi and Donald L. Wyman, *Manufacturing Miracles: Paths of Industrialization in Latin America and East Asia* (Princeton, NJ: Princeton University Press, 1990), 98. Suk-jun Lim adopts a different slant by analyzing the historically specific way that Korean leaders approached their problems of legitimacy as compared to Taiwan's. See his "Politics of Industrialization: Formation of Divergent Industrial Orders in Korea and Taiwan," (Paper presented at the annual American Political Science Conference, San Francisco, CA, September 1, 1996).

[55] Wade, 1990, 156; also, see Laurence J. Lau, "The Role of Government in Economic Development: Some Observations from the Experience of China, Hong Kong, and Taiwan," in Mashiko Aoki, Hyung-ki Kim, and Masahiro Okuno-Fujiwara, *The Role of Government in East Asian Economic Development* (New York: Oxford University Press, 1996), 48.

[56] Wade, 1990, 27-28.

state's push for industrial upgrading has been incremental, intermittent, and reliant on state-controlled enterprises."[57] Yet in other sectors, such as petrochemicals or information technology, the state's role has been more prominent.[58] To the present, scholars have not conducted comprehensive studies of Taiwan's major industrial sectors over the half-century of nationalist rule.

The case of Taiwan is essentially an argument over whether the glass is half empty or half full. Private entrepreneurs had greater freedom from direct government control, and the state did curb the formation of huge conglomerates for largely political reasons. In these respects, advocates of the neo-classical economics or *laissez-faire* approach are correct. However, as Karl Fields notes in his summary comparing Taiwan's economic development with South Korea's, the dominant intervening influence was the state. Although the Taiwan government had different reasons for its actions, nonetheless it imposed "institutional constraints, obligations, and incentives" on the economy.[59]

Our judgment varies slightly from Fields', in that the state has applied more incentives than constraints to industry. Describing his work with the chemical industry, a section chief of Taiwan's IDB commented:

> We use no compulsory means. We have incentives and for high value products, we offer assistance—for example, tax exempt status. We help big business firms with special incentives and offer SMEs help in product development, usually a 50-50 split for new developments. But we can advise only. Our plans are very general and by no means so specialized as the Japanese. We have studied from the Japanese, but our relationship to businesses is much more distant.[60]

In summary, we can say that Taiwan has an industrial policy, but it is relatively weak as compared to those of South Korea and Japan; its strength varies by sector and is highly reliant on incentives.

CONCLUSIONS

At the start of this article we asked whether and to what extent Taiwan's democratization process has influenced economic policy-making. Specifically, we directed attention to the concentration of elite power and the closed nature of decision-

---

[57] Yun-han Chu, "Industrial Change and Developmental State in Two East Asian NICs: A Case Study of the Automotive Industries in South Korea and Taiwan," *Proceedings of the National Science Council*, vol. 3, no. 2 (July 1993), 218.

[58] See, for example, Sung Gul Hong, *The Political Economy of Industrial Policy in East Asia: The Semiconductor Industry in Taiwan and South Korea* (Cheltenham, UK: Edward Elgar, 1998).

[59] Fields, 1995, 243.

[60] Personal interview with Ya-ger Wang, Section Chief, 3rd Division, Industrial Development Bureau, Ministry of Economic Affairs, May 11, 1996.

making processes before democratization began. Table 2 summarizes some of these dimensions of economic policy-making:

Table 2. Dimensions of Economic Policy-Making

Dimension	Monetary	Fiscal	Regulatory	Industrial
Degree of Centralization	high	moderate	moderate	moderate
Degree of Inclusiveness	low	high	moderate	moderate
Degree of Openness	closed	open	part open	part open
Impact of Social Groups on	low	high	high	moderate
Autonomy of Technocrats	high	moderate	moderate	moderate

Of the policy areas under review, monetary policy-making showed the least influence of democratic forces. It is typically the case in industrial democracies, however, that central banks operate behind a curtain and make decisions independently; the lack of significant change in this area is not an indictment of the democratic process. Moreover, in several small ways, the Central Bank of China has become more responsive. Legislators have resisted its drive for autonomous budgetary powers, and the bank now publicizes its decisions (and promises to release the decision-making record in the future).

In fiscal policy, the bottom line proposed by the executive is little affected by the legislature, but this is attributable to Taiwan's constitutional arrangements. However, the composition of the budget has changed. Defense spending now takes a smaller slice out of central government spending than at any time in Taiwan's post-war history. Conversely, social welfare spending comprises a higher share of government dollars than at any time in Taiwan's history. Legislators are partly responsible for these changes (although the trends were evident before the legislature became influential). A quickly aroused and attentive mass public, which is no longer hesitant to place demands on the state, is a factor, too.

Detractors complain that the Legislative Yuan is a collection of grandstanding, credit-claiming, frivolous politicians who compromise the public interest when they delay or deny executive requests for action. The deliberative function, however, is time consuming and messy, and legislators have used it to expand public protections and benefits. Most legislators are responsive to clear constituent demands, and they show this when pressures heat up. One area reflecting responsiveness is tax policy, and most legislators are reluctant to increase taxes without producing clear benefits.

Regulatory policy-making shows the impact of democratic forces very clearly. Popular concerns now are translated into law within a relatively short period of time. Although social regulatory movements got off to a slow start, if they developed a ground-swell of support, both legislators and executives responded to them. The series of 1990s laws protecting workers' rights, improving consumer product safety, and tightening pollution standards are evidence of this.

It is the case that the public will is sometimes frustrated by economic interests. Some of the economic interests speak in the voice of Taiwan's richest and most powerful, who are able to convert public resources to private benefits (as, for example, in public construction). However, CEOs of conglomerates are not the sole clients of the state. Established economic interests such as farmers, laborers, and professionals have access to economic and social regulatory policy-making, too, and newer public interest groups that have organized well and mobilized many followers also have been able to gain access and some influence. The analysis of regulatory policy in terms of four quite different political process allows us to focus on the kinds of issues likely to be subject to the influence of economic groups.

Industrial policies typically do not involve mass publics; their constituents are business firms and factories, which benefit if they are included within the state's strategic development plan. In the early days of nationalist rule on Taiwan, the business sector was co-opted into the corporate state, and lacked autonomy to influence industrial development policies. Since democratization, business firms and factories and their representatives—the industrial and peak associations—have gained influence vis-à-vis the economic bureaucracy. Business associations are not yet equal to the technocrats, but the playing field is relatively more equal than at any time in Taiwan's modern history. The remaining question with respect to industrial policy is whether the state has the capacity to enforce one, and here the evidence is mixed.

We cannot say that Taiwan has become a state with freely competing and relatively well-balanced economic interests sharing influence over policy-making. No state satisfies this idealistic conception. Taiwan does demonstrate signs of decentralization in economic policy-making, however, and the decisional system has become more open to public view. These are clear results of the democratic process.

Chapter 5

CHINA-U.S.-TAIWAN ECONOMIC RELATIONS

WAYNE M. MORRISON
WILLIAM COOPER

The heightened tensions between the People's Republic of China (PRC) and Taiwan[1] reached a peak in March 1996 when the Chinese military conducted maneuvers off the coast of Taiwan just before Taiwan's first fully democratic presidential elections. Although the tensions seem to have subsided for the time being, the differences between China and Taiwan are fundamental and are likely to continue to be the source of friction from time to time. Both China and Taiwan have a policy that Taiwan is a province of China and not an independent state. But recently, Taiwan's official actions seem to be moving in the opposite direction.[2]

These differences pose a foreign policy dilemma for the United States. On the one hand, the United States has operated under the "one China policy" since completion of the Shanghai Communique in 1972 during President Nixon's first visit. In conformance with that policy, the United States withdrew diplomatic recognition of Taiwan as the Republic of China in January 1979, when it recognized the People's Republic of China. Since 1979, the United States has developed relations with China on many fronts.

Yet, the United States has also reserved the right to continue "unofficial" relations with Taiwan, including military sales and economic ties. Furthermore, Taiwan has become a full fledged democracy after years of martial law, a trend the United States would like to see continue. Thus, the United States has strong interests in both China and Taiwan. When responding to incidents of heightened tension or confrontation between China and Taiwan, U.S. policymakers must weigh American interests in the region.

U.S. economic relations with China and Taiwan are a significant element of those interests. This report explores the complex China-U.S.-Taiwan economic relationship by examining its various elements. The report provides: overviews and comparisons of the Chinese and Taiwanese economies; analyses and comparisons of overall trends in U.S. trade and investment relations with China and Taiwan; examinations of the major issues in U.S.-China and U.S.-Taiwan economic relations; and an analysis of the growing economic interdependence between China and Taiwan. The appendix at the end of this report provides various data on U.S.-China-Taiwan economic relations.

---

[1]Taiwan is also commonly referred to as the Republic of China and Chinese Taipei.

[2]For an explanation of broader U.S. interests with China and Taiwan, see: U.S. Library of Congress, Congressional Research Service, *China-U.S. Relations*, by Kerry Dumbaugh, IB94002 (regularly updated); and *Taiwan: Recent Developments and U.S. Policy Choices*, by Robert G. Sutter, IB94006 (regularly updated).

Among this report's major findings are that:

- China and Taiwan rank among the world's fastest growing economies. China's economy is much larger than Taiwan's. However, China is a developing country with a relatively low living standard compared to that of Taiwan. China and Taiwan also rank among the world's major traders. In terms of trade volumes, China is a larger trader than Taiwan. On the other hand, Taiwan's trade on a per capita basis greatly exceeds that of China's.

- The United States has strong and growing economic ties with China and with Taiwan. Both China and Taiwan are significant markets for U.S. exports, sources of U.S. imports, and destinations for U.S. investment. Currently, Taiwan is a larger market for U.S. exports than China, while China is a larger supplier of U.S. imports than Taiwan. China's importance as a U.S. trading partner, at least in terms of volume of trade, is growing much faster than Taiwan's.

- The United States faces problems of market access and intellectual property rights (IPR) protection with China and Taiwan, although U.S. concerns with China are currently much greater, while the relationship with Taiwan has become less tense over the years as Taiwan has made substantial efforts to liberalize its economic and trade regimes. Admission to the World Trade Organization (WTO) is a high priority for both China and Taiwan and is a process in which the United States plays a significant role. The United States and China also face the issues of China's transshipments of textile exports and U.S. most-favored-nation (MFN) status for China.

- Despite the absence of formal political and economic links, China and Taiwan have established indirect trade and investment ties which have grown substantially over the past few years. China is Taiwan's largest destination for overseas investment and the second largest market for its exports. Taiwan is China's fourth largest trading partner and the second largest foreign investor in China. It is likely that, barring major political disruptions, economic integration between China and Taiwan will continue to expand rapidly in the near future. Such ties may help to diminish political tensions between Taiwan and the mainland. Chinese threats (or use) of military force against Taiwan could lead to a reduction or termination of Taiwanese investment in, and trade with, the mainland, which could have damaging effects on both economies.

- The growing interdependence between China and Taiwan is changing the character of the U.S. economic relationship. It is becoming less a bilateral one and more a triangular one. This trend will affect U.S. policy choices.

- Taiwan firms have invested heavily in a wide variety of labor-intensive and export-oriented industries (such as consumer electronics, shoes, textiles, toys, plastics, etc.) in the mainland. It is estimated that about 70% of the products exported by Taiwan-invested firms in China are shipped to the U.S. market.

- A U.S. withdrawal of China's MFN status, or other trade sanctions against China, could negatively impact the Taiwanese economy (as well as those of the United States and China). For example, the Taiwan government estimates that U.S. trade sanctions against China over IPR issues, if implemented, could cost Taiwan-invested firms in China over $600 million.

OVERVIEW OF CHINA'S ECONOMY

CHINA'S ECONOMIC REFORMS

Prior to 1978, China maintained a centrally planned economy, where most of the country's production was directed and controlled by the central government. Beginning in 1978, China launched several economic reforms, including the introduction of price and ownership incentives for farmers and the establishment of four special economic zones in China for the purpose of attracting foreign investment, boosting exports, and importing high technology products into China. Additional reforms which sought to decentralize economic policymaking in several economic sectors (especially trade) followed in stages. Economic control of various enterprises was given to provincial and local governments, foreign-funded joint ventures, and private enterprises. Such enterprises were generally allowed to operate and compete on free market principles, rather than under the direction and guidance of state planning. In addition, state price controls on a wide range of products were eliminated. Finally, the government established additional economic zones in several Chinese coastal cities which were given extensive autonomy to experiment with various free-market reforms.[3]

Chinese officials state that the goal of China's free market reforms is to create a "socialist market economy" in which market forces become increasingly important in determining production and prices, but where the state continues to maintain overall control of the economy as well as over key economic sectors. In a sense, China maintains a dual economy. About half of China's industrial production is produced by non-state enterprises which are relatively free from control by the central government, while the other half is produced by state-controlled enterprises, according to specified production quotas and prices. A significant number of China's state enterprises are unprofitable and must be heavily subsidized.

---

[3]For additional information on China's economic reforms, see: U.S. Library of Congress, Congressional Research Service. *China's Changing Conditions*, by Robert G. Sutter, IB93114 (regularly updated).

China's economic reforms and open investment policies have contributed to a surge in economic growth. Between 1979 (when reforms began) and 1995, China's real gross domestic product (GDP) more than quadrupled. Over the past 10 years, China's real GDP has grown by an average rate of 9.6% annually, making it one of the world's fastest growing economies. China's real GDP grew by 9.9% in 1995. Over the next 5 years (1996-2000) China's real GDP is projected by DRI/McGraw Hill to average over 8.2% (see figure 1). At this rate of growth, China will more than double its GDP in less than 10 years.

FIGURE 1. China's Real Annual GDP Growth Rates: 1986-1995 and
Projections Through 2000

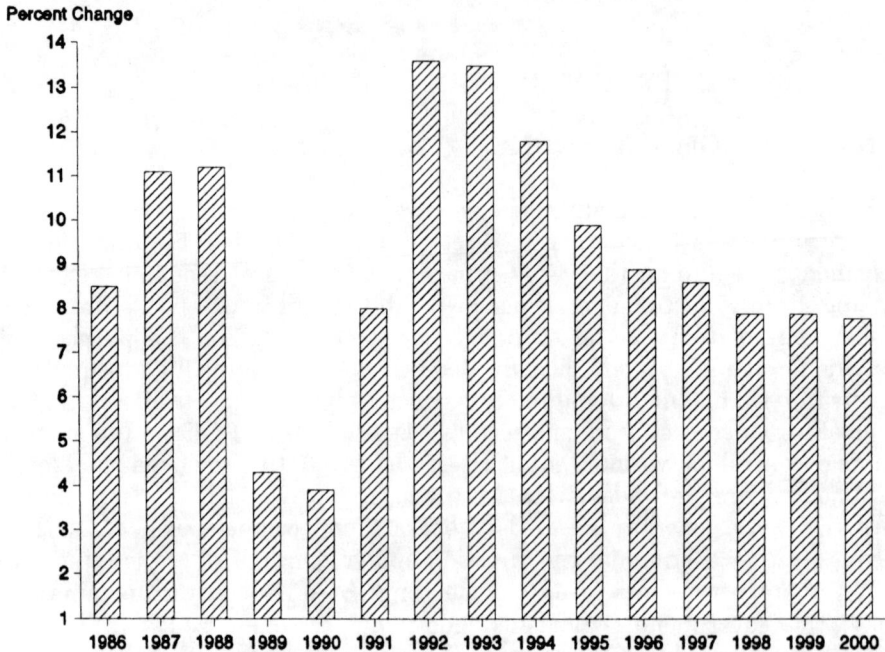

Percent Change

Source: DRI/McGraw Hill. *World Markets Country Summaries, Fourth Quarter 1995*; and, *World Markets Reports*. February 1996.

FOREIGN TRADE AND INVESTMENT

China's economic reforms and open investment policies have quickly made it a major world trader and a recipient of foreign investment. China rose from being the 27th largest trading country in 1978 to 11th largest in 1995. Over the past 10 years, China's trade has increased substantially: Merchandise exports grew from $31.4 billion in 1986 to $148.8 billion in 1995 (up 374%), while imports grew from $43.2 billion to $132.1 billion (up 206%). China's exports in 1995 increased by 23.2% over the previous year's levels, while imports grew by 14.3%. Over the past 10 years, China's balance of trade has swung from deficits to surpluses. In 1995, China had a $16.7 billion trade surplus.

Chinese trade data for 1995 indicate its top trading partners (based on total trade) were Japan ($57.5 billion), Hong Kong ($44.6 billion), the United States ($40.8 billion), and the European Union ($40.3 billion). However, Chinese trade data differ significantly with that of many of its trade partners.[4] For example, according to Chinese trade data, Chinese exports to the United States in 1995 totalled $24.7 billion, making the United States China's third largest export market (after Hong Kong/Macau and Japan). However, U.S. trade data show U.S. imports from China in 1995 at $45.6 billion. These data would indicate that the United States was by far China's largest export market in 1995.[5]

China's abundance of cheap labor has made it internationally competitive in many labor-intensive industries. As a result, manufactured products (as opposed to primary products such as food and live animals, raw materials, and mineral fuels) comprise an increasingly larger share of China's trade. The share of Chinese manufactured exports to its total exports rose from 50% in 1980 to 84% in 1994, while manufactured imports as a share of total imports rose from 65% to 86%. A large share of China's manufactured imports are comprised of intermediates (such as chemicals and related products, iron and steel, and textile yarn) used in manufacturing products there.[6]

The large influx of foreign direct investment (FDI) in China, much of which has gone into export-oriented production facilities, has been a key factor in China's rapid economic growth. Utilized (or actual) FDI in China has grown from $916 million in 1983 to $37.5 billion in 1995, making China the second largest world destination for foreign investment (after the United States).[7] Cumulative FDI in China at the end of 1995 was $136.1 billion. A significant share of China's foreign investment has come from overseas Chinese: Hong Kong/Macau was the largest investor in 1994 (59.7% of total utilized FDI), followed by Taiwan (10%). The United States and Japan were the third and fourth largest investors in China. According to Chinese data, about 39% of China's foreign trade is conducted by foreign invested firms in China.[8]

---

[4]A large share of China's exports pass through Hong Kong and are re-exported to other countries; China records such exports as Chinese exports to Hong Kong. However, many nations, such as the United States, treat such re-exports as having come from China, not Hong Kong.

[5]Chinese exports to the United States constituted about 31.1% of total Chinese exports in 1995. This figure was calculated using U.S. trade data on imports from China (treating these figures as Chinese exports to the United States) and official Chinese trade data on total Chinese exports. The U.S. share as a destination of total Chinese exports rose from 15.3% in 1986 to 34.3% in 1993, but declined to 32.1% in 1994 and to 31.1% in 1995.

[6]*The Economist Intelligence Unit, Country Profile: China and Mongolia, 1995-1996.* 1995, p. 34-35.

[7]Data supplied by the PRC embassy, Washington, D.C.

[8]*China News Service,* February 2, 1996, World Wide Web Page.

ECONOMIC CHALLENGES FACED BY CHINA

Despite China's recent economic success, it faces a wide variety of economic problems, such as high inflation, infrastructure bottlenecks, uneven economic growth, growing unemployment, official corruption, and inefficient (and financially burdensome) state-run enterprises. The lack of effective macroeconomic institutions and policy instruments has caused the economy to experience boom-to-bust cycles. Implemented economic reforms have contributed to rapid economic growth at the beginning of the cycle. However, the lack of effective macroeconomic controls has often led the economy to become overheated, resulting in high inflation. In the past, the central government has attempted to rein in inflation by restricting credit, re-imposing price controls on some products, and suspending or rolling back certain economic reforms. Such efforts, however, have often caused a sharp decline in economic growth. Once inflation has significantly slowed, the government has eased control over credit and allowed economic reforms to resume.

The government is currently considering adopting a variety of macroeconomic measures intended to promote long-term stable economic growth, including a major overhaul of its banking system.[9] Such reforms would strengthen the central government's ability to assert macroeconomic controls while continuing to decentralize its control over major sectors of the economy (i.e., exposing a greater share of the economy to free-market forces). In addition, the government is considering reforms which would gradually reduce subsidies to state-owned enterprises and expose them to market forces.[10]

OVERVIEW OF TAIWAN'S ECONOMY

Taiwan is often grouped with South Korea, Hong Kong, and Singapore as one of the Four Asian Tigers, Four Dragons, or Newly Industrializing Economies (NIEs). While no set standards define these economies, the terms are generally used to denote developing countries that have made rapid progress towards industrialization and economic growth. They have advanced ahead of most developing countries and are poised to become fully developed or industrialized economies.

---

[9]In November 1993, the Chinese Communist Party adopted a broad framework for China's transition to a "socialist market economy" in which market forces become increasingly important in determining production and prices, but where the state would continue to exercise overall control of the economy as well as over key economic sectors.

[10]The Chinese government has been reluctant to cut off financial support of such enterprises in the past out of concern that doing so would lead to employment disruptions which could lead to social unrest.

During the past 30 years, Taiwan's real GDP growth rate has averaged 9% per year.[11] In recent years, that growth rate has dropped, although it remains impressive. It averaged around 6.5% from 1992-1994 and fell slightly in 1995 to 6.1%, due in part to military tensions with the mainland.[12] DRI/McGraw Hill projects that Taiwan's real GDP will grow at an average annual rate of 5.6% over the next five years (**see figure 2**). Taiwan's per capita GDP on a purchasing power parity (PPP) basis[13] is $14,402 (1995) compared with the industrialized countries such as the United States ($26,814), Japan ($20,840), and Spain ($13,501), and compared with developing countries such as Mexico ($6,772), and China ($2,786).[14]

---

[11] Central Intelligence Agency. *World Factbook -- 1995*. World Wide Web Version. 1996. Washington.

[12] DRI/McGraw-Hill. Data Resources. *World Market Summaries --Fourth Quarter 1995*. p. 133.

[13]Purchasing Power Parities (PPP) are foreign exchange rates used to convert foreign economic data to U.S. dollars that reflect relative price differences in the two countries. This allows the actual purchasing power of a nation's GDP (relative to U.S. GDP) to be measured.

[14] DRI/McGraw Hill. *World Markets Executive Overview, Fourth Quarter 1995*, p. A-12.

FIGURE 2. Taiwan Real Annual GDP Growth Rates: 1986-1995 and
Projections Through 2000
(Percent)

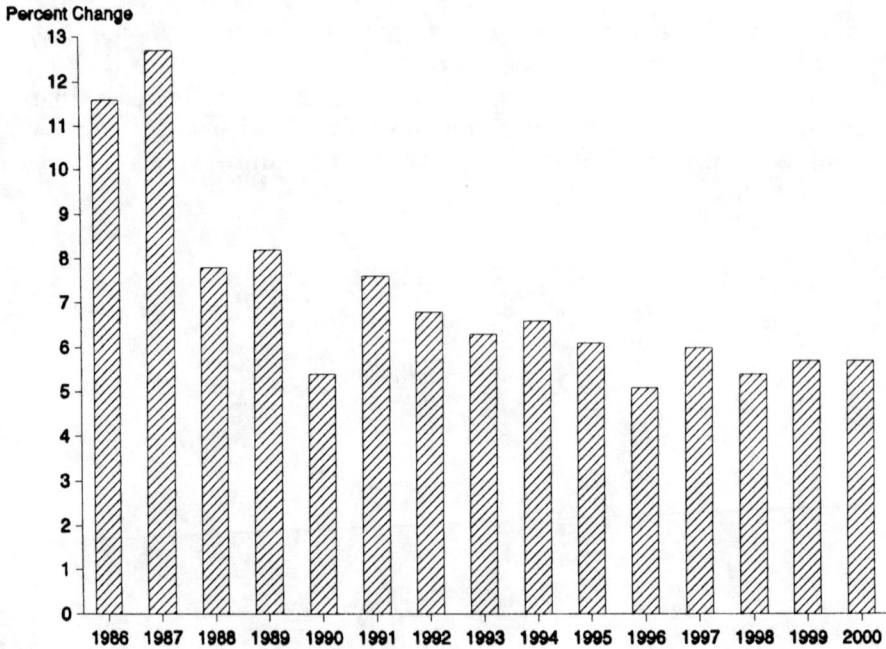

Source: DRI/McGraw Hill. *World Market Summaries, Fourth Quarter, 1995.* p. A–3, B–4; and,
world Markets Report: Taiwan. April 1996. p. 2.

A recent study by the Organization of Economic Cooperation and
Development (OECD) attributes Taiwan's rapid economic growth and
development to several factors. The study attributes 40% of the growth to
investment and the country's ability to accumulate large amounts of capital for
investment. In the early 1950s, through most of the 1960s, American aid was
an important source of the capital. But from the late 1960s to the present, the
economy has drawn on its population's high savings rate for capital. The OECD
study attributes another 40% of the growth to the continuous improvement of
productivity in all factors of production over a long span of time. The increase
in productivity resulted from government policies and cultural traits that place
a high premium on education. It also resulted from government policies that
encouraged labor mobility.[15]

In addition, factor productivity improvements have resulted from the
government's export-led policies that have encouraged gradual trade and foreign
investment liberalization. Taiwan turned to export-led development in the

---

[15] The OECD study attributes the remaining 20% of economic growth to increase in total
labor supply. OECD. *Development Centre Studies Long Term Growth Series. Chinese Taipei:
The Origins of the Economic "Miracle."* Paris. 1995. p. 9-12.

1960s, after undertaking highly protectionist import-substitution development policies in the 1950s.[16]

As a small island that lacks natural resources, Taiwan has had to depend on foreign trade as a source of economic growth. In 1994, the ratio of Taiwan exports of goods and services to GDP was 46.8%, and the ratio of imports to GDP was 43.7%. (In comparison, the ratios for the U.S. economy, a large, resource-rich economy, were 12.4% and 14.2.% in 1994, respectively.)[17]

From the 1950s to the 1960s, Taiwan developed from a primarily agricultural economy into a producer of mostly light industrial goods. In the 1960s, Taiwan's exporting industries relied mainly on labor-intensive products, such as wearing apparel, footwear, and toys. Later Taiwan developed its heavier industries, including steel and shipbuilding, and became a major producer of consumer electronics goods, such as televisions and sound equipment. Since the 1980s, the appreciation of the local currency (the New Taiwan dollar), rising wage rates, and strengthening competition from Malaysia, Thailand, and China, have forced Taiwan to shift its production to more capital and technology-intensive industries. Taiwan is now the world's largest producer of computer peripherals, such as keyboards and mouses, and is further developing its high-technology sectors. Taiwan producers have shifted much of their labor-intensive production offshore through foreign investments in other, less industrialized advanced Asian countries, especially mainland China.

Taiwan ranks as the world's 14th largest trader (1995).[18] Taiwan has consistently incurred trade surpluses. The surpluses were particularly large in the mid-1980s, having peaked at $18.7 billion in 1987. Since then, Taiwan imports have grown much faster than exports and the surpluses have declined to $8.1 billion in 1995. Nevertheless, the surpluses have contributed to Taiwan's accumulation of large foreign reserves that reached $100 billion by the summer of 1995. However, China's threats of military force led to a decrease in the foreign reserves to about $90 billion as of the end of February 1996 and $83 billion by the end of March 1996.[19]

Foreign trade has served Taiwan's economic, but also political, objectives. Since the 1970s, Taiwan has had official diplomatic relations with only a handful of small countries. China's and Taiwan's "one China" policy made most diplomatic recognition mutually exclusive. The major powers, including the United States, maintain diplomatic ties with the PRC while conducting "unofficial ties" with Taiwan.

---

[16]Ibid., p. 14-17. See also Lasater, Martin. L. *U.S. Interests in the New Taiwan.* San Francisco. Westview Press. 1993. p. 71-79.

[17]DRI/McGraw Hill. *World Markets Executive Overview, Fourth Quarter 1995.* p. A-29, A-31.

[18] *World Trade Organization*, World Wide Web Page.

[19] Telephone conversation with Taiwan analyst at DRI-McGraw Hill, April 25, 1996.

A key element of these unofficial ties is foreign trade, investment, and overall economic relations, which Taiwan has used in building relations with major countries, such as the United States, Japan, and the countries of the European Union. Taiwan has also used economic ties as a key to entering international organizations. Taiwan has become a member with the PRC in the Asian Development Bank and belongs (with the PRC) to the Asian-Pacific Economic Cooperation (APEC) forum,[20] and has applied for membership in the World Trade Organization. Taiwan is thus regaining some international status through its position as a major economic power.

COMPARISON OF CHINA'S AND TAIWAN'S ECONOMIES

China's economy is significantly larger than Taiwan's. In nominal dollar terms, China's GDP in 1995 was $658 billion, compared to $266 billion for Taiwan. When these data are converted to U.S. dollars in purchasing power parities (i.e., the actual purchasing power of GDP), China's GDP is $3.4 trillion, while Taiwan's GDP is $308 billion. Based on these measurements, China's economy may be nearly 10 times that of Taiwan's.[21] However, China's population (at 1.2 billion) is nearly 57 times greater that of Taiwan's (21.4 million).[22]

China and Taiwan are similar in some aspects. Both have experienced rapid economic growth over the past few years. From 1986 to 1995, the average annual real GDP growth for China and Taiwan was 9.6% and 8.0%, respectively. Both rank among the world's major trading countries, and both economies are heavily dependent on trade. Both China and Taiwan have high rates of savings and investment -- important factors for supporting economic growth. Finally, both China and Taiwan maintain large foreign exchange reserves, which will enable them to finance a high level of imports in the near future.

On the other hand, China and Taiwan are at vastly different stages of economic development. For example, China's per capita GDP in PPPs in 1995 was $2,786 compared with $14,402 for Taiwan, indicating that Chinese living standards are well below those of Taiwan's. In terms of trade, Taiwan's per capita exports and imports in 1995 were $5,220 and $4,841, respectively; compared with $122 and $109, respectively, for China. Finally, Taiwan has been

---

[20] APEC is group of 18 counties that includes the United States, Canada, Chile, Mexico, Brunei, Malaysia, Philippines, Thailand, Indonesia, Singapore, South Korea, Hong Kong, Papua New Guinea, China, Taiwan, Thailand, Australia, and New Zealand. The group, as established, coordinates mutual economic relations and has set out an agenda for trade and investment liberalization.

[21]These measurements also indicate that China may be the world's third largest economy (after the United States and Japan), although precise PPP measurements are difficult to make for China because it is not a fully market economy (prices for many goods and services are distorted).

[22]DRI/McGraw Hill. *World Markets Country Summaries*. Fourth Quarter 1995, p. 93 and 137.

able to achieve high economic growth, while keeping the rate of inflation relatively low and stable. China, on the other hand, has experienced problems with high and volatile rates of inflation over the past 10 years (**see table 1**).

In sum, China has the world's largest population, and by some measurements, the world's third largest economy. Yet, China is still a developing economy; its living standards are far below that of Taiwan's. In contrast, while Taiwan has a relatively small population, its economy is significantly more developed, and its living standards are much higher, than China's.

Table 1. Selected Economic and Trade Data For China and Taiwan

	China	Taiwan
Population, Millions of Persons (1995)	1,215	21
Nominal GDP, Billions of U.S. Dollars (1995)	658	266
GDP in PPPs, Billions of U.S. Dollars: 1995	3,386	308
Per Capita GDP in Nominal U.S. Dollars: 1995	541	12,480
Per Capita GDP in PPPs, U.S. Dollars: 1995	2,786	14,402
Per Capita GDP in PPPs Relative to U.S. Level (1995) (%)	10.7	55.3
Average Annual Real GDP Growth: 1986-1995 and projected average annual growth for 1996-2000 (%)	9.6 [7.1]	8.0 [5.6]
Average Annual Consumer Price Inflation: 1986-1995 (%)	12.1	3.2
Total Trade: 1995 ($Billions & World Rank)	280 [11th]	215 [14th]
Exports: 1995 ($Billions & World Rank)	149 [11th]	111 [14th]
Imports: 1995 ($Billions & World Rank)	132 [12th]	104 [15th]
Exports as a Share of GDP: 1995 (%)	22.6	42.0
Imports as a Share of GDP: 1995 (%)	20.1	38.9
Exports Per Capita: Nominal U.S. Dollars, 1995	122	5,220
Imports Per Capita: Nominal U.S. Dollars, 1995	109	4,841
Year End Foreign Exchange Reserves, 1995, ($Billions)	73.9	90.7
National Savings as a % of GDP, 1995 (%)	42.6	27.3
Nominal Investment as a % of GDP, 1995 (%)	36.4	24.3

Purchasing Power Parities (PPP) are foreign exchange rates used to convert foreign economic data to U.S. dollars that reflect relative price differences in the two countries. This allows the actual purchasing power of a nation's GDP (relative to U.S. GDP) to be measured.

Sources: DRI/McGraw-Hill: *World Markets Report*, various issues; and *World Trade Organization*, World Wide Web Site.

U.S.- CHINA ECONOMIC RELATIONS

U.S.-CHINA TRADE

U.S. trade with China rose rapidly after the two nations provided mutual most-favored-nation (MFN) status beginning in 1980. Total trade (exports plus imports) between the two nations rose from $4.8 billion in 1980 to $57.3 billion in 1995. Over the past few years, the U.S. trade deficit with China has grown significantly, due largely to a surge in U.S. imports of Chinese goods relative to U.S. exports to China, and has been rising at a faster rate than that of any other major U.S. trading partner. From 1986 to 1995, the U.S. trade deficit with China rose from $1.7 billion to nearly $34 billion, making China the second largest U.S. deficit trading partner after Japan. Many trade analysts contend that the U.S. trade deficit with China is likely to surpass that with Japan sometime in the near future.

While China in absolute terms is a smaller market for U.S. exports than various other East Asian markets (such as Hong Kong, Singapore, South Korea, and Taiwan), it has been, over the past few years, one of the fastest growing markets. Between 1990 and 1995, U.S. exports to China grew by over 144%; they grew by 26.5% in 1995 alone over the previous year. U.S. exports to China in 1995 totalled $11.7 billion, accounting for 2.0% of total U.S. exports to the world. Major U.S. exports to China in 1995 included fertilizers, aircraft and parts, agricultural products, textiles fibers, and telecommunication equipment **(see table 2)**.

Table 2. Top Five U.S. Exports to China: 1986, 1990, and 1995
($Millions)

SITC Commodity	1986	1990	1995
Total All Commodities	3,105	4,807	11,748
Fertilizers (except crude of group 272)	46	544	1,204
Transport equipment, n.e.s. (mainly aircraft and aircraft parts)	467	755	1,189
Cereals and cereal preparations	11	513	1,147
Textile fibers & their wastes (excluding wool tops etc.)	18	385	1,041
Telecommunication & sound recording & reproducing appliances & equipment	66	81	724

Commodities sorted by top five exports in 1995.
N.e.s. means not elsewhere specified.
Source: U.S. Department of Commerce.

China is a relatively large source for U.S. imports. In 1995, imports from China accounted for 6.1% of total U.S. imports. The top five U.S. imports from China in 1995 are shown in **table 3**. A large share of these imports are comprised of low-value, labor-intensive products, such as toys and games, clothing, and shoes.

Table 3. Top Five U.S. Imports From China: 1986, 1990, 1995
($Millions)

SITC Commodity	1986	1990	1995
Total All Commodities	4,771	15,224	45,555
Miscellaneous manufactured articles (such as toys, games, etc.)	673	3,243	10,332
Articles of apparel and clothing accessories	1,710	3,469	5,854
Footwear	77	1,477	5,824
Telecommunication & sound recording & reproducing appliances & equipment	57	1,163	4,308
Electrical machinery, apparatus & appliances, n.e.s.	42	657	3,099

Commodities sorted by top five imports in 1995.
N.e.s. means not elsewhere specified.
Source: U.S. Department of Commerce.

U.S. DIRECT INVESTMENT IN CHINA

The United States is the largest non-Chinese investor in China. From 1979-1995, utilized (or actual) U.S. foreign direct investment (FDI) in China was estimated at $10.7 billion (or 7.8.% of total FDI in China). Of this amount, over $7.6 billion (or 72% of total U.S. FDI in China) was invested in China between 1993 and 1995. It is estimated that new U.S. FDI in China in 1995 alone totalled $3.1 billion. (**see table 4**).[23] The largest sectors for U.S. investment in China include manufacturing, petroleum, and wholesale.[24]

There are a number of reasons why U.S. FDI in China has surged in recent years. China is one of the world's fastest growing economies, and U.S. firms

---

[23]The U.S.-China Business Council. *The U.S.- China Business Council: Forecast '96, Foreign Direct Investment*, March 1996. Data for 1995 are estimates based on actual data for January-September 1995. All investment data are taken from official Chinese statistics.

[24]United States Trade Representative. *1996 National Trade Estimate Report on Foreign Trade Barriers*, 1996, p. 45.

have sought to increase their presence there to take advantage of a potentially large market for their goods and services. In addition, U.S. firms have been attracted by China's recent investment reforms, which have made it easier to do business there. Furthermore, U.S. companies may also be trying to skirt Chinese trade barriers (such as quotas, high tariffs, restrictive license requirements, etc.) by shifting production to China in order to obtain easier access to the Chinese market.

TABLE 4. Utilized U.S. Foreign Direct Investment in China and as a % of Total Foreign Direct Investment : 1979-1995*

Year	U.S. FDI ($Millions)	All Countries FDI ($Millions)	U.S. FDI as a % of Total (%)
1979-1986	946	7,937	11.9
1987	263	2,647	9.9
1988	236	3,194	7.4
1989	284	3,774	7.5
1990	456	3,487	13.1
1991	323	4,366	7.4
1992	511	11,008	4.6
1993	2,063	27,515	7.5
1994	2,491	33,767	7.4
1995*	3,097	37,521	8.3
Cumulative total: 1979-1995*	10,657	136,054	7.8

*Data for 1995 are estimates based on actual data for January-September 1995.

Source: The U.S.-China Business Council. *The U.S.- China Business Council: Forecast '96, Foreign Direct Investment*, March 1996. All investment data are taken from official Chinese statistics.

U.S.-TAIWAN ECONOMIC RELATIONS

The United States and Taiwan have a strong economic relationship, beginning in 1949 when the Kuomintang (Nationalist) Republic of China Government led by Chiang Kai-Shek retreated to the island after the

Communists defeated them and drove them off the mainland.[25] As previously discussed, on January 1, 1979, the United States switched diplomatic recognition from Taiwan to the PRC.

As a condition of its recognition of the Beijing regime, however, the United States reserved the right to maintain unofficial ties with Taiwan. To provide the domestic authority for such relations, the Congress passed the Taiwan Relations Act (TRA), P.L. 96-8, which was signed April 10, 1979. The TRA provided for the establishment of the American Institute on Taiwan (AIT) to represent U.S. interests in Taiwan, and for the establishment of the Coordination Council for North American Affairs (CCNAA) (renamed in 1994 the Taipei Economic and Cultural Representative (or TECRO) to represent Taiwan's interests in the United States.

Because official diplomatic links are restricted, economic links have become the strongest channels of communication between Taiwan and the United States. The TRA authorizes the United States to maintain economic relations with Taiwan and apply U.S. laws, including trade laws, to Taiwan, as it would any other foreign country, despite the lack of diplomatic ties. Therefore, the United States extends MFN tariff treatment to imports from Taiwan. In addition, U.S. exporters and investors have access to U.S. official credit facilities, including the U.S. Export-Import Bank, the Commodity Credit Corporation (CCC), and the Overseas Private Investment Corporation (OPIC), as incentives to trade with and invest in Taiwan.

The U.S.-Taiwan economic relationship has been characterized by growing linkages in the form of two-way trade and investment, but has also been characterized by periods of friction. The United States responded to rapidly growing trade deficits during the 1980s by pressing Taiwan to reduce barriers to imports. In addition, the United States has pressed Taiwan to reduce barriers to foreign investment and to improve its protection of U.S.-origin intellectual property rights.

U.S.-TAIWAN TRADE

Trade flows between the United States and Taiwan have grown appreciably over the past 10 years. Largely as a result of strong economic growth and development in Taiwan, U.S. exports soared between 1986 and 1995, from $5.2 billion to $19.1 billion. U.S. imports from Taiwan over the same period rose from $19.7 billion to $26.5 billion. The United States is Taiwan's most important export market as of 1995, although the relative importance of the U.S. market has been slipping. From 1983 to 1995, the share of Taiwan's exports going to the United States dropped from 48% to 24%. The United

---

[25] For more information on overall U.S. Taiwan relations, see U.S. Library of Congress. Congressional Research Service. *Taiwan: Recent Developments and U.S. Policy Choices.* Issue Brief 94006 by Robert G. Sutter. [Continually updated.]

States is Taiwan's second largest source of imports, accounting for 20% in 1995. Japan, the largest source, accounted for 29%.[26]

The United States has experienced persistent deficits in its trade with Taiwan. These deficits rose sharply in the mid-1980s, largely as a result of a rapidly appreciating U.S. dollar in the early 1980s. (Trade flows generally respond to changes in exchange rates with some time lag.) The deficits peaked in 1987 at $17.4 billion and declined to $9.7 billion by 1995.

In 1995, the top U.S. imports from Taiwan included office and automatic data processing machines (mostly computers and computer accessories), electrical machinery and appliances, miscellaneous manufactured products, manufactured metals, and clothing (**see table 5**).

Table 5. Top Five U.S. Imports From Taiwan: 1986, 1990, 1995
($Millions)

SITC Commodity	1986	1990	1995
Total All Commodities	19,791	22,667	28,975
Office machines and automatic data processing machines (mainly computers and parts)	1,216	3,092	7,395
Electrical machinery, apparatus & appliances, n.e.s.	1,366	2,194	5,180
Miscellaneous manufactured articles, n.e.s.	2,577	2,992	2,499
Manufactures of metals, n.e.s.	1,254	1,561	2,175
Articles of apparel and clothing accessories	2,588	2,489	2,151

Commodities sorted by top five imports in 1995.
N.e.s. means not elsewhere specified.
Source: U.S. Department of Commerce.

In 1995, electrical machinery and appliances, organic chemicals, transportation equipment (mostly aircraft and aircraft parts), road vehicles, and cereals were the most important U.S. exports to Taiwan (**see table 6**).

---

[26] Republic of China (Taipei). *Republic of China Yearbook -- 1996*. World Wide Web version.

Table 6. Top Five U.S. Exports to Taiwan: 1986, 1990, 1995
($Millions)

SITC Commodity	1986	1990	1995
Total All Commodities	5,183	11,482	19,295
Electrical machinery, apparatus & appliances, n.e.s.	546	1,440	3,427
Organic chemicals	476	867	1,794
Transport equipment, n.e.s. (mainly aircraft and aircraft parts)	220	430	1,727
Road vehicles (including air-cushion vehicles)	60	847	1,074
Cereals and cereal preparations	413	659	945

Commodities sorted by top five exports in 1995.
N.e.s. means not elsewhere specified.
Source: U.S. Department of Commerce.

U.S.-TAIWAN INVESTMENT

In 1995, the United States replaced Japan as the largest foreign investor in Taiwan. The cumulative value of U.S. investment at the end of 1995 was estimated by the Taiwan government at $6.3 billion, accounting for 28.3% of total foreign investment in Taiwan; Japanese investors accounted for $6.0 billion, or 27.1%.[27] New U.S. investment in Taiwan in 1995 was $1.3 billion, an increase of 300% over the previous year. The surge in U.S. investment in 1995 was due in part to recent steps taken by the Taiwan government to liberalize its investment regime.[28]

U.S. data for 1994 show that most U.S. investment (63%) has gone into Taiwan's manufacturing sector (see table 7).[29] Within manufacturing, the most prominent American investors are in autos (Ford), high technology and

---

[27] Taiwan measures foreign direct investment according to investments that have been approved. Data are from Taiwan Investment Commission, Ministry of Economic Affairs. *Statistics on Overseas Chinese & Foreign Investment, January 1996.*

[28] *Free China Journal* (Taiwan), January 19, 1996, World Wide Web Page.

[29] U.S. foreign direct investments abroad are measured as the direct investment position on an historical-cost basis. U.S. Department of Commerce. Bureau of Economic Analysis. *Survey of Current Business*, June 1995. p. 63.

electronics (Texas Instruments, General Instrument, Motorola, IBM), and chemicals (AMOCO, Dupont, Uniroyal).[30]

TABLE 7. U.S. Foreign Direct Investment in Taiwan, Year-end 1994
(Millions of U.S. Dollars)

All Industries	3,882
Petroleum	D
Manufacturing	2,459
Wholesale Trade	528
Banking	435
Finance	168
Services	160
Others	D

Source: U.S. Department of Commerce. Bureau of Economic Analysis. *Survey of Current Business*, June 1995. p. 63. Foreign direct investment is valued on an historical-cost basis. "D" indicates data was suppressed to avoid identification of individual companies.

The United States is the second largest destination of Taiwan overseas investment (after China).[31] According to U.S. data, investments from Taiwan were valued on a historical-cost basis (through 1994) at $1.4 billion.[32] These investments were spread over various sectors of the U.S. economy.

COMPARISONS OF U.S.-CHINA TRADE WITH U.S.-TAIWAN TRADE

U.S. EXPORTS

Both China and Taiwan have increased in importance as markets for U.S. exports. China's ranking as a destination for U.S. exports rose from 18th in 1986 to 13th in 1995, and Taiwan's export ranking rose from 11th to 7th. Taiwan is currently (1995) larger than China as an export market for U.S. products, $19.3 billion and $11.7 billion, respectively (**see table 8 and figure 3**). However, in recent years, U.S. exports to China have risen faster than those

---

[30]Taiwan data cited in U.S. Department of Commerce. International Trade Administration, *Country Market Reports, Taiwan*, 1995.

[31]Official Taiwan investment data list the United States as the largest destination for Taiwan overseas investment. However, Taiwan investment in China (which is done indirectly) far exceeds its investment in the United States.

[32]*Survey of Current Business*, June 1995. p. 67.

to Taiwan. For example, over the past five years, U.S. exports to China increased by 144.4% while those to Taiwan rose by 68.0%. U.S. exports to China and Taiwan in 1995 rose by 26.5% and 13.0%, respectively, over the previous year. Should these trends continue, it is likely that China will overtake Taiwan in importance as a U.S. export market.

Table 8. U.S. Exports to China and Taiwan: 1986, 1990, and 1995
($Millions and U.S. Export Ranking)

Year	China		Taiwan	
	U.S. Exports ($Millions)	U.S. Export Ranking	U.S. Exports ($Millions)	U.S. Export Ranking
1986	3,105	18	5,183	11
1990	4,807	18	11,482	9
1995	11,748	13	19,295	7

Source: U.S. Department of Commerce.

FIGURE 3. U.S. Exports to China and Taiwan: 1986–1995

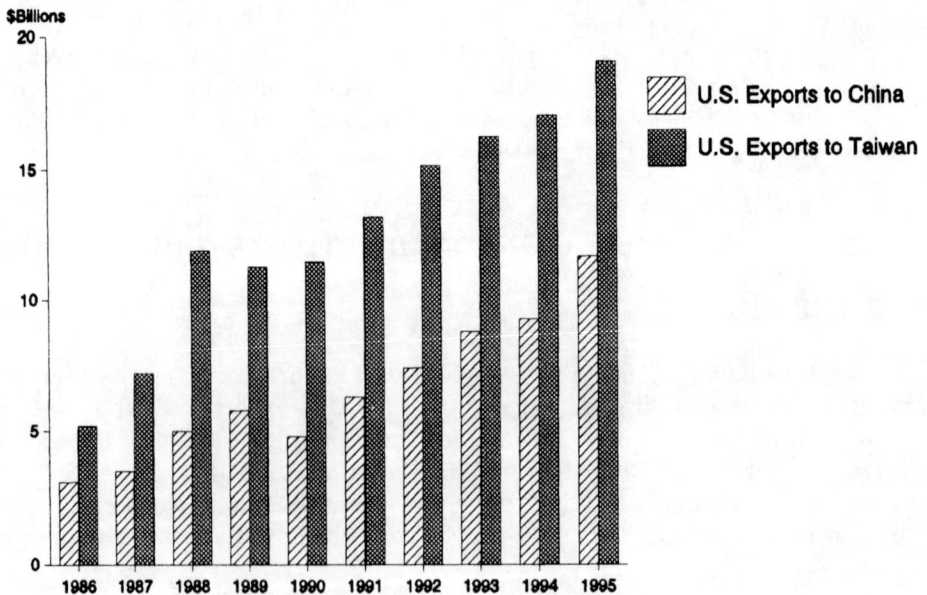

Source: U.S. Department of Commerce.

U.S. IMPORTS

From 1986 to 1995, U.S. imports from China increased significantly faster than those from Taiwan (855% versus 46%, respectively). China's ranking as a source of U.S. imports surged from 18th to 4th, while Taiwan's import ranking fell from 4th to 6th (**see table 9 and figure 4**).

Table 9. U.S. Imports From China and Taiwan: 1986, 1990, and 1995
($Millions and U.S. Import Ranking)

	China		Taiwan	
Year	U.S. Imports ($Millions)	U.S. Import Ranking	U.S. Imports ($Millions)	U.S. Import Ranking
1986	4,771	18	19,791	4
1990	15,224	8	22,667	4
1995	45,555	4	28,975	6

Source: U.S. Department of Commerce.

FIGURE 4. U.S. Imports from China and Taiwan: 1986–1995

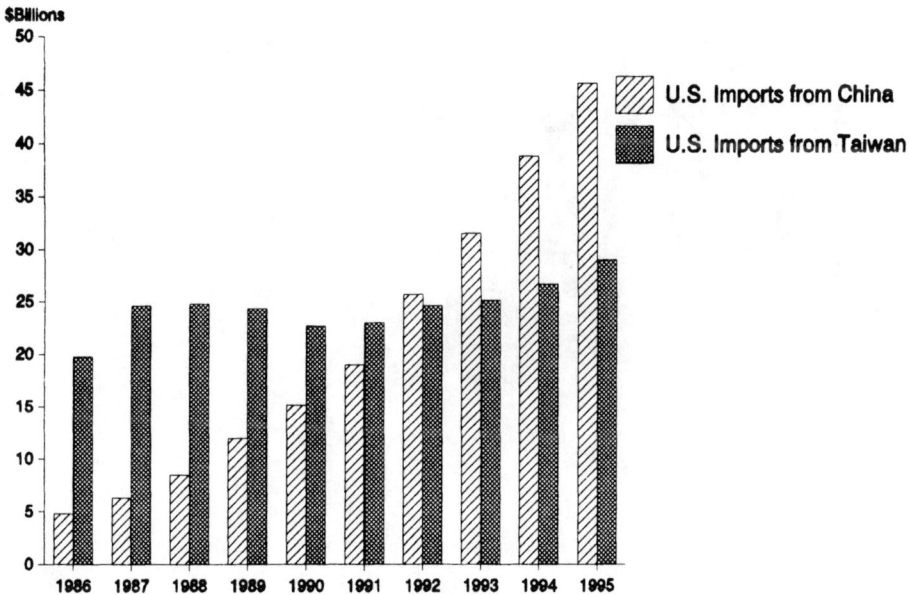

Source: U.S. Department of Commerce.

U.S. TRADE BALANCES

The U.S. trade deficit with China has risen sharply over the past 10 years, from $1.7 billion to $33.8 billion; while the U.S. trade deficit Taiwan has fallen, from $14.6 billion to $9.7 billion over the same period. China rose from being the 17th largest U.S. deficit trading country in 1986 to the second largest in 1995; Taiwan's trade deficit ranking fell from 3rd to 6th over the same period (**see table 10 and figure 5**).

Table 10. U.S. Trade Balances With China and Taiwan:
1986, 1990, and 1995
($Millions and U.S. Trade Deficit Rankings)

Year	China		Taiwan	
	U.S. Trade Balance	U.S. Trade Deficit Ranking	U.S. Trade Balance	U.S. Trade Deficit Ranking
1986	-1,666	17	-14,608	3
1990	-10,417	3	-11,184	2
1995	-33,807	2	-9,680	6

Source: U.S. Department of Commerce.

FIGURE 5. U.S. Trade Balances with China and Taiwan: 1986–1995

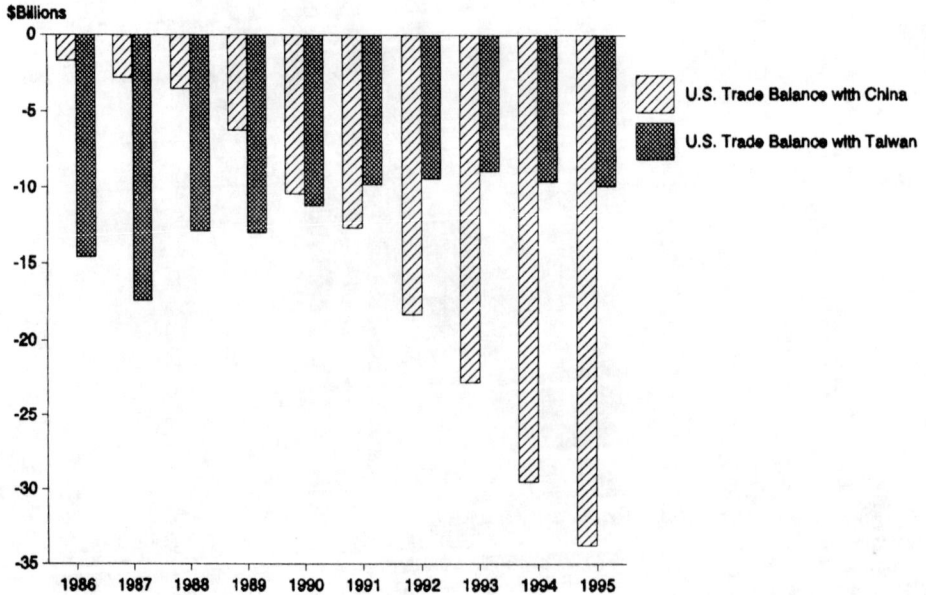

Source: U.S. Department of Commerce.

CHANGES IN U.S. IMPORTS FROM CHINA AND TAIWAN

The level and composition of U.S. imports from Taiwan and China have changed markedly over the past 10 years. Table 11 indicates the top five U.S. commodity imports from Taiwan in 1986 and compares them with U.S. imports of the same commodities from China in that year. U.S. imports of the same five commodities from Taiwan and China are also shown for 1995. In addition, the table indicates the rankings of the five commodities in terms of U.S. imports from China and Taiwan for both years.

The top five U.S. imports from Taiwan in 1986 were: (1) apparel and clothing; (2) miscellaneous manufactured products; (3) footwear; (4) telecommunications, sound, and recording equipment; and (5) electrical machinery and appliances. The value (and U.S. import rankings) of U.S. imports of each of these commodities (with the exception of electrical machinery and appliance) from Taiwan declined in 1995 over 1986 levels. On the other hand, U.S. imports of each of these five commodities from China rose sharply over the same period. The commodities which were the top five U.S. imports from Taiwan in 1986 were the top five U.S. imports from China in 1995.

For example, U.S. imports of Taiwan footwear fell from $2.2 billion (1986) to $400 million (1995), and the ranking of this commodity in terms of U.S. imports from Taiwan fell from 3rd to 13th. On the other hand, U.S. imports of Chinese footwear rose from $100 million in 1986 to $5.8 billion in 1995, and the U.S. import ranking of this commodity (in terms of U.S. imports from China) rose from 7th to 3rd.[33]

As previously indicated in table 5, a large share of U.S. imports from Taiwan in 1995 were comprised of computers and peripherals and electrical machinery. This trend reflects the shift in production (and export) by Taiwan from primarily labor-intensive goods to capital-intensive products. On the other hand, China has substantially boosted its production and export of labor-intensive commodities.

---

[33]U.S. imports of electrical machinery and appliances from Taiwan and China rose between 1986 and 1995, both in terms of value and U.S. import rankings from both economies.

TABLE 11. U.S. Imports of Selected Commodities From Taiwan and China: Totals and Rankings of Commodities in Relation to U.S. Imports From Each Entity, 1986 and 1995 ($Billions)

Commodity	1986 Taiwan $	1986 Taiwan U.S. Import Rank	1986 China $	1986 China U.S. Import Rank	1995 Taiwan $	1995 Taiwan U.S. Import Rank	1995 China $	1995 China U.S. Import Rank
All Commodities	19.8	--	4.8	--	29.0	--	45.6	--
Articles of Apparel and clothing accessories	2.6	1	1.7	1	2.2	5	5.9	2
Miscellaneous manufactured articles, n.e.s.	2.6	2	0.7	2	2.5	3	10.3	1
Footwear	2.2	3	0.1	7	0.4	13	5.8	3
Telecommun & sound & record & reproduce app & equip	1.9	4	0.1	12	1.2	6	4.3	4
Electrical Machinery, apparatus & appliances, n.e.s.	1.4	5	*	16	5.2	2	3.1	5
Total Five Commodities	10.7	--	2.6	--	11.5	--	29.4	--

*Less than 100 million
Commodity listing based on the top 5 U.S. imports from Taiwan in 1986.
N.e.s. means not elsewhere specified.
Import ranks are the ranking of each commodity in relation to U.S. imports from China and Taiwan.
Source: U.S. Department of Commerce.

The sharp increase in U.S. imports from China (especially in labor-intensive commodities) in recent years, relative to those from Taiwan, may be partially attributed to Taiwan investment in China in export processing operations.[34] Data do not exist on exports to the United States of commodities produced by Taiwan-owned firms in the mainland. However, Chinese data estimate that Taiwanese firms invested over $11 billion in China between 1990 and 1995 (see discussion on China-Taiwan economic relations beginning on page 37). A large

[34]Hong Kong and Macau firms have also invested heavily in export-oriented industries, which have also contributed to the surge of U.S. imports from China. However, such investment is not discussed in this report.

portion of that investment has gone into labor-intensive industries, many of which produce commodities mainly for export. In many cases, several export-oriented Taiwan firms have simply closed down labor-intensive production facilities in Taiwan and moved them to the mainland.[35] For example, a large portion of Taiwan's footwear industry is believed to have transferred its production facilities to the mainland. The United States was a major export market for the Taiwan footwear industry before such facilities were transferred to China, and it is likely that the United States remains a major market for shoes produced by transplanted Taiwan firms in China.[36] The Taiwanese Board of Foreign Trade estimates that 70% of all exports by Taiwan-funded factories in China are shipped to the U.S. market.[37]

MAJOR ISSUES IN U.S.-CHINA TRADE RELATIONS[38]

Despite the introduction of various economic and trade reforms over the past decade, the Chinese government attempts to regulate the level and composition of China's imports. It attempts to promote the import of priority products which are considered important to China's economic development (such as capital equipment, high technology products, and inputs used in the production of products for export). Many imports are limited or restricted in order to protect domestic industries or due to balance of trade considerations (i.e., to prevent trade deficits). To those ends, China has utilized import bans, high tariffs, restrictive license requirements, import substitution regulations, restrictive standards and inspection requirements, and foreign exchange controls to manage the level and composition of imports. The United States Trade Representative (USTR) has often described China as "one of the most protectionist trade regimes in the world."

Some trade analysts have attributed the growing U.S.-China trade deficit to Chinese trade and investment barriers. It is also estimated that U.S. firms suffer significant trade losses due to Chinese pirating of U.S. intellectual property rights (IPR) products. Other trade issues of concern to the United States include China's transshipments of textiles to the United States in violation of U.S. textile quotas, issues concerning China's accession to the World Trade Organization (WTO), and China's MFN status.

---

[35]Hickey, Dennis Van Vranken. Will Inter-China Trade Change Taiwan or the Mainland? *Orbis*, V. 35, Fall 1991, p. 519.

[36]Taiwan's shift of a large share of its labor-intensive production to China has allowed it to concentrate a greater share of domestic production and export of more capital-intensive products, such as computers and electrical machinery.

[37]*The Free China Journal* (Taiwan), May 24, 1996, World Wide Web Site.

[38]For a comprehensive discussion of U.S.-China trade relations, see U.S. Library of Congress, Congressional Research Service. *China-U.S. Trade Issues*, by Wayne M. Morrison (regularly updated).

MARKET ACCESS

On October 10, 1991, the USTR initiated a Section 301 investigation of four major Chinese trade barriers, including (1) import prohibitions and quotas, (2) restrictive import license requirements, (3) restrictive standards and certification requirements for imports, and (4) lack of transparency of Chinese trade laws.[39] The Section 301 case against China was highly unusual due to its breadth of coverage; it was essentially aimed at inducing China to reform its entire trade regime. In addition, the USTR linked U.S. support for China's re-entry into the General Agreement on Tariffs and Trade (GATT) to a successful resolution of the trade dispute.

On August 21, 1992, the USTR determined that negotiations had failed to resolve the trade dispute and threatened to impose $3.9 billion in U.S. trade sanctions (the highest level ever issued by the USTR under a Section 301 case up to that time) unless an agreement was reached by October 10, 1992. China in turn threatened retaliation against a comparable level of U.S. products.

On October 10, 1992, the United States and China reached an agreement. China pledged to reduce or eliminate a wide variety of trade barriers over the next 5 years (according to specific timetables), including tariffs, quotas, import restrictions, import licenses, and import substitution laws. In addition, China agreed to take a number of specified steps to make its trade regime more transparent, such as publishing its trade laws and regulations. Finally, China agreed to establish a joint working group to eliminate agricultural import barriers in the form of scientific standards and testing. For its part, the United States pledged to "staunchly support" China's entry into the GATT and to reduce exports controls on computer and telecommunications equipment exports to China.

USTR officials have noted that China has made some progress in recent years in reforming its trade regime by making its trade regime more transparent, lowering tariffs, and eliminating many quotas and license restrictions. However, the USTR contends that China has failed to remove all trade barriers to certain commodities and, in some cases, has erected new barriers. In addition, China has failed to eliminate discriminatory sanitary regulations on imported food products.[40] On several occasions, the USTR has threatened to impose trade sanctions against China for failing to comply with certain aspects of the agreement.

---

[39]Section 301 refers to provisions in the 1974 Trade Act (as amended) which authorizes the USTR to take certain measures in response to unfair trade practices.

[40]United States Trade Representative. *1996 National Trade Estimate Report on Foreign trade Barriers*, 1995. p. 46-59.

INTELLECTUAL PROPERTY RIGHTS PROTECTION

The United States has pressed China over the past several years to improve its enforcement of U.S. intellectual property rights (IPR) in China and to afford greater market access to intellectual property-related products, such as computer software, compact disks (CDs), and audio-visual products. Concerns over China IPR protection led the USTR to place China on its Special 301 *priority watch list* in 1989 and 1990.[41]

On April 26, 1991, the USTR designated China as a *priority foreign country* under Special 301 for failing to provide adequate protection for U.S. intellectual property rights IPR. Under the threat of $1.8 billion in U.S. sanctions, China agreed in January 1992 to enact new laws to strengthen its patent, copyright, and trade secret laws, and to improve protection of U.S. intellectual property, including computer software, sound recordings, agrichemicals, and pharmaceuticals. The USTR placed China on its Special 301 *watch list* in 1992 and 1993.

In June 1994, the USTR again designated China as a *priority foreign country* under Special 301 for failing to enforce its IPR laws and for restricting market access of intellectual property–related products. On February 4, 1995, the USTR announced that about $1 billion in sanctions would be imposed against China by February 26, 1995, unless a new agreement was reached. A preliminary agreement was subsequently reached on February 26, 1995. Under the agreement, China pledged to:

- **Begin a "Special Enforcement Period" over the course of the next several months** to stem IPR piracy in China by taking action against large-scale producers and distributors of pirated materials, and prohibiting the export of pirated products such as CDs, LDs, and CD-ROMs. Chinese officials pledged that if such firms were found to be in violation of IPR laws, they would be shut down, their business licenses revoked, and their pirated-making machinery destroyed.

- **Establish mechanisms to ensure long-term enforcement of IPR laws,** such as banning the use of pirated materials by the Chinese government, establishing a coordinated IPR enforcement policy among each level of government, enhancing IPR enforcement agencies, creating an effective customs enforcement system, establishing a title

---

[41]Special 301 refers to provisions in the 1974 Trade Act (as amended) which authorizes the USTR to take certain actions against nations which fail to provide adequate protection of U.S. IPR. Since 1989, the USTR has issued a three-tier Special 301 list of countries which are considered to maintain inadequate regimes for the protection of U.S. IPR or deny market access: (1) *Priority foreign countries* which are considered to be the worst violators of U.S. IPR and are subject to Section 301 investigations and possible U.S. trade sanctions; (2) *priority watch list countries* which are considered to have serious deficiencies in their IPR regime, but do not currently warrant a Section 301 investigation; and (3) *watch list countries* which have been identified because they maintain IPR practices or barriers to market access that are of particular concern, but do not yet warrant higher level designations.

verification system in China to ensure that U.S. audio visual works are protected against unauthorized use, reforming China's judicial system to ensure that U.S. firms can obtain access to effective judicial relief, establishing a system of maintaining statistics concerning China's enforcement efforts and meeting with U.S. officials on a regular basis to discuss those efforts, improving transparency in Chinese laws concerning IPR, and strictly enforcing IPR laws.

- **Provide greater market access to U.S. products** by removing import quotas on U.S. audio visual products, allowing U.S. record companies to market their entire works in China (subject to Chinese censorship concerns), and allowing U.S. intellectual property-related industries to enter into joint production arrangements with Chinese firms in certain Chinese cities.

Some U.S. firms have charged that IPR piracy in China has worsened during the past year, despite the U.S-China IPR agreement, and have pressed the USTR to take tougher action against China. The International Intellectual Property Alliance (IIPA), a U.S. IPR business association estimates U.S. trade losses from IPR piracy in China in 1995 at $2.3 billion.[42]

On April 30, 1996, USTR the designated China as a *priority foreign country* under Special 301 (signifying that the United States regards China as one of the worst violators of U.S. IPR) for failing to fully implement the February 1995 agreement on IPR, and warned that U.S. sanctions may be imposed against China if the IPR piracy and market access issues are not adequately addressed. The USTR noted that, while China had made some progress in cracking down on IPR violations, especially at the retail level, it has failed to: (1) take effective action against the major factories in China that are producing pirated products, (2) establish an effective border enforcement mechanism within its customs service to prevent the export of pirated products, and (3) provide sufficient market access to U.S. firms, such as removing high tariffs and permitting U.S. firms to establish joint-ventures in China.

On May 15, 1996, the USTR published a preliminary list of Chinese products which were under consideration for U.S. sanctions, and warned that the United States would impose 100% prohibitive tariffs on approximately $2 billion worth of Chinese products (drawn from the preliminary list) by June 17, 1996, unless China takes more effective action to fully implement the IPR agreement.[43] The preliminary lists mainly targets clothing, consumer electronics, and various miscellanies manufactured products. The Taiwanese Board of Foreign Trade estimates that U.S. sanctions, if imposed, would cost

---

[42]Reported in the *Journal of Commerce*, April 12, 1996, p.2.

[43]The USTR's preliminary sanctions list contains sanctions valued at $3 billion. The USTR will hold public hearings on the proposed list, after which, a final sanctions list will be developed (barring a U.S-China agreement) which is likely to total approximately $2 billion. (Source: *USTR press release, May 15, 1996*. Obtained from the USTR World Wide Web Page.)

Taiwan-invested firms (especially those making consumer electronic products) in China over $600 million in lost sales.[44]

TEXTILE TRANSSHIPMENTS

The U.S. Customs Service has found evidence on several occasions that China has attempted to circumvent U.S. textile quotas by transshipping Chinese products through other countries to the United States using false country of origin labels, and through misclassification of textile and apparel products. In January 1994, the USTR threatened to significantly reduce China's textile and apparel quotas, because of China's refusal to accept a new textile agreement containing anti-circumvention provisions. However, later that month, China accepted such provisions and concluded a new textile agreement with the United States. The agreement effectively slows the growth rate of China's textile exports to the United States and allows the United States to reduce China's quotas (under certain conditions) if China violates the agreement through transshipments. The textile agreement is effective for 3 years through 1997.

U.S. officials allege that transshipments continue to occur, despite Chinese assurances that such practices have been effectively halted. On several occasions, the United States has charged certain textile imports against China's quota levels on products U.S. officials alleged were transshipped by China through other countries.

WORLD TRADE ORGANIZATION (WTO)

The Chinese government has made China's accession to the WTO a major priority. China believes that its accession would enable it to gain nondiscriminatory treatment in its trade relations with WTO members and provide it with access to the multilateral trade dispute resolution process. Supporters of China's WTO membership argue that it would bring China's trade regime in line with other WTO members and would result in a significant reduction of Chinese trade barriers. Currently at issue are the specific steps China would be required to take to gain accession to the WTO.

The Chinese government has argued that China is a developing country and hence should be allowed to implement reforms gradually over a period of time and be allowed to protect certain industries. The United States and certain other WTO members argue that China is a major trading power and hence should be made to bring its trade regime more in line with basic multilateral trade rules once it is brought into the WTO. Specifically, it is argued that China should make its trade regime more transparent, afford national treatment to foreign firms in China, create a fully market-oriented exchange rate system, remove investment and import restrictions, provide adequate protection of IPR, phase out price controls, and limit government protection of infant industries.

---

[44]*The Free China Journal*, May 24, 1996, World Wide Web Site.

Talks between Chinese officials and a GATT working party failed to yield an agreement on a protocol for China's accession to the WTO before the end of 1994. This prevented China from becoming a founding WTO member. Chinese officials viewed the United States as having posed the greatest impediment to its entry into the WTO. Subsequently, China broke off WTO negotiations and announced that it would suspend implementation of the October 1992 market access MOU with the United States. However, following the March 1995 signing of the U.S.-Chinese IPR agreement, China pledged to resume implementing the market access MOU, while the United States pledged to hold talks with China on its accession to the WTO on a "flexible, pragmatic, and realistic basis, and to address realistically the issue of China's developing country status on the basis of the Uruguay Round Agreement." If China eventually accedes to the WTO, it might be brought in under a clause which would allow it to be recognized as a founding WTO member.[45]

CHINA'S MFN STATUS

Under Title IV of the 1974 Trade Act, as amended (commonly referred to as the "Jackson-Vanik Amendment"), China's MFN status is subject to annual renewal (through a presidential waiver, which is subject to possible congressional action).[46] Prior to 1989, renewal of China's MFN status was generally non-controversial and automatic. However, the Tiananmen Square massacre in June 1989, and subsequent Chinese government crackdown on the exercise of human rights, generated support among many Members of Congress to terminate China's MFN status.

Subsequently, the annual renewal of China's MFN status has been a source of considerable debate in the Congress. In addition, China's annual MFN status renewal has been used by Members to express concerns over the growing U.S. trade deficit with China, unfair Chinese trade practices, inadequate IPR protection, weapons proliferation, prison labor exports, as well as human rights and foreign policy issues. On several occasions over the past six years, Congress has considered legislation which would revoke China's MFN status, terminate MFN status for products produced by certain Chinese government entities, or condition MFN status on a presidential certification that China has made improvements in specified areas. Legislation to terminate or condition China's MFN status has passed one or both Houses, but such bills have not been enacted into law.

President Clinton in May 1993, specifically linked renewal of China's MFN status to specific improvements in human rights, but abandoned this policy in

---

[45]For additional information on China's accession to the GATT/WTO, see U.S. Library of Congress, Congressional Research Service. *China and the General Agreement on Tariffs and Trade*, by George D. Holliday. CRS Report 94-723E, September 12, 1994.

[46]For a discussion of China's MFN status, see U.S. Library of Congress, Congressional Research Service. *Most-Favored-Nation Status of the People's Republic of China*, by Vladimir N Pregelj, IB92094 (updated regularly).

May 1994 in announcing his decision to renew China's MFN status for another year. The Administration determined that such linkage had proved relatively ineffective in improving human rights in China and that a termination of China's MFN status was not in the interests of the United States. Subsequently, the Clinton Administration has supported renewing unconditional MFN status for China.

China's recent threats of possible military action against Taiwan are likely to be one of many issues examined by Congress in the next round of debate over the renewal of China's MFN status in 1996. A termination of China's MFN status would lead to substantially higher import duties on many Chinese products, and would likely lead to a significant reduction in U.S. imports of Chinese goods. In addition, it is likely that China would retaliate against U.S. exporters and investors in China.

PROSPECTS FOR FUTURE U.S.-CHINA ECONOMIC RELATIONS

Economic and trade reforms have helped to make China one of the world's fastest growing economies. This has led many analysts to predict that China will become an increasingly important market for many U.S. products. The Chinese government has announced extensive plans to upgrade and modernize its economy. It has made infrastructure development (including transportation, energy, and telecommunications), in particular, a major priority, and the Chinese government has announced that foreign firms will be allowed to participate in a wide variety of projects. The Department of Commerce has estimated that China's infrastructure needs through the year 2000 will require it to spend over $250 billion on imports. China's sharp economic growth, along with its massive infrastructure needs, has led the Department of Commerce to designate China as one of the top 10 emerging markets which offer the greatest future opportunities for U.S. exports. It projects the top five best commercial prospects (based on size and growth potential) for U.S. firms in China for 1996 will be aircraft and parts, electric power systems, computers and peripherals, telecommunications equipment, and automotive parts and service equipment.

While China has taken steps to liberalize its trade regime, U.S. firms continue to face a wide variety of trade barriers and restrictive business requirements in China. The Chinese government often attempts to pressure foreign firms to set up joint venture operations in China and to share technology as conditions for entering the Chinese market, rather than allowing such firms to export their products directly. In other cases, U.S. firms are allowed to establish operations in China only if they produce products for export. Problems doing business in China itself include government policies and regulations which discriminate against foreign firms in favor of Chinese firms, lax enforcement of IPR, and restrictions on the establishment and the scope of U.S. business offices in China. The extent and pace of China's future economic reforms, and China's willingness to implement its trade agreements with the United States fully, are likely to be major factors in determining the extent of future U.S. business opportunities in China.

Trade disputes between the United States and China are likely to arise often in the near future. While China has opened several sectors of its economy to foreign competition, several of its sectors (such retail and banking) remain relatively closed to foreign firms. In addition, China has targeted different sectors for development. For example, it recently announced that it intends to make autos a "pillar industry." It appears that China intends to develop its auto industry by erecting high tariffs and other barriers on foreign imports, while pressuring foreign firms to invest in joint venture operations in China. Chinese officials believe that, without trade protection measures, it cannot promote the development of indigenous industries it deems important to its economic future. China is also concerned that opening too many sectors to foreign competition could cause economic disruptions, especially for state-owned enterprises, many of which are very inefficient and would likely go out of business if subjected to foreign competition. U.S. officials have argued that free trade and open investment policies offer the best methods for promoting China's economic development.

The U.S. trade deficit with China is likely to continue to rise over the near term, possibly exceeding the U.S. trade deficit with Japan in the near future. Should this occur, it is likely that Congress may press the Executive branch to take greater action against Chinese trade barriers. Such pressures are likely to generate trade conflicts over a number of issues.

MAJOR ISSUES IN U.S.-TAIWAN ECONOMIC RELATIONS

For decades, the Taiwanese government protected domestic agriculture and industries against foreign competition through a variety of import barriers as part of its economic development strategies. These barriers included restrictions at the border, such as high tariffs, quotas, and import licenses. The barriers also included internal regulations such as safety and certification requirements, that favored domestic products over imports. The Taiwan government also barred imports of products like cigarettes and alcohol through its state monopoly control over production and distribution of these products. In addition to restricting imports, Taiwan closely limited foreign investment.

Until the 1980s, the United States tolerated these restrictions, especially when national security concerns, in the form of the Soviet Union and China, took priority over foreign trade. Beginning in the 1980s, however, U.S. relations with China, including commercial relations, developed and the security threat from China receded. In addition, as imports from, and the U.S. trade deficit with, Taiwan soared in the 1980s, U.S. producers were demanding greater access for their products in the Taiwan market. The U.S. government, therefore, placed increasing pressure on Taiwan, through threats of retaliation, to remove import barriers. These market access issues had been the subject of many series of often tense bilateral negotiations.

U.S.-Taiwan trade relations were especially tense in the mid- to late-1980s. The United States was particularly concerned about its trade deficits. Because of the importance of the United States as an export market (accounting for close to 50% of Taiwan exports at that time), Taiwan was very vulnerable to U.S. pressures. In the 1980s, the Taiwan government sent "Buy America" missions to the United States in a public effort to increase its American imports and reduce U.S. pressure.

The peak of bilateral tension to date was reached with the enactment of the Omnibus Trade and Competitiveness Act of 1988 (P.L. 100-104). Congressional concerns over rising trade deficits with Japan, South Korea, and Taiwan, led the Congress to enact provisions aimed at countries that practice unfair trade ("Super 301"), do not protect U.S. IPR ("Special 301"), and manipulate their currencies to achieve an unfair advantage for their exports.

In April 1989, Taiwan announced an action plan that included commitments to reduce its trade surplus with the United States, cut tariffs on a number of products, and to strengthen IPR protection.[47] The announcement came shortly before the USTR was to determine which countries would be labeled as "priority countries" under the first "Super 301" list. Taiwan avoided being named. But Taiwan, along with South Korea, had been cited for manipulating its currency.[48]

U.S.-Taiwan trade relations have become much less tense in recent years. This is in part because of the reduction of the U.S. trade deficit with Taiwan. Taiwan has also made great strides in opening its markets and has greatly liberalized foreign investment.

Nevertheless, some barriers remain a concern of the U.S. business community and, therefore, of U.S. policymakers. These issues are now largely addressed in the context of Taiwan's application to join the WTO. The United States is also concerned about Taiwan's IPR practices.

GATT/WTO

On January 1, 1990, the government of Taiwan filed its application to join the General Agreements on Tariffs and Trade (GATT). Because of its preoccupation with the Uruguay Round negotiations and because of the political difficulties of having to consider applications from China and Taiwan at the same time, the GATT did not establish a working party until September 1992. A working party is a group of GATT member-countries selected to study Taiwan's application and to produce a Protocol of Accession outlining Taiwan's obligations for becoming a GATT member. Taiwan's application has now been taken up by the WTO, the successor to the GATT.

---

[47] Bayard, Thomas O. and Kimberley Ann Elliott. *Reciprocity and Retaliation in U.S. Trade Policy.* Institute for International Economics. Washington. September 1994. p. 184.

[48] The U.S. Treasury Department made such a determination in October 1988. *International Trade Reporter*, vol. 5, October 26, 1988. p. 1415.

Taiwan has several factors in its favor as it pursues its application to the WTO. It has applied as a fully developed country rather than as a developing country. It, therefore, has agreed to adhere to the strictest rules WTO membership which should make WTO members more inclined to approve the application. (The WTO allows developing countries exceptions to some of the WTO obligations.) In addition, by some measurements, Taiwan is the 19th largest economy in the world, much larger than many of the current WTO members. Membership in the WTO would require Taiwan to liberalize its trade regime breaking down barriers that would benefit exporters from Japan, the United States, the European Union and other major trading countries. The United States supports Taiwan's application.

China opposed Taiwan's membership when Taiwan first applied, but now only demands that it be admitted ahead of Taiwan. Taiwan has applied as a "separate customs territory" rather than as a country, thus skirting the political issue of Taiwan as an integral part of China.

The working party is studying Taiwan's trading system and is drawing up a Protocol of Accession that will list the conditions under which Taiwan can join the WTO. The WTO admission process also requires that Taiwan conduct bilateral negotiations with its major partners to satisfy their concerns about its trade policies and regime. The United States is a member of the working party on Taiwan and is one of the countries with which Taiwan is negotiating bilaterally. Through the WTO accession process, the United States is promoting its concerns with Taiwan on a number of market access issues and on other aspects of Taiwan's trade and investment regime.

The timing of Taiwan's admission to the WTO will likely depend on that of China. Taiwan's negotiations with the working party members and with its bilateral trade partners continue, but this stage of the accession process seems to be nearly completed. The United States, however, still has some outstanding concerns.

High tariffs. The United States has pressed Taiwan to reduce tariffs on 2,786 products that cover roughly 55% of U.S. exports (as measured in the 1989-91 period) and has sought a reduction on tariff peaks or a binding of tariffs on the other 45%. Of particularly concern to U.S. exporters are high tariffs on a variety of agricultural products, such as fresh fruits, processed fruits, processed vegetables, breakfast cereals, and chocolate. Taiwan also maintains high tariffs on auto parts, passenger cars, and trucks. Taiwan has made commitments to reduce tariffs on some of the products, but negotiations continue over tariffs on the others.[49]

Import Licensing. Taiwan has radically reformed its import licensing regime during the last decade. At one time, it maintained a "positive" list system, that is, the government would only permit those products on the list to be imported

---

[49] Office of the United States Trade Representative. *1995 National Trade Estimate Report on Foreign Trade Barriers.* Washington. April 1995. p. 289-290.

without licenses. This system restricted most products and was burdensome to foreign exporters. In July 1994, Taiwan adopted a "negative" list system that has reduced the portion of product categories requiring licenses from 66% to 15%.[50]

Taiwan still requires licenses for imports of over 700 product categories. Some products only require notification. Others require approval from the government's Board of Foreign Trade. But some 243 products are completely banned from importation, including rice, chicken meat, certain fruits (including bananas), and certain arms and munitions. Often, products that can be legally imported require the approval of various government agencies that attempt to protect domestic producers, thereby effectively prohibiting the imports.

Standards, Testing, Labeling, and Certification. The United States has argued that the Taiwan government applies more restrictive criteria on imported than domestic products for approval for sale in Taiwan.[51]

Government Procurement. The Taiwan government has applied a very restrictive "Buy Taiwan Policy" in its procurement. Government agencies must buy locally unless the product, or an acceptable substitute, is not produced locally. It also has applied very selective criteria to firms bidding for government contracts that virtually prevent foreign firms from competing for government contracts.[52]

If Taiwan becomes a member of the WTO it will have to adhere to multilateral codes on import licensing, customs valuation, and standards. Taiwan has agreed also to adhere to the WTO code on government procurement, although not required to do so. These codes bind their signatories to rules designed to ensure that the measures they cover are not applied in a manner that discriminates against imports.

INTELLECTUAL PROPERTY RIGHTS PROTECTION

For many years, Taiwan had a reputation, along with other Asian newly industrializing economies, for poor protection of foreign IPR. Local firms routinely produced goods that violated foreign registered copyrights, trademarks, and patents. The United States has pressured the Taiwan government to develop statutory protection for intellectual property and to enforce the laws. In April 1992, the USTR designated Taiwan as a Special 301 *priority foreign country*.[53]

---

[50] Ibid., p. 291.

[51] Ibid., p. 292.

[52] Ibid., p. 293.

[53] *International Trade Reporter*, vol. 9, May 6, 1992. p. 784.

According to the U.S. government, Taiwan's record on IPR has greatly improved. But, some problems remain. For example, U.S companies have reported that Taiwan producers pirate and export counterfeit computer software, including video games. The USTR placed Taiwan on its Special 301 *priority watch list* in 1993, and on its Special 301 *watch list* in 1994 and 1995. In 1996, no designation was given to Taiwan by the USTR under Special 301. If Taiwan joins the WTO, it will be required to adhere to the WTO agreement on trade-related intellectual property rights (TRIPs) that requires member countries to recognize and protect foreign IPR.

PROSPECTS FOR U.S.-TAIWAN ECONOMIC RELATIONS

The United States and Taiwan have overcome many earlier obstacles in their economic ties and have built a strong relationship. Barring major changes in policy on either side, it seems likely that the relationship will remain strong for the foreseeable future.

Taiwan has maintained a pattern of substantial economic growth for a long period of time. It is unlikely that Taiwan will be able to maintain such high growth rates in the long term as its economy matures. Nevertheless, DRI/McGraw Hill projects that for the remainder of the decade, Taiwan will maintain growth rates of about 6%.[54] This trend, plus the continuation of trade liberalization in Taiwan, indicates that Taiwan should remain a strong market for U.S. exports and investment.

Taiwan will continue to depend on imports for many of its food products. Opportunities for U.S. food producers should increase as Taiwan implements tariff reductions on food products as part of the WTO admission's process. Taiwan should also remain a good market for U.S. manufactured exports. The U.S. Department of Commerce has identified a number of categories of manufactured products as the best export prospects for the next two years. These categories include electronic components, such as integrated circuits; aircraft and aircraft parts; computer software; equipment for electronic power systems; laboratory scientific instruments; and chemical production machinery.[55] U.S. agricultural producers will face competition in the Taiwan market from Asian producers. U.S. manufacturers particularly of high technology based goods, will likely face competition from Japan.

The relative importance of the United States as a market for Taiwan's exports will continue to recede as Taiwanese exporters concentrate on building markets in Asia, particularly China, and shifting production offshore. Nevertheless, the U.S. market, given its size, is one that Taiwan cannot ignore. American consumers can expect Taiwan to be the source of increasingly

---

[54] DRI/McGraw Hill, Inc. *World Markets Country Summaries -- Fourth Quarter 1995.* p. 133.

[55] U.S. Department of Commerce. International Trade Administration. *Commercial Guides - - Taiwan*, 1995.

sophisticated consumer goods, such as computers, as the level of technology in these industries advances.

CHINA-TAIWAN ECONOMIC RELATIONS

China and Taiwan do not maintain official relations, and Taiwan forbids direct trade with, and investment in, the mainland. As a result, trade and investment flows between the two entities is generally done indirectly, mainly through Hong Kong and other countries. Taiwan imposes significant restrictions on the import of Chinese products, attempts to limit those imports which might be disruptive to domestic industries, and seeks to regulate Taiwan investment in China.

Prior to 1980, trade and investment flows between Taiwan and China were virtually nil, due largely to Taiwanese policies that generally forbade most trade and investment relations with the mainland. However, during the early 1980's, wage demands and the appreciation of Taiwan's currency made many labor-intensive and export-oriented industries (especially small and medium-sized firms) less competitive and led many Taiwan producers to invest in production facilities outside Taiwan -- especially in China. The mainland was viewed by many Taiwanese firms as a source of cheap labor for sunset (declining) industries (such as shoes, textiles, plastic products, toys, and consumer electronics) and as a potential market for Taiwan exports. These factors induced the Taiwan government to adopt measures to slowly increase and liberalize indirect trade with and investment in the mainland.

In 1987, the Taiwanese government removed restrictions on (indirect) travel to the mainland, which led Taiwanese investors to travel there seeking investment opportunities.[56] In 1989, the Taiwan government promulgated regulations permitting indirect trade, indirect investment, and cooperation with the mainland, and expanding (from 30 to 92 items) the number of products which could be imported from the mainland. In 1990, the Taiwan government issued regulations requiring Taiwan firms to register investments in China and specified the types of investments (mainly labor-intensive industries) that would be allowed.[57] Over the past 5 years, the Taiwan government has gradually expanded the types of investments that can be made in China and the list of products that can be imported from the mainland (including a wide range of semi-finished industrial goods).

China, since implementing economic reforms in 1978, has actively sought to encourage trade with and investment from Taiwan for economic as well as

---

[56]Chang, Maria Hsia. *Taiwan and the Mainland: A Shifting Competition.* Global Affairs, Volume 7, Summer 1992, p. 21.

[57]Chiu, Lee-in Chen. *The Pattern and Impact of Taiwan's Investment in Mainland China.* In Emerging Patterns of Asian Investment in China: From Korea, Taiwan, and Hong Kong. 1995, p. 145.

political reasons. For example, in 1985, it formally opened its domestic market to Taiwan investors and designated 10 coastal ports for Taiwan investment, shipping, and trade. In 1988, the Chinese government promulgated regulations to encourage Taiwan investment by providing special tax incentives to Taiwan investors.[58]

The absence of direct trade and investment links makes it difficult to obtain comprehensive and accurate data on China-Taiwan trade and investment links. China's data on trade with Taiwan include only trade that occurs through Hong Kong, which constitutes about 88% of China-Taiwan trade. The Taiwan government does not include indirect trade with China in its official trade statistics, although the government, since 1989 (when indirect trade was first permitted), has attempted to estimate the total level of China-Taiwan trade. China collects data on Taiwanese investment in the mainland, although this data may be somewhat overstated because some foreign investors attempt to register their investments as Taiwanese in order to take advantage of preferential trade and investment treatment afforded to Taiwanese firms in China. Taiwan's data on indirect investment in China is limited to Taiwan firms which have officially registered with the government or have received government approval for *proposed investment* in the mainland.[59] Due to government controls on Taiwanese investment, it is likely that a significant amount of Taiwanese investment in China is not reported to the Taiwan government.

Taiwanese and Chinese bilateral trade and investment data are surveyed below. Both these data sources show a trend of increasingly interdependency and integration between the two economies.

CHINA-TAIWAN TRADE

Chinese Trade Data

According to Chinese data, China-Taiwan merchandise trade (through Hong Kong) has grown grew significantly over the past 15 years (**see figure 6**). Total China-Taiwan trade between 1980 and 1986 rose gradually, from $300 million in 1980 to $1.0 billion in 1986. Since 1986, trade has risen sharply, due mainly to Chinese investment and trade incentives, and Taiwan's liberalization of its trade and investment regulations with the mainland. Total trade rose from $1.0 billion in 1986, to $4.0 billion in 1990. China-Taiwan trade appears to have surged between 1990 and 1995 (**see table 12**), growing by nearly 348% to $17.9 billion in 1995. The largest annual increase in bilateral trade occurred in 1992-1993 when total trade grew from $7.4 billion to $14.4 billion. From 1994 to 1995, total trade increased by 9.8%. Based on these data, China's trade with

---

[58]Chinese government officials held that promoting greater economic relations with Taiwan was the first step towards national re-unification.

[59]Taiwanese investment data reflect the value of contracted investment, as opposed to actual investment.

Taiwan (through Hong Kong) now constitutes about 6.4% of China's total trade, making it China's fourth largest trading partner (1995).[60]

Chinese data indicate that China imports substantially more from Taiwan than it exports. In 1995, Chinese imports from Taiwan (through Hong Kong) totalled $14.8 billion, while exports to Taiwan totalled $3.1 billion. As a result, China incurred a $11.7 billion trade deficit with Taiwan.

FIGURE 6. China–Taiwan Trade Through Hong Kong: 1980–1995

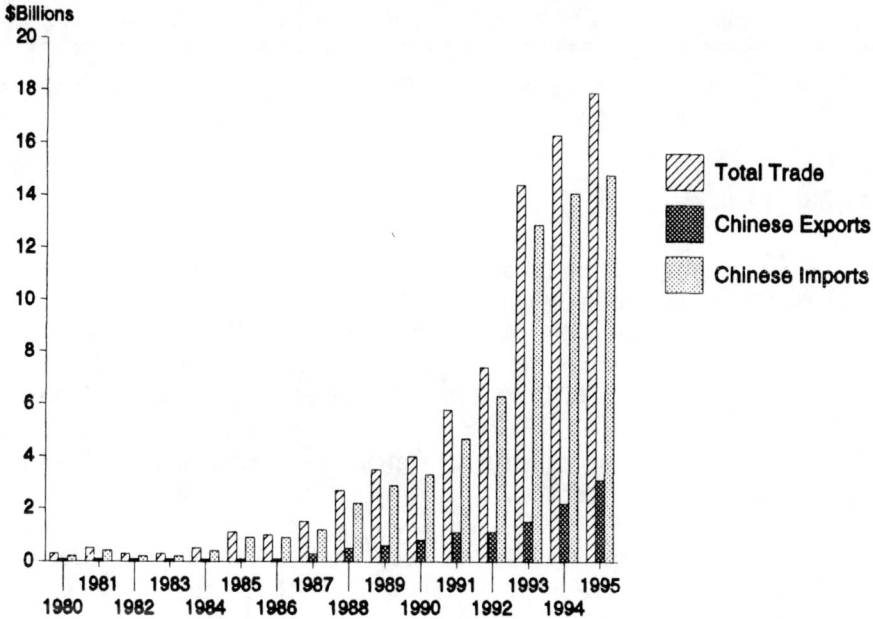

Source; Data supplied by Chinese Embassy, Washington, D.C.

---

[60]Data supplied by the Chinese Embassy, Washington, D.C.

Table 12. China-Taiwan Trade Through Hong Kong:
1980, and 1990-1995 ($Billions)

	1980	1990	1991	1992	1993	1994	1995
Total Trade	0.3	4.0	5.8	7.4	14.4	16.3	17.9
Exports	0.1	0.8	1.1	1.1	1.5	2.2	3.1
Imports	0.2	3.3	4.7	6.3	12.9	14.1	14.8
Trade Balance	-0.1	-3.2	-3.6	-5.2	-11.4	-11.9	-11.7

Source: Embassy of the People's Republic of China, 1993 *China Statistical Yearbook*, and official Hong Kong trade statistics.

Taiwan Trade Data

Taiwan's Mainland China Council estimates that Taiwan's total trade with China rose from $5.2 billion in 1990 to $21.0 billion in 1995 -- an average annual increase of about 39%. Total trade grew by 17.3% in 1995 over 1994.[61] In particular, Taiwanese indirect exports to the mainland have grown sharply, from $4.4 billion in 1990 to $17.9 billion in 1995; and the share of Taiwan's exports going to China over this period rose from 9.8% to 16.0%, respectively, making China the fastest growing market for Taiwanese exports. Based on these figures, China is currently Taiwan's second largest export market after the United States, and will likely be the largest in the near future.[62] Taiwan's indirect exports to China in 1995 were over two-thirds as large as those to the United States. Despite recent political tensions with the mainland, Taiwanese officials project that Taiwan-China trade will rise by about 20% in 1996.[63]

Taiwanese trade data indicate that Taiwan's imports from the mainland grew from $800 million in 1990 to $3.1 billion in 1995, reflecting a gradual liberalization of Taiwan's policies on Chinese imports. Taiwan has enjoyed a growing trade surplus with China; that surplus rose from $3.6 billion in 1990 to $14.8 billion in 1995 (**see table 13**).

---

[61]Taiwan data attempts to measure all indirect trade with China, which includes trade through Hong Kong, Singapore, Japan, and other countries.

[62]Taiwan's official trade data show Hong Kong as the second largest export market. However, nearly 60% of Taiwan's exports to Hong Kong are re-exported to China. Combining these re-exports with other Taiwanese indirect trade with China makes China the second largest destination for Taiwan exports.

[63]*China Economic News* (CEN) Home Page (Taiwan). March 15, 1996.

TABLE 13. Taiwan Estimates of Indirect Taiwan-China Trade:
1990-1995 ($Billions)

	1990	1991	1992	1993	1994	1995
Total Trade	5.2	8.6	11.7	15.1	17.9	21.0
Exports	4.4	7.5	10.5	14.0	16.0	17.9
Imports	0.8	1.1	1.1	1.1	1.9	3.1
Trade Balance	3.6	6.4	9.4	12.9	14.1	14.8

Source: Mainland Affairs Council (Taiwan).

Taiwanese trade data for 1994, (the most current year in which data are available), indicate the top Taiwan exports to China were textile fibers (32% of total exports), electrical and electronic parts (13.2%), raw plastic materials (12.8%) and industrial machinery (9.1%). Major imports from China included herbal medicines, footwear semi-products, polyester staple with cotton, and furs and feathers.[64]

TAIWAN INVESTMENT IN CHINA

Chinese Data

Chinese data indicate that Taiwanese investment in China was small prior to 1990, but increased sharply thereafter. Taiwan investment in China grew from $222 million in 1990 to $3.4 billion in 1994. In 1995, Taiwan investment fell to $3.0 billion, although the amount of contracted investment with the mainland increased (from $5.4 billion in 1994 to $5.8 billion in 1995). Through the end of 1995, Taiwanese businesses have invested in over 32,000 projects in China, with a contracted value of $30.1 billion, and actual investment at over $11.4 billion (**see table 14**). Chinese data indicate that Taiwan is the second largest investor in China (after Hong Kong/Macau), accounting for about 10% of total actual investment.

[64]*1996 Taiwan Yearbook*, Homepage.

TABLE 14. Chinese data on Indirect Taiwan Investment in China: 1978-1995 (Total Projects and $Billions)

	No. of Projects	Contracted Value ($Billions)	Actual Investment ($Billions)
Cumulative 1978-1988	437	0.60	0.02
1989	540	0.55	0.15
1990	1,103	0.89	0.22
1991	1,735	1.39	0.47
1992	6,430	5.54	1.05
1993	10,948	9.97	3.14
1994	9,247	5.40	3.39
1995	4,778	5.78	3.00
Cumulative: 1978-1995	32,218	30.1	11.44

Source: Data supplied by the Chinese Embassy, Washington, DC.

Taiwan Data

The Taiwanese government did not officially allow investment in China until 1991, although indirect investment in China had occurred (technically illegally) prior to that time. In 1991, the Taiwanese government established regulations governing the types of investment which could be made, and required investors to submit investment proposals for approval. The government sought to limit Taiwan investment in the mainland to low-tech production of such items as plastics, foodstuffs, footwear, and apparel. The guidelines also provided a general amnesty to Taiwanese firms and individuals who had made investments in China before the change in government policy as long as they reported their investments to the government by 1993.[65]

According to Taiwanese data on government approved and registered indirect investment in China, industries with the greatest Taiwanese investment in China from 1991-1994 have been electronic and electronic appliances, food and beverage processing, plastic products, basic metal and metal products,

---

[65]Hickey, Dennis Van Vranken. Will Inter-China Trade Change Taiwan or the Mainland? *Orbis*, V. 35, Fall 1991, p. 519.

precision instruments, and chemicals.[66]   The main provinces for Taiwan's investment have mainly been the southeastern coastal regions of China, especially Guangdong and Fujian provinces.

Officially, the Taiwanese government began collecting data on indirect investment in China, based on the amount of investment registered (and approved) with the Taiwanese Investment Commission, Ministry of Economic Affairs. These data put the total amount of registered Taiwanese investment in China through 1995 at about $5.6 billion (**see table 15**).[67]   Taiwan investment data indicate that China is the largest destination for overseas Taiwan investment.[68]

TABLE 15. Registered and Approved Indirect Investment
by Taiwanese Firms in China: 1991-1995

	Number of Projects	Amount ($Billions)
1991	237	$0.17
1992	264	0.25
1993*	9,329	3.17
1994	934	0.96
1995	560	1.09
Cumulative Total: 1991-1995	11,324	5.64

*1993 was the deadline for Taiwan businesses to register their mainland investments or face fines, which led to a surge in reported projects.

Source: Taiwan Ministry of Economic Affairs.

OUTLOOK FOR CHINA-TAIWAN ECONOMIC RELATIONS

Taiwanese have invested in China for several economic reasons: to gain access to China's vast and growing market, to take advantage of China's abundant labor and relatively low production costs, and to gain access to raw

[66]Investment Commission, Ministry of Economic Affairs, Republic of China. *Statistics on the Republic of China*, November 1995, p. 74-77.

[67]These data appear to differ significantly from Chinese data on the value of contracted Taiwanese investment in China from 1991-1995 ($28.1 billion). This implies that a large amount of Taiwan investment is probably not reported to the Taiwanese government.

[68]This is based on Taiwan data for approved investment in 1995. Approved investment for China was $1.1 billion, compared to $793 million for the United States (the second largest destination for Taiwanese investment).

materials. China has actively sought Taiwan investment to obtain technology, hard currency, technical know-how, and to provide employment and training opportunities to its citizens. Hence, the economic relationship has proved beneficial for both sides.

It is likely that China-Taiwan economic relations will continue to grow in the near future, barring a military conflict in the region, or efforts by either government to impose restrictions on trade and investment. As Taiwan's economy becomes more modernized, it is likely that a greater share of its GDP will comprise capital-intensive, high-tech, and service industries, while the importance of labor-intensive industries will continue to diminish. China will likely continue to be an attractive source of investment for many of Taiwan's sunset industries.

China is also likely to become an increasingly important source for parts and components used in the production of Taiwan products, which could make many Taiwan products more internationally competitive.[69] Sourcing production in China will also make the mainland an important market for Taiwan capital equipment, such as machinery and parts.

China's rapid economic growth is likely to continue in the near future, which will increase domestic demand for foreign goods and services. Taiwan's close proximity to the mainland, its common language and cultural bonds, and its extensive investment in China, provide it with several unique advantages over foreign competitors in gaining access to China's growing market. These factors suggest that economic integration and interdependence between China and Taiwan is likely to move rapidly in the years ahead.

Chinese leaders have stated on several occasions that political factors will not affect China's economic relations with Taiwan, and have thus continued to promote greater economic ties with Taiwan, despite political tensions.[70] The Fujian provincial government in April 1996 called for greater economic cooperation with Taiwan, stating that it would seek to obtain Taiwan investment in large-scale projects, including various service sectors (such as retailing and banking) which are currently closed to foreign investors.[71]

The Taiwan government, on the other hand, appears to be moving somewhat cautiously in expanding economic relationship with the mainland. On the one hand, some Taiwan government officials, have expressed concern that

---

[69]Increased investment in China will enable Taiwanese firms to shift a greater share of its low-skilled, labor-intensive, production to China, allowing Taiwan firms to concentrate a greater share of their production on high-skilled, capital intensive, and service-related industries.

[70]*Reuters*. March 16, 1996. According to the report, An Min, Director General of the Chinese Ministry of Foreign Trade and Economic Cooperation, was quoted as saying: "No matter what happens, the legal rights of Taiwan business people in the Chinese mainland will always be protected and encouraged."

[71]*The Hong Kong Standard* (Hong Kong). April 4, 1996. World Wide Web Homepage.

growing economic ties with the mainland could make Taiwan too financially dependent on China. They argue that a disruption in trade (due to political reasons, or if China's economy became volatile) would seriously affect Taiwan's economy.[72] Such concerns have led the Taiwan government to limit and regulate the amount and types of trade and investment that can legally take place with the mainland. In addition, the Taiwan government in 1993 advocated a "Southern Investment Strategy" to encourage and assist Taiwan investors to diversify their investments into other Asian markets such as Vietnam, Malaysia, the Philippines, and Indonesia to avoid overdependency on the Chinese economy.[73] The Taiwanese government is also attempting to establish Taiwan as an operations center for manufacturing, transportation, finance, and telecommunications for the Asia-Pacific region over the next 10 years.[74]

On the other hand, the Taiwan government appears to be taking several steps to promote greater economic relations with China:

- In February 1996, the Taiwan government announced plans to provide trade and investment assistance to Taiwan firms seeking to enter the Chinese market.[75]

- In March 1996, the Taiwan government indicated that it was studying various alternatives to help establish direct business relations (including trade, investment, and travel) with the mainland.[76] The removal of restrictions on direct trade, travel, and investment would significantly lower business costs and thus would likely lead to an increase in bilateral trade and investment flows. For example, it is estimated that indirect trade routes result in 20% to 50% in additional shipping costs for exporters.[77] A removal of such restrictions would also likely lead to a greater dispersion of Taiwan trade and investment throughout the mainland, since Taiwan firms would no longer be

---

[72]Chinese military threats led to a downturn in Taiwan's economy in 1995 and may affect future near-term economic growth.

[73]*1996 Republic of China Yearbook* (Taiwan), World Wide Web edition.

[74]*The Government Information Office, R.O.C. (Taiwan)* World Wide Web Site.

[75]*Reuters.* February 27, 1996.

[76]*Free China Journal* (Taiwan) March 28, 1996 World Wide Web Page.

[77]Hickey, Dennis Van Vranken. Will Inter-China Trade Change Taiwan or the Mainland? *Orbis*, V. 35, Fall 1991, p.525.

required to go through Hong Kong and other countries to conduct business with the mainland.[78]

- In April 1996, the Taiwan government announced that it would expand the list of products which could legally be indirectly imported from the mainland, from 2,900 to 3,900, beginning in July 1996.[79]

Efforts by the Taiwanese government to expand investment and trade links with the mainland appear to be motivated by two main factors. Some Taiwan officials believe that greater economic ties with the mainland will foster more stable political relations. They contend that greater economic ties with the mainland makes China more economically dependent on Taiwan, hence reducing the likelihood of the use of force by China against Taiwan. In addition, many Taiwanese businesses are pushing the government towards expanding economic links with the mainland because such ties are viewed as highly profitable.

Several trade and investment issues could likely prove contentious in the near future, however. First, Chinese officials have increasingly sought to attract capital-intensive and high-tech industries into investing in China. As a condition for access to the Chinese market, foreign firms are often pressured into investing and sharing technology. China is currently attempting to encourage investment by Taiwan's capital-intensive and high-tech industries. The Taiwan government may seek to block such investment, due to concerns that domestic workers will be displaced, and that technology transfers will increasingly make China a competitor of Taiwan in important export industries. Second, China may attempt to put pressure on Taiwan to provide greater market access for its products, and to allow Chinese firms to make investments in Taiwan. While Taiwan has liberalized its restrictions on Chinese imports in recent years, it will likely continue to ban those products that it deems may harm domestic industries. Finally, while Chinese laws offer some protection for Taiwan investment, the two entities have not signed an investment treaty or agreement which would provide comprehensive legal safeguards to Taiwan investors. The lack of such safeguards adds a level of uncertainty (and costs) to Taiwan's investment in China.

CONCLUSIONS

The United States has significant economic interests in China and Taiwan, and their importance is growing in any formulation of U.S. policy in the region. Both economies are important U.S. export markets for agricultural and manufactured goods and are platforms for U.S. foreign investment in

---

[78]The issue of direct trade and investment is also being driven by Hong Kong's reversion to Chinese sovereignty in July 1997. Since a large share of Taiwan-China trade, and Taiwan investment in China, takes place through Hong Kong, it may soon no longer be possible to conduct indirect business relations through Hong Kong.

[79]*The Free China Journal* (Taiwan), April 19, 1996, World Wide Web Site.

manufactures and services sectors. Both economies are important sources of imported goods that provide American consumers with a variety of relatively low-cost goods (although some imports have competed with U.S. import-sensitive industries).

Both China and Taiwan appear to be on economic development paths that promise substantial future economic growth, and therefore, greater opportunities for U.S. involvement. In this regard, Taiwan's is the more developed of the two economies and will likely grow less rapidly than China. That trend, plus China's size, would indicate that China will at some point become a more important export market for U.S. products than Taiwan in terms of volume. However, rising living standards, increased spending for infrastructure development, and continued reductions in trade and investment barriers will likely make Taiwan an important market for many U.S. goods and services in the near future.

U.S. economic ties with China and Taiwan have been fraught with friction. Currently, the relationship with Taiwan appears the more stable one. Over the years, Taiwan has substantially opened its markets to imports and foreign investment and has improved its protection of IPR alleviating many of the concerns that U.S. exporters and investors had. Taiwan's petition for admission to the WTO as a fully developed country implies a commitment to reduce trade and investment barriers even further. U.S. relations with China, on the other hand, currently contain a number of sources of friction, including U.S. concerns over market access and China's IPR. The continued increase in the size and growth of the Chinese economy, and increases in the U.S. trade deficit with China, are likely to generate greater U.S. pressure for China to adopt multilateral rules on trade, investment, and IPR, and to afford greater market access to U.S. goods and services. China may resist such pressures as it attempts to promote the development of industries it deems important to future economic development. In addition, U.S. concerns over China's human rights policies and foreign policy practices continue to play a role in the debate over MFN status and other trade matters with China. These problems would indicate more friction ahead.

As the report has shown, the Taiwan and China economies are becoming increasingly more interdependent. As a consequence, the character of the U.S. economic relationship with them is becoming increasingly less bilateral and more triangular. The integration is evident in the sharp growth of Taiwan investments in China and China's importance as a Taiwan export market. Trade data would seem to indicate that many of the labor-intensive products once produced in Taiwan and exported to the United States are now produced by Taiwan-owned companies in China and exported to the United States. This trend will affect U.S. policy choices. A U.S. removal of MFN status for China, or other types of trade sanctions against China, may negatively impact production facilities in China that are largely owned by Taiwan investors (as well as other foreign investors). Therefore, the calculation of U.S. interests in both China and Taiwan is becoming increasingly complex.

The rapid economic integration between China and Taiwan may, in the long-run help to reduce military and political tensions, because both entities have a growing economic stake in maintaining peaceful and stable bilateral relations. Chinese continued use of threats (or use) of military force against Taiwan could greatly harm Taiwan's economy. However, such actions would likely lead to a sharp reduction in Taiwanese investment in the mainland, which would have a negative impact on China's economy, especially the coastal regions where Taiwanese investment is concentrated.

APPENDIX: U.S.-CHINA-TAIWAN TRADE AND ECONOMIC DATA

TABLE A1. China's World Trade: 1986-1995
($Billions)

	Exports	Imports	Trade Balance
1986	31.4	43.2	-11.9
1987	39.4	43.2	-3.8
1988	47.6	55.3	-7.7
1989	52.9	59.1	-6.2
1990	62.9	53.9	9.0
1991	71.9	63.9	8.1
1992	85.5	81.8	3.6
1993	91.6	103.6	-11.9
1994	120.8	115.6	5.2
1995	148.8	132.1	16.7

Source: International Monetary Fund, Direction of Trade Statistics.

TABLE A2. Taiwan World Trade, 1986-1995
($Billions)

	Exports	Imports	Trade Balance
1986	39.6	24.2	15.4
1987	53.5	34.8	18.7
1988	60.5	49.8	10.7
1989	66.1	52.5	13.6
1990	67.1	54.8	12.3
1991	76.2	62.9	13.3
1992	81.5	72.0	9.5
1993	85.1	77.1	8.0
1994	93.1	85.4	7.7
1995	111.7	103.6	8.1

Source: World Trade Organization. *International Trade: Trends and Statistics -- 1995.*

TABLE A3. U.S. Merchandise Trade with China: 1986-1995
($Billions)

Year	U.S. Exports	U.S. Imports	U.S. Trade Balance
1986	3.1	4.8	-1.7
1987	3.5	6.3	-2.8
1988	5.0	8.5	-3.5
1989	5.8	12.0	-6.2
1990	4.8	15.2	-10.4
1991	6.3	19.0	-12.7
1992	7.4	25.7	-18.3
1993	8.8	31.5	-22.8
1994	9.3	38.8	-29.5
1995	11.7	45.6	-33.8

Source: U.S. Department of Commerce,

TABLE A4. U.S. Merchandise Trade with Taiwan, 1986-95
(Billions of U.S. Dollars)

	U.S. Exports	U.S. Imports	U.S. Trade Balance
1986	5.2	19.8	-14.6
1987	7.2	24.6	-17.4
1988	11.9	24.8	-12.9
1989	11.3	24.3	-13.0
1990	11.5	22.7	-11.2
1991	13.2	23.0	-9.8
1992	15.2	24.6	-9.4
1993	16.3	25.1	-8.9
1994	17.1	26.7	-9.6
1995	19.3	29.0	-9.7

Source: U.S. Department of Commerce.

TABLE A5. Chinese Exports to the United States and as a % of Total Chinese Exports*: 1986-1995

Year	Total Chinese Exports ($Billions)	Chinese Exports to the United States ($Billions)	Chinese Exports to the United States as a % of Total Exports (%)
1986	31.4	4.8	15.3
1987	39.4	6.3	16.0
1988	47.7	8.5	17.8
1989	52.9	12.0	22.7
1990	62.8	15.2	24.2
1991	71.9	19.0	26.4
1992	85.5	25.7	30.0
1993	91.6	31.5	34.3
1994	120.8	38.8	32.1
1995	148.8	45.6	31.1

*Note: Data on total Chinese exports to the world are official Chinese trade statistics. Data on Chinese exports to the United States are U.S. data, reported as U.S. imports (customs value) of Chinese products into the United States).

Sources: International Monetary Fund, *Direction of Trade Statistics*; U.S. Department of Commerce, and official Chinese government statistics.

TABLE A6. China's Real GDP Growth Rates: 1986-1995
and Projections to 2000
(%)

	Annual % Change in Real GDP
Actual	
1986	8.5
1987	11.1
1988	11.2
1989	4.3
1990	3.9
1991	8.0
1992	13.6
1993	13.5
1994	11.8
1995	9.9
Projections	
1996	8.9
1997	8.6
1998	7.9
1999	7.9
2000	7.8

Source: DRI/McGraw Hill, World Markets Country Summaries,
Fourth Quarter 1995; and World Markets Reports, February 1996.

TABLE A7. Taiwan's Real GDP Growth Rates: 1986-1995
and Projections Through 2000
(Percent)

	Annual % Change in Real GDP
Actual	
1986	11.6
1987	12.7
1988	7.8
1989	8.2
1990	5.4
1991	7.6
1992	6.8
1993	6.3
1994	6.6
1995	6.1
Projections	
1996	5.1
1997	6.0
1998	5.4
1999	5.7
2000	5.7

Source: DRI/McGraw Hill. *World Market Summaries, Fourth Quarter, 1995*. p. A-3, B-4; and *World Markets Report: Taiwan*, April 1996, p.2.

TABLE A8. China-Taiwan Trade Through Hong Kong: 1980-1995
(\$Billions)

	Trade Turnover	Chinese Exports	Chinese Imports
1980	0.3	0.1	0.2
1981	0.5	0.1	0.4
1982	0.3	0.1	0.2
1983	0.3	0.1	0.2
1984	0.5	0.1	0.4
1985	1.1	0.1	0.9
1986	1.0	0.1	0.9
1987	1.5	0.3	1.2
1988	2.7	0.5	2.2
1989	3.5	0.6	2.9
1990	4.0	0.8	3.3
1991	5.8	1.1	4.7
1992	7.4	1.1	6.3
1993	14.4	1.5	12.9
1994	16.3	2.2	14.1
1995	17.9	3.1	14.8

Source: Data supplied the Chinese Embassy, Washington, DC.

Chapter 6

CHINA AND THE MULTILATERAL DEVELOPMENT BANKS

JONATHAN SANFORD

SHOULD THE MDBS LEND TO CHINA?

The World Bank and Asian Development Bank (ADB) have been large and growing sources of loans for China. In 1985, the World Bank and ADB agreed to lend China $1.1 billion. Ten years later, the annual total for their loan commitments to China had quadrupled, to $4.3 billion in both 1995 and 1996.

Today, many debate what role the MDBs should play in the world's most populous country. Resources are scarce at the multilateral development banks (MDBs) and there are many alternative claimants for available funds. China has one of the fastest growing economies in the developing world, yet it is also the home of many very impoverished people. Some people ask whether the United States, Japan, and other major countries should help finance the development of a country that may be their international rival in the coming century. Should the MDBs stop making low-cost concessional rate loans to China? Should they make these loans only for activities that promote poverty alleviation, environmental preservation, and economic reform? Should they lend at all, given China's questionable record as regards official respect for internationally recognized human rights, its military buildup, and its apparent readiness to use force in settling international disputes? Alternatively, can the MDBs justify *not* lending to China, given its low per capita income, the prevalence of poverty in its less developed regions, and the Chinese government's apparent orientation towards development?

This paper does not attempt to answer these questions. Strong arguments can be made on several sides of each issue. Rather, it provides a brief analysis of China's relationship with the MDBs to highlight some issues and help observers better understand the context in which events occur.

WHAT ACTIVITIES DO MDB LOANS SUPPORT IN CHINA?

China borrows more from both the World Bank and ADB than any other country. Its share in World Bank loan approvals increased from 9.8% in 1985 to 17% in 1996. More dramatically, ADB loan commitments for China grew from zero in 1985 to 30% in 1995 (47% in 1994) of total lending. China has rapidly increased its access to foreign credit -- receipts from new disbursements from all sources of long-term foreign debt grew from $5.3 billion in 1985 to $18.3 billion in 1994.[1] MDB disbursements accounted for 14% of China's new loan receipts in 1994.

---

[1] World Bank. *World Debt Tables, 1996*. Vol. 2, p. 99. Disbursements by MDBs totalled $2.559 billion. Concessional loans comprised less than a third ($704 million) of the total.

Table 1. MDB Loans to China, 1985-95
(millions of U.S. dollars)

| | World Bank Group | | | Asian Development Bank | |
	IBRD	IDA	IFC	Reg Loans	Priv Sector
1985	659.6	442.3	17.0	-.-	-.-
1986	687.0	450.0	-.-	-.-	-.-
1987	867.4	556.2	8.0	133.3	-.-
1988	1,053.7	639.9	15.0	282.9	3.0
1989	833.4	515.0	3.0	39.7	-.-
1990	-.-	590.0	-.-	50.0	-.-
1991	601.5	977.8	-.-	498.3	14.3
1992	1,577.7	948.6	16.4	853.0	50.0
1993	2,155.0	1,017.0	43.2	1,050.0	-.-
1994	2,145.0	925.0	83.4	1,167.0	-.-
1995	2,369.5	630.0	104.2	1,201.0	-.-
1996	2,490.0	480.0	184.5	1,040.0	102.0

Excludes guarantees not involving some allocation of MDB resources.
Source: Annual reports of the World Bank, IFC, and ADB, relevant years.

The World Bank provides aid to China through all four of its "windows:" the International Bank for Reconstruction and Development (IBRD), the International Development Association (IDA), and the International Finance Corporation, and the Multilateral Investment Guarantee Agency (MIGA). The IBRD, the original World Bank, lends on market-based terms.[2] IDA, the Bank's concessional loan affiliate, lends on low-cost terms,[3] mainly to countries with per capita incomes below $869 annually. Most have per capita income levels below $400. The IFC primarily helps private domestic firms in developing countries.[4] MIGA insures or guarantees foreign investors in developing countries against various non-commercial risks (expropriation, etc.). Its exposure in China totals about $112 million and is not discussed here.

The ADB lends to China through its market-based loan "window" and through that facility's private sector loan and equity investment program. By agreement among the ADB member countries, neither China nor India receive concessional assistance from the Asian Bank, though their levels of per capita income might qualify them for such aid.

---

[2] The IBRD's repayment period varies from 12 to 25 years, depending on the nature of the project. Its floating interest rate is pegged one-half of 1% higher than the average price the IBRD pays to borrow money in world commercial capital markets. In recent years, it has generally been around 7.5%.

[3] IDA loans for China are repayable over 35 years, including a 10 year grace period. No interest is charged but the borrower pays a 3/4 of 1% service charge on the disbursed balance.

[4] IFC loans carry commercial rates of interest. IFC equity investments involve no IFC participation in the management of the developing country firm. Most IFC loans or equity investments in China have been in the industrial or mining sectors. In some countries (but not China), the IFC also lends to or invests in private utility companies.

What is China's Per Capita Income?

There are two methods for calculating a country's per capita income. Both are valid but they are not interchangeable.

Per Capita GNP in Dollars. The first method, which the World Bank uses for determining IDA eligibility, calculates a developing country's per capita income in dollars through a simple conversion process. The per capita Gross National Product (GNP) is measured in local currency and converted to dollars using the average exchange rate for the past three years as adjusted for inflation. China's annual per capita GNP in 1995 was about 5,200 yuan. On the basis of this calculation, the World Bank said in 1996 that China's per capita annual income the previous year was $620.

This system is useful for comparing the income levels of countries when the ability to buy imported goods is a consideration. It gives an unrealistic picture of local living standards, however, since products not traded internationally (services, rent, etc.) are valued by an exchange rate applicable only to traded goods. Actual living standards can be much higher than implied in this dollar figure.

The system is also subject to technical problems and relies on GNP calculations that may not be very accurate. For example, many transactions are outside the purview of official data collection. The Bank made adjustments in the base data for China in 1994 and 1995. Earlier World Bank data reported that China's per capita GNP stood at $370 in 1993. Two years later, according to World Bank figures, China's per capita GNP was $620. China's economy was not two-thirds larger in 1995 than it had been in 1993. Technical changes in the method of calculation account for much of the apparent change in the Bank's figures for China's per capita annual income. The Bank made no similar recalculation of income figures for other countries.

Purchasing Power Parity. The second method seeks to establish purchasing power parity (PPP) using a fixed market basket of goods and services to compare income levels in different countries. People's ability to purchase the items in the basket will vary from country to country. However, the items are valued according to a common standard, regardless of their local price. The World Bank says China's PPP income in 1995 was $2,920 (slightly higher than those of El Salvador and the Philippines).

The PPP system allows better comparisons of living standards among countries. However, it prices the income generated in a country's domestic economy as though it were useable in the international economy and it does not take the varying quality of goods sold in different countries into account. Thus, it tends to blur the differences in countries' relative capacity to purchase imported goods. The World Bank uses the per capita GNP in dollars method as its benchmark for determining countries' eligibility for IDA aid. IDA loans mainly finance the purchase of foreign goods. The World Bank has not specified an alternative measure using the PPP methodology for determining whether countries are eligible for IDA loans.

China is what the World Bank calls a "blend" country. That is, it receives loans from both the IBRD and IDA. Theoretically, the projects the Bank finances in China could be funded by either the IBRD or IDA, depending whether the Bank decides China can afford to service additional non-concessional debt. In practice, the World Bank has used its market-rate loans and its concessional loans in China to finance activity in different sectors. The IBRD has concentrated mainly on infrastructure or industrial projects, whereas IDA has focused much more on agriculture and social development activities.

Between 1985 and 1996, as Figure 1 shows, the IBRD lent most (83%) of its funds to finance the construction of infrastructure or industrial facilities, with the former accounting for most of the total. (See also Table 2, page 7.) Most of these projects have been located in areas experiencing rapid economic growth, mainly in urban or coastal regions. About 6% of total IBRD lending has financed agricultural development projects.[5] Roughly twice this proportion has gone for social and environmental projects (mainly the latter).[6]

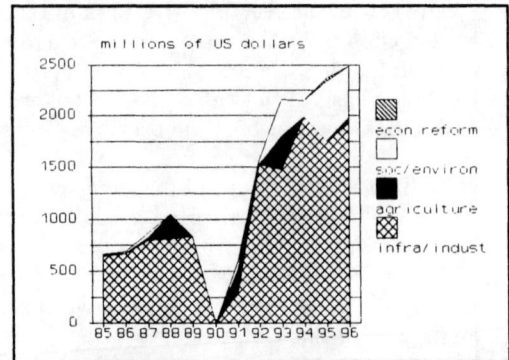

Figure 1 IBRD Assistance to China, Types of Activity

Only about one-fifth of 1% of IBRD aid has financed economic reform.

By contrast, as Figure 2 reveals, IDA has lent only 12% of its funds in China to finance infrastructure and industry. Most (45%) went to finance agricultural development, mainly in the poorer or less developed regions. Another 38% of IDA lending went to fund social sector and environment projects (mainly the former). Economic reform accounted for the remaining 4%.

---

[5] The agriculture proportion would be slightly higher if two IBRD loans in 1996 ($80 million for seed sector commercialization and $150 million to strengthen the animal feed industry) were counted as agriculture rather than industry. The World Bank lists them among its agriculture loan. The published descriptions of the projects suggest, however, that they are more industrial in their focus and they have been included in that category here. The parallel $20 million IDA loan for seed sector commercialization has been treated here similarly.

[6] The proportion lent by the IBRD for social sector projects in 1996 would be higher if the $250 million sewerage project in Shanghai and the $125 million wastewater and solid waste disposal project in Hubei were counted in the urban development category (per the World Bank categorization). However, the published project descriptions show that environmental measures comprise the bulk of the activities funded by the projects. Thus, they are treated as environmental projects here, as is the parallel $25 million IDA project in Hubei.

The pattern of ADB activity in China resembles that of the IBRD. As Figure 3 shows, infrastructure and industry account for 82% of ADB lending to China, while agriculture comprised less than 4% of the total. Moreover, one ADB agriculture loan to China (1992) funded a commercially oriented project developing tropical crops. Two others (1990 and 1995) helped the state agricultural bank modernize agro-industrial firms in China's poorer regions. These could just as easily be called loans to promote industrial growth. The most recent "agriculture" loan (1996) funded a marine aquaculture project. Social and environmental projects accounted for the other 14% of ADB aid to China. Most of this (11%) consisted of environmental projects funded in recent years. The one social project (1994) financed an urban water system.[7]

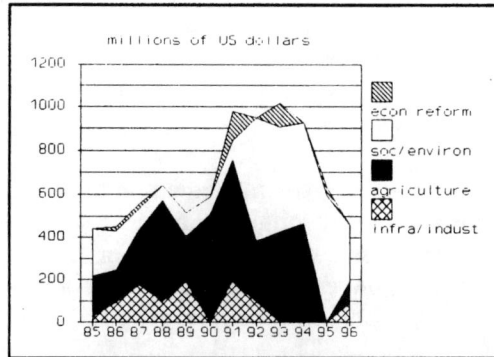

Figure 2 IDA Assistance to China, Types of Activity

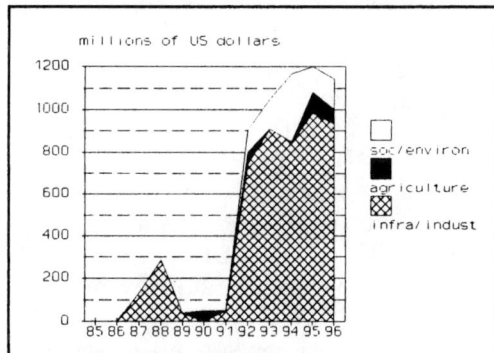

Figure 3 ADB Assistance to China, Types of Activity

The ADB has not lent directly to fund economic reform in China. The promotion of reform -- for example, better management or accounting practices and more market-oriented policies or procedures for state firms -- has been built into many ADB and World Bank loans and is not reflected in the sectoral statistics. The Chinese government has been willing to adopt economic reforms when it sees that these will strengthen its economic situation. China is particularly sensitive to any appearance that it was compelled to adopt reforms as a result of conditions in MDB loans or other leverage applied by the multilateral agencies.

TIANANMEN SQUARE AND MDB LENDING TO CHINA

The Tiananmen Square bloodshed in June 1989 caused a sharp (albeit temporary) break in MDB treatment of China. Lending fell substantially. The United States and other major member countries urged the MDBs to stop lending in light of the human rights situation in China. Although the World

---

[7] The figure for environment would be a few percentage points higher and the figure for industry a few percentage points lower if two large loans (1996) promoting energy conservation and pollution control in industry were put in the former category. Because of their dual focus, one loan was assigned to each category for present purposes.

Bank and ADB have no provisions in their Articles of Agreement specifically taking human rights conditions into account, World Bank and ADB management justified their suspension of new lending for China on grounds they were waiting to see if the crackdown on political expression would be followed by a slowdown or reversal of China's support for economic liberalization and reform.

The Chinese crackdown on dissidents came in the last month of the World Bank's July-through-June fiscal year, a time when many new projects would normally be sent to its Board of Executive Directors for final approval. Top Bank management withdrew its plans to recommend several new China loans that month and the volume of IBRD, IDA, and IFC lending to China fell considerably. The ADB, whose fiscal year runs from January to December, had lent only a small amount to China in 1989 when further action on new loans was suspended, as management waited to see what was happening in China.

In early 1990, representatives of the Group of Seven leading developed countries (G-7) -- who together with other countries in the European Union own well over a majority of the World Bank and ADB's voting stock -- agreed that their representatives at the MDBs could support a limited flow of lending to China so long as the loans were targeted to fund activities meeting basic human needs (BHN). The IBRD made no loans to China during its fiscal 1990, while IDA made six loans (for earthquake reconstruction, agricultural development in poor provinces, vocational education, and afforestation) between February and June 1990. The ADB made only one loan (to support an agricultural development bank) in late November.

At the Houston summit meeting in mid-1990, leaders of the G-7 countries decided to maintain their policy of limited support for MDB aid to China. However, they added two new criteria that would garner their support -- loans to facilitate economic reform and loans for projects benefiting the environment. Following the Houston summit, the volume of MDB lending to China increased substantially. By 1992, it was almost one-quarter larger in dollar terms than the amount lent in 1988.

According to the Treasury Department, the United States continues to support the policy approved at the Houston summit. To do otherwise would contradict the requirements of U.S. law as well as Administration and congressional preferences. Other countries, however, have broadened their attitude towards MDB lending for China in subsequent years. Two factors seem to be at work.

First, the determination of the G-7 countries to only support MDB loans that would promote basic human needs, environmental protection or economic policy reform has proven hard to sustain. Many MDB loans to China have some link to economic policy reform or an environmental component. Thus, in the absence of a clearer definition of the terms, those criteria could be used to justify G-7 support for a wide variety of loans.

Table 3. MDB Lending to China, by Bank and Type of Activity
(millions of U.S. dollars)

World Bank (IBRD)	infra-structure	industry	agri-culture	social sectors	environ-ment	economic reform
Total	$9,861	$2,869	$885	$558	$1,240	$28
1985	$545	$97	$17	$0	$0	$0
1986	$583	$87	$0	$17	$0	$0
1987	$355	$448	$20	$45	$0	$0
1988	$624	$190	$240	$0	$0	$0
1989	$243	$591	$0	$0	$0	$0
1990	$0	$0	$0	$0	$0	$0
1991	$100	$200	$222	$79	$0	$0
1992	$1,450	$82	$0	$46	$0	$0
1993	$1,330	$151	$325	$0	$349	$0
1994	$1,984	$0	$0	$0	$161	$0
1995	$1,128	$623	$0	$360	$230	$28
1996	$1,520	$400	$60	$10	$500	$0

Intl Develop Assoc (IDA)	infra-structure	industry	agri-culture	social sectors	environ-ment	economic reform
Total	$743	$230	$3,638	$2,449	$774	$317
1985	$30	$0	$187	$225	$0	$0
1986	$70	$25	$150	$185	$0	$20
1987	$125	$50	$260	$100	$0	$21
1988	$99	$0	$474	$67	$0	$0
1989	$191	$0	$215	$109	$0	$0
1990	$0	$0	$510	$80	$0	$0
1991	$131	$65	$562	$89	$0	$131
1992	$97	$0	$287	$450	$115	$0
1993	$0	$0	$427	$330	$149	$110
1994	$0	$0	$465	$110	$350	$0
1995	$0	$0	$0	$485	$110	$35
1996	$0	$90	$100	$220	$50	$0

Asian Develop Bank (ADB)	infra-structure	industry	agri-culture	social sectors	environ-ment
Total	$2,711	$1,283	$205	$160	$518
1985	$0	$0	$0	$0	$0
1986	$0	$0	$0	$0	$0
1987	$0	$133	$0	$0	$0
1988	$0	$283	$0	$0	$0
1989	$40	$0	$0	$0	$0
1990	$0	$0	$50	$0	$0
1991	$28	$22	$0	$0	$0
1992	$407	$338	$55	$0	$103
1993	$610	$300	$0	$0	$140
1994	$773	$77	$0	$160	$158
1995	$853	$130	$100	$0	$118
1996	$652	$280	$70	$28	$112

Second, as the events of June 1989 recede, most G-7 countries are giving other foreign policy and trade factors higher precedence in their MDB policy calculations. Many seem to have abandoned the Houston criteria entirely, as these seem to apply only tangentially to many of the MDB loans approved in recent years.

U.S. LAW AND U.S. VOTES ON MDB CHINA LOANS

Section 701(a) of the International Financial Institutions (IFI) Act (P.L. 95-118), adopted in 1977, requires the United States to oppose MDB loans to countries evidencing a pattern of gross violations of internationally recognized human rights. The U.S. representatives at the MDBs may vote for loans to such countries only if they are deemed to meet basic human needs (BHN). Other countries do not appear to have similar directives governing their votes on MDB loans. Sections 701(c) and 1701(b)(9) of the IFI Act require the Administration to submit quarterly and annual reports to Congress indicating whether it supported or opposed any MDB loans and whether those loans meet basic needs.

Table 4. U.S. Votes on MDB Loans to China, 1985-1995

	Total Loans		Supported by U.S.	
	WB	ADB	WB	ADB
1985	12	0	12	0
1986	10	0	10	0
1987	15	2	13	2
1988	15	4	15	3
1989	14	1	14	1
1990	11	1	10	0
1991	22	13	11	0
1992	19	14	11	0
1993	20	14	7	0
1994	22	18	9	5
1995	21	25	7	4

These reports show that between 1985 and 1995, the United States supported 111 of 182 loans approved by the World Bank Group (including the IFC) and 15 of 92 loans approved by the ADB. (See Table 3.) Before the Tiananmen square events in 1989, the United States supported 70 of 74 approved by the two banks. Later, it voted for only 56 of 200 MDB loans.[8] The

---

[8] The U.S. Administration is required by law to report annually to Congress and the public how it votes on MDB loans. The last report submitted covers 1991. Lack of staff reportedly has prevented the Treasury Department from both filing the required reports and monitoring U.S. participation in the MDBs. For U.S. votes between 1985 and 1991, see: [U.S. Treasury Department] *International Finance: Annual Report of the Chairman of the National Advisory Council on International Monetary and Financial Policies [NAC] to the President and to the Congress* The unpublished quarterly reports to Congress show that the United States voted subsequently in the World Bank to support the following loans: (1992) educational development for poor provinces, Tianjin urban development and environment, and Sichuan agricultural development; (1993) Chingchan water and environment, effective teaching, Zhejiang municipal development, agricultural support services, South Jiangsu environment, rural health workers, and Tangshan/Chengde environmental improvement; (1994) red soils development, Songliao Plain agricultural development, Xiaolongdi resettlement, loess plateau watershed rehabilitation, forest resource development, enterprise housing and social security reform (2), Liaoning environment, and basic education for poor and minority areas; (1995)

BHN exception was the criterion justifying these 56 votes. The United States abstained or voted "no" on all other loans to China. The U.S. representative abstained on a World Bank rural water and sanitation loan for China in January 1992 even though the Administration's quarterly report to Congress said it had a BHN orientation.

The concept "basic human needs" has no clear meaning in U.S. law. The human rights guidelines for U.S. votes in the MDBs were adopted in 1977. The concept "basic human needs" was borrowed from laws governing the U.S. bilateral foreign aid program. Section 102(b)(4) of the Foreign Assistance Act (FAA) of 1961 (which governs U.S. bilateral aid) says that activities aimed at improving health conditions (particularly infant mortality), education (particularly literacy), control of population growth, increased income equality, reduced unemployment or underemployment, and agricultural development aid for the rural poor could be defined as meeting basic human needs.

Other provisions of the FAA of 1961 say that alternative criteria -- equitable growth, better conditions for women, improved development administration, protection of the environment and natural resources, promotion of private investment, economic policy reform designed to achieve economic growth with equity, etc. -- may also be key elements of U.S. development aid policy. It is not clear, however, whether these other criteria exemplify the concept "basic human needs". Some might argue that the context is sufficiently general that any criteria promoting growth with equity or poverty alleviation might be included in the term. In recent years, the Clinton Administration has made "sustainable development" a key component of U.S. development aid policy. Environmental considerations are a major element of this concept.

Since the G-7 conference in Houston in 1992, the MDBs have increased considerably the number of their projects in China and in other countries that are labeled "environmental". The Treasury Department indicates, though, that some "environment creep" in loan titles is evident. Projects categorized under this label today might have been listed otherwise in prior years. In addition, MDB environment projects now often contain funding for many related activities. Some -- water and sewerage or toxic waste disposal, for example -- are clearly BHN activities. Others are not. Some aspects -- reclamation or alteration of watercourses in the context of flood control or industrial upgrades at steel plants, for example -- may not even be "environmental".

It would seem that the inclusion of BHN activities in a multi-purpose environmental loan may be deemed sufficient to justify U.S. support, providing the other components in the loan are not blatantly unacceptable. In large part, the prospect for U.S. support depends on the way the MDBs "package" their

---

southwest poverty reduction (2), iodine deficiency disorders control (2), disease prevention, and labor market development (2). In the ADB, the United States voted to support: (1994) northern grassland ecosystem improvement technical assistance (TA), Dalian water supply, comprehensive maternal and child health, Beijing urban transport TA, and Beijing environmental improvement; (1995) agricultural development bank, commercial finance and management TA, Fujian soil conservation and rural development, and Fujian soil and water conservation TA.

loans. Thirteen of the MDB loans for China that the U.S. supported -- citing the BHN provisions in Section 701(a) -- were environmental projects. However, the published descriptions of at least ten of them make no mention of activities focusing primarily on public health or assistance to the poor. These include four general environment projects, an afforestation project, a watershed rehabilitation project, and two urban environmental improvement projects. The ADB soil conservation project was linked to rural development. Several ADB loans for small amounts of money, which the United States supported, were intended to provide technical assistance to the Chinese agencies responsible for soil or water conservation and grassland management, and provided no direct assistance to the public. If this trend continues, the BHN waiver in Section 701(a) could be used (if the Administration wished) to justify U.S. votes in favor of a broad range of MDB assistance for China.

PROSPECTIVES ON THE FUTURE

The U.S. government has opposed long MDB concessional aid to China on grounds that it can afford to borrow more of its foreign credit on commercial terms and its potential for absorbing the lion's share of existing MDB resources. Even before the Tiananmen Square crackdown, when U.S. relations with China were less complicated, the U.S. Administration opposed the extension of ADB concessional aid to China when lending began in 1987. Other countries, however, were willing to see China borrow concessional funds from the ADB. However, they eventually acquiesced to the U.S. argument that Asian Development Bank concessional funds were too scarce and that little would be left over for the smaller Asian countries if India and China were eligible to borrow those funds.

In the World Bank, the U.S. Administration has argued for a reduction in IDA lending to China. In part, the U.S. view has been justified on grounds that IDA resources are limited and the poor countries in Africa and the other low-income countries in Asia have fewer alternatives than do China and India. More pointedly, though, the U.S. view has been buttressed with arguments that China's favorable balance of payments situation, its substantial foreign reserves ($75 billion in December 1995) and its growing capacity to attract foreign investment and commercial credit obviate China's need for IDA aid.

In the agreement among the donor countries undergirding the IDA ninth replenishment (signed in 1990), the World Bank's major member countries agreed that the combined lending to IDA's two largest borrowers (China and India) should not exceed 30% of IDA resources during the three-year replenishment period. In late 1992, in the IDA tenth replenishment agreement, the IDA donors declined to reduce these countries combined share of IDA further. They did agree, however, that lending to the "blend" countries (China being arguably the most prominent member of that group) should see their combined access to IDA resources reduced from the 40% level approved in 1990 to a lower combined total of 30-to-35%. Given the strong pressure for continued IDA lending to some of the other countries in the "blend" group (Egypt, Pakistan, and India, for example), the IDA 10 agreement seemed to put clear limits on IDA's ability to provide aid to China.

In the IDA eleventh replenishment agreement, initialled March 19, 1996, in Tokyo, the other donor countries finally agreed that IDA lending to China should stop. China will be eligible to borrow from IDA 11, but the lending framework the World Bank presented to justify the new replenishment indicated it would receive only about 4% of IDA lending during the IDA 11 period. China would graduate from IDA in 1999.

Japan was reportedly one of the countries that most stoutly resisted the effort to reduce and ultimately terminate IDA assistance to China. The Japanese reportedly believe that efforts on their part to facilitate strong economic growth in China and to strengthen their economic relationship with China should be an important aspect of their foreign policy. In recent years, China has been the largest single recipient of Japan's foreign aid. For example, in 1994-95, China received almost 20% of the net $10 billion Japan disbursed annually for bilateral development aid.[9] China also receives many export credits and other near-market rate official loans from Japan.

The Chinese government has agreed this would be its last replenishment. The question whether China's borrowing from IDA would taper down to zero or whether it would continue at a constant level throughout the replenishment period was not resolved. The United States is the principal sponsor of the plan to end China's eligibility for IDA aid. If U.S. influence in the World Bank remains strong, one may expect to see the volume of IDA lending to China decline in the next few years. If U.S. influence wanes and that of Japan grows, the plan to reduce or terminate IDA aid to China may be reconsidered.

Member countries such as the United States can delay by a few weeks the consideration of any loan (including China loans) by the MDB executive boards. However, no country has a veto over World Bank or ADB lending.[10]

Congress will be considering legislation in 1997 to formally authorize U.S. participation in IDA 11. The other IDA donor countries approved their comparable legislation in 1996. Congressional efforts to bar IDA from using U.S.-contributed funds for China have a low chance of success. The World Bank made it clear in the past (as for example the struggle in the late 1970s about

---

[9] Development Assistance Committee (DAC), *Development Cooperation, 1996 Report.* Paris: Organization for Economic Cooperation and Development (OECD), 1997, pp. A30 and A76. The United States, by comparison, gave China almost none of the average $6.45 billion in net bilateral development aid it disbursed during those two years. Ibid., pp. A36 and 82. The Peace Corps, at about $900,000 annually, is the only foreign aid the United States currently provides to China. Compensation to volunteers comprises most of those funds.

[10] The United States is the largest single member of the World Bank, with a 17% voting share in the IBRD, 15.3% in IDA, and 22.7% in the IFC. In the ADB, it is the second largest member, with a 8% voting share. Japan has a 15.6% share in the ADB. The U.S. share would be equal to Japan's if the United States purchased all the stock available to it.

IDA aid to Vietnam[11]) that it will not accept earmarked contributions that direct or restrict the way it can use those funds. If Congress wished to legislate on this issue, however, it could make the reduction or termination of IDA lending to China a condition for U.S. participation in IDA 11. The other donors might acquiesce if (as stipulated in the new IDA agreement) this merely sought a guarantee that China's eligibility would end with IDA 11. A crisis would likely ensue, and many other major donors would stoutly resist, if the United States sought to end Chinese borrowing from IDA any earlier than now planned.

The effects of a termination of IDA lending to China can only be surmised. On the one hand, if the Chinese government decides to rely more on foreign investment and commercial credit to fund China's development, it may well adopt more market-oriented economic policy and institutional reforms in order to make it more attractive to lenders. On the other hand, the Chinese government may feel it needs to intervene more in the economy in order to deal with the consequences of increased reform. Private capital would probably flow mainly to the fast-growing urban and coastal regions, rather than to the poorer inland provinces. This could magnify existing social and economic strains and inter-regional tensions. One concern is whether the central government will have the authority and capacity to control or mitigate these tensions. Another is whether the exercise of such authority would be compatible with efforts to allow individuals and localities more autonomy and a larger role in the economic and public policy process.

It is unlikely that private capital will fund the kinds of projects IDA has financed in recent years. The question is whether China will be willing to borrow regular IBRD and ADB money to fund these activities. As noted before, IDA has emphasized poverty-alleviation, agricultural development, and other social sector programs. The IBRD and ADB have lent relatively little for these purposes. Many other countries (Indonesia, for example) use MDB market-rate money for these purposes. The Chinese government showed little indication in 1996 that it is prepared to do this also. IBRD lending for social sector, poverty alleviation, and agriculture projects may increase as the volume of IDA lending declines. The descriptions of projects under consideration for China, however, provide only slight support for this conclusion.[12]

---

[11] See: Jonathan E. Sanford, "Restrictions on United States Contributions to the Multilateral Development Banks" in *The George Washington Journal of International Law and Economics*, 15:3 (1981), pp. 561-573.

[12] The World Bank's *Monthly Operational Summary* dated December 6, 1996 shows 42 projects for China at various stages of preparation. Most will come to the Bank's executive board for approval in the next two years. Of these 18 (accounting for most of the money) are for power or transport infrastructure, with funding from the IBRD. Eight others are for environmental (mainly pollution control) projects, 7 with IBRD funding and one (afforestation with an anti-poverty element) with minority IDA funding. Another 5 will promote enterprise reform (mainly for state firms or finance institutions). Two of these (with no discernable poverty orientation) will be partly funded by IDA. All this seems to replicate the previous pattern. A possible change may be found in the funding for planned projects in the agriculture and social sectors. Of the 4 planned agriculture projects, three have a commercial or market orientation and are scheduled for IBRD funding. The last, a $150 million poverty and environment project in the

It is doubtful, in any case, whether China will be able to replace the funds it previously borrowed from IDA with increased borrowing from the IBRD. The World Bank's rules stipulate that no country may account for more than 10% of the IBRD's outstanding loans over a period of time. The Bank has made exceptions, as in the case of Indonesia and Mexico, which accounted for 10.7% and 11.6% respectively of the IBRD's outstanding loans at the close of the Bank's fiscal 1996. It makes such exceptions reluctantly, however. At the end of 1996, total lending to China comprised 6.6% of the IBRD's outstanding credits. However, if loans approved but not yet effective (i.e., not formally signed) and loans not yet disbursed are included in the total, China's share of total IBRD lending rises to 9%.

If the IBRD continues lending to China at its current rate, the share of its total approved loans allocated to China would likely exceed 10% within two years. The IBRD member countries could raise the loan ceiling for China. However, this step would be controversial and a number of major countries might oppose it.[13] China may not wish to risk its prestige on an application of this sort. Still, some sort of waiver will be necessary if China is to retain its current access to IBRD resources, not to mention any increase in IBRD lending to cover the expected reduction in IDA credit. If IBRD lending to China must be scaled back in the future because of this ceiling, one can doubt whether the Chinese government will use its remaining MDB credit to finance mainly social sector and agricultural development projects.

China may be willing to use loans from the IBRD to finance more social projects if its access to IBRD credit is not restricted, its foreign trade situation remains positive, and its net income from exports to the United States and other developed countries remains strong. To repay its growing debt to multilateral and commercial lenders, China will need to increase its net income from foreign trade. In relation to its annual import bill, China's foreign exchange reserves

---

Tarim Basin, however, will be funded by the IBRD (60%) and IDA (40%). The prior Tarim Basin project (1992) was financed solely by IDA. Likewise, the IBRD seems slated to play a larger role in funding the 6 planned projects in the social sector. Two health projects will be financed solely by IDA. However, one of the two water and sewerage projects and one of the two education undertakings (for higher education reform) will receive partial IBRD funding, as will the Qinba Mountains poverty reduction project. Even so, total IBRD funding for these social sector projects is not expected to exceed $150 million. In effect, the share of IBRD lending for social and poverty-oriented projects would grow slightly (to perhaps $240 million over two years) if all the projects in the MOS are implemented. Total World Bank lending for these kinds of project would fall, however, as the volume of IDA lending diminishes.

[13] *The Economist* concluded that the prospects for an increase in China's loan ceiling are doubtful, saying "Not all rich-country members of the G7 are yet convinced that China's economic reforms are irreversible. They would probably object to a still greater share of the Bank's lending going to China." See: "China: A problem with the Bank." July 13, 1996, pp. 32-33.

at the end of 1995 were comparable to those of India, Bolivia, and Egypt, all of them current IDA borrowers.[14]

If China's export situation declines, because of a turndown in the world economy or because of foreign policy-induced restrictions on its trade opportunities, the Chinese government's willingness to borrow market-rate World Bank funds for agriculture and social sector projects may decline. In sum, it seems likely that a reduction in future IDA lending to China will lead to a diminution in MDB lending for social projects and other programs aimed at the direct alleviation of poverty.

---

[14] China's total reserves minus gold (a standard IMF benchmark) in December 1995 totalled $75.38 billion while its annual imports (c.i.f.) were $115.68 billion. In other words, its total reserves were sufficient to finance 58.4% of its import bill. India's reserves would have funded 56.6% of its imports that year. The comparable figures for Bolivia and Egypt were 46.4% and 40.6%. There is no significant effort underway to graduate these countries from IDA. To be sure, most poor developing countries have much lower reserve-to-import ratios. Those for Senegal, Pakistan, and Honduras, for example, were 12.8%, 16.4% and 21.5%, respectively, in 1995. See: International Monetary Fund. *International Financial Statistics*, December 1996, relevant pages for each country cited.

Chapter 7

THE EFFECTIVENESS OF THE PRC'S ECONOMIC MEASURES FOR FOREIGN DIRECT INVESTMENT, THE ASIAN FINANCIAL CRISIS, AND THE REFORM OF STATE-OWNED ENTERPRISES

DANIEL K. T. LI,
Lingnan College
Hong Kong
MIKE GOLDSTEIN
University of Technology
Sydney, Australia
GORDON WALKER
University of Canterbury
New Zealand

INTRODUCTION

An immense body of literature has emerged in the last 37 years to explain the rapid growth of foreign direct investment (FDI). Each theory typically explains why FDI occurs in certain industries or in particular types of firms. Although many theories have been proposed and tested, none has been able to explain FDI for all types of industries, firms, and countries. Under the socialist system, the People's Republic of China (PRC) has a number of peculiar features in its system of market, finance, banking, foreign trade, foreign exchange, enterprises, industrial policies, taxation, etc., which are quite different from those of other developed and developing markets. FDIs are motivated by a wider and more complicated set of strategic, behavioral, and economic considerations. The application of FDI theories to the FDI in the PRC since the "Open Door Policy" in 1978 by multinational companies (MNCs) are even more complex owing to a continual series of economic reforms.

To explain the emergence of MNCs, numerous theories have been produced since 1950s by prior researches which include (1) *the strategic motives FDI theory* of Hogue

[1967][1] and Nehrt and Hogue [1968];[2] (2) *the behavioral motives FDI theory* of Aharoni [1966];[3] (3) *the economic motives FDI theory* which can be sub-classified into (i) the *product and factor market imperfections FDI theory* of Hymer [1960][4] and Kindleberger [1969];[5] (ii) the *internalization FDI theory* of Rugman [1980];[6] (iii) the *economies of scale FDI theory* of Horst [1972][7] and Wolf [1975];[8] (iv) the *managerial and marketing expertise FDI theory* of Servan-Schreiber [1968];[9] (v) the *technology strength FDI theory* of Vernon [1966],[10] Gruber, Mehta, and Vernon [1967],[11] and of Severn and Laurence [1974];[12] (vi) the *financial strength FDI theory* of Lee and Kwok [1988];[13] (vii) *differentiated products FDI theory* of Caves [1971];[14] (viii) the *product cycle FDI theory* of Vernon [1966]; (ix) the *defensive FDI theories* of Knickerbocker [1973],[15] who developed a *follow the leader theory* and Belassa [1966], who developed a *growth to survive theory*.[16] All these theories have been proposed and tested by numerous prior

[1] Hogue, W. Dickerson, 1967. " The Foreign Investment Decision Making Process," *Association for Education in International Business Proceedings*, December 29, 1967, pp.1-2.

[2] Nehrt, Lee and Hogue, W. Dickerson,1968. "The Foreign Investment Decision Process," *Quarterly Journal of AISEC International,* February-April 1968, pp. 43-48.

[3] Aharoni, Yair, 1966. *The Foreign Investment Decision Process*, Boston : Harvard Graduate School of Business Administration, Division of Research, 1996.

[4] Hymer, Stephen H.. 1976. *The International Operations of National Firms : A Study of Direct Foreign Investment*, Cambridge, Mass: MIT Press.

[5] Kindleberger, Charles P.,1969. *American Business Abroad : Six Lectures on Direct Investment,* New Haven, Conn. : Yale University Press, 1969.

[6] Rugman, A.M.1980. *Internalization as a General Theory of Foreign Direct Investment : A Reappraisal of the Literature.* Weltwitschaftliches Archive; pp. 1051-60.

[7] Horst, Thomas. 1972. "Firm and Industry Determinants of the Decision to Invest Abroad : An Empirical Study," *Review of Economics and Statistics*, August, pp. 258-266.

[8] Wolf, Bernard N. 1975. "Size and Profitability among U. S. Manufacturing Firms : Multinational versus Primarily Domestic Firms," *Journal of Economics and Business*, Fall, pp. 15-22.

[9] Servan-Schreiber, J. J. . 1968. *The American Challenge*, London : Hamish Hamilton.

[10] Vernon, Raymond, 1966. International Investment and International Trade in the Product Cycle, *Quarterly Journal of Economics*, May 1966, pp. 190-207.

[11] Gruber, W., D. Mehta, and R. Vernon, 1967. "The R & D Factor in International Trade and International Investment of United States Industries," *Journal of Political Economy*, February, pp.20-37.

[12] Severn, A. and M. M. Laurence. 1974. "Direct Investment, Research Intensity, and Profitability," *Journal of Financial and Quantitative Analysis*, March, pp. 181-190.

[13] Lee, Kwang Chul and Chuck C. Y. Kwok. 1988. "Multinational Corporations vs. Domestic Corporations : International Environmental Factors and Determinants of Capital Structure," *Journal of International Business Studies*, Summer, pp. 195-217.

[14] Caves, and S.K. Mehra. 1986. Entry of Foreign Multinationals into U.S. Manufacturing Industries. In M. Proter, ed., *Competition in Global Industries*. Boston : Harvard Business School.

[15] Knickerbocker, Fred T. , 1973. *Oligopolistic Reaction and the Multinational Enterprise*, Boston: Harvard Graduate School of Business Administration, 1973.

[16] Belassa, Bela. 1966. "American Direct Investment in the Common Market," Banca Nazionale del Lavoro, *Quarterly Review*, June, pp. 121-146.

researches in the last 40 years to explain the rapid growth of FDI. The findings of the immense body of literature have one theme in common: to explain why a firm resorts to 100%-owned FDI rather than relying on exporting, licensing, joint ventures, or management contracts. As for the case of the PRC, most of these FDI theories are applicable, as revealed by the fact that the PRC is currently second only to the United States as a recipient of FDI.

Since July 1997, foreign multinational corporations (FMNCs) with investments in the PRC are most concerned about the implications of the Asian financial crisis and the PRC's reform in State-owned enterprises (SOEs) for their investments. The anticipated positive implications of the reform in SOEs for both foreign direct investments (FDIs) and the PRC's investment environment will mainly be derived from four factors : (i) the Joint-stock Company System providing FMNCs with attractive financing options for their FDI in the PRC; (ii) the golden opportunity for FMNCs to establish an operating presence in the PRC through acquisitions of small SOEs; (iii) the banking system reform and the injection of government subsidy for Renminbi (RMB) Yuan 1,000 billion to SOEs in the forthcoming three years; and (iv) the tax reform for aligning the PRC's tariff practices with international norms to establish the preconditions for joining the World Trade Organization as well as create a fairer business environment and trading mechanisms etc.

As far as the Asian financial crisis is concerned, most FMNCs showed great concern about the potential devaluation of the RMB and the Hong Kong dollar which may make a great impact on their investments in the PRC and the Hong Kong. In terms of gross national product (GNP), the market value of the stock exchange market and the depletion of foreign exchange reserves, the financial crisis pushes Asian countries' economic conditions backward by seven to ten years. For instance, as at 18th May, 1998, the Indonesia Rupiah has devaluated by 80 per cent against the US dollar. In the meanwhile, the Thailand Baht, South Korea Won, Malaysia Ringgit and Philippines Peso have individually devaluated from 35 per cent to 50 per cent.

Due to the Won's devaluation by 50 per cent as in May 1998, the economic strength of South Korea has gone downward from the twelfth to the seventeenth position among Asian countries. As a consequence, South Korea's gross national product per capita has been reduced form US$10,548 in 1996 to US$6,664 in May 1998. Its economic condition has accordingly gone backward by, at least, 7 years. Overall, the Asian financial crisis causes a great financial loss in Southeast Asia which amounts to approximately US$1,000 billion, including the sharp diminution in value of the stock exchange market by US$600 billion. However, the impact of the Asian financial crisis on the PRC is the lightest among Asian countries as a result of its semi-open financial system. Typical examples include (i) the severely intervened and managed float exchange rate system under which only a narrow array of defined shares are available for foreign investors, i.e. the B share of SOEs in the Shenzhen Stock Exchange and the Shanghai Stock Exchange, and the H share in Hong Kong Stock Exchange, (ii) the huge amount of foreign exchange reserve boosting investors' confidence, (iii) the PRC's appropriate monetary and financial policy to stabilize the exchange rate of RMB, etc.. On the other hand, there are also a number of added business risks and adverse impacts on FDI as a consequence of the reform of SOEs and the Asian financial crisis. This study will investigate the implications of these two important economic factors for FDI in the PRC.

Table 1 below shows the foreign exchange reserves of the top ten countries in descending order during the period from December 1997 to March 1998 which reveals the amounts of the PRC and Hong Kong reaching US$140.6 billion and US$96.8 billion and ranking second and third respectively in the order.

TABLE 1

The Foreign Exchange Reserve of the Top Ten Countries / Regions for the Period from December, 1997 to March 1998

Place	Countries / Regions	US$ Billion	Period End
1	Japan	223.6	31st March 1998
2	People's Republic of China	140.6	28th February 1998
3	Hong Kong	96.8	31st March 1998
4	Taiwan	84.0	28th February 1998
5	Germany	82.2	28th February 1998
6	Singapore	74.1	28th February 1998
7	U. S. A.	71.3	31st January 1998
8	Spain	69.0	28th February 1998
9	Italy	57.8	28th February 1998
10	Brazil	51.0	31st December 199

Source : Hong Kong Monetary Authority, International Monetary Fund and Reuters

THE RECENT GLOBAL SITUATION OF FOREIGN DIRECT INVESTMENT

In 1996, the sum of foreign direct investment established in the People's Republic of China was US$42.3 billion, which was the largest one among prevalent developing countries. The PRC has become the second largest recipient of foreign capital after the United States of America and the largest recipient among developing countries. In descending order, the FDI amounts of other major developing countries in 1996 were US$6.4 billion in Mexico, US$6.2 billion in Malaysia, US$5.8 billion in Indonesia, US$5.5 billion in Brazil, US$4.2 billion in Poland, US$ 2.9 billion in Thailand, US$2.2 billion in Chile, US$2 billion in Argentina, and US$1.7 billion in Hungary. In general, the common characteristics of their congenial investment environments include a stable macro-economy, a good regulatory framework, a dependable legal system and fine infrastructural facilities, and a large and fast-growing market[17]. The factors account for the PRC's rapid absorption of FDI in the last 19 years since 1978 are (i) political stability and the continuing open door policy; (ii) the policy of offering attractive preferential treatments to FDI; (iii) the adoption of the "Economic Contract Law" concerning

---

[17]" *The World Competitiveness Yearbook 1997.* Switzerland: International Institute for Management Development.

overseas interests; (iv) improved legislation and regulatory work; (v) continual improvement in infrastructural facilities; (vi) low labor and land costs, and (vii) large and fast-growing market.[18] Due to the above-mentioned factors, leading foreign multinational corporations (FMNCs) are moving aggressively in the PRC to set up their operations and to build up a dominant market share to preempt the entry of big rivals. The number and size of their ventures in the PRC are rapidly expanding. For example, the number of approved FDIs contracts grew from 1,856 to 37,011 and the actual value of FDIs from US$1.258 billion to 41.726 billion in 1996. The trend of FDI growth during the period 1979-1996 can be seen from statistical data as set out in Table 2 below.

TABLE 2
**The Trend of Foreign Direct Investment in the PRC
for the Period from 1979 to 1996**

Year	Actually Utilized FDI in US$ Million	Annual Percentage Growth
1978 - 1983	1,802	N/A
1984	1,258	N/A
1985	1,661	32.03
1986	1,874	12.83
1987	2,314	23.48
1988	3,194	38.03
1989	3,392	6.20
1990	3,487	2.80
1991	4,365	25.18
1992	11,007	152.16
1993	27,515	149.98
1994	33,767	22.72
1995	37,521	11.12
1996	41,726	11.21

Source : China Statistical Yearbook, 1997 and various issues.

---

[18]Hu, F. 1997. "The Factors for Inducing Foreign Direct Investment," *Hong Kong Economic Journal*, July 17. p. 30. (in Chinese).

THE IMPORTANT ROLE OF FOREIGN DIRECT INVESTMENTS IN THE ECONOMIC REFORM OF THE PRC

Since the adoption of the open door economic policy in 1979, FDIs have played an increasingly important role in promoting the PRC's economic and trade development through technology transfer and the provision of funds. The FDI's portion in total value of imports and exports of the whole country grew from 34.27 per cent in 1993 to 39.1 per cent in 1995. On the contrary, the portion of that of the State-owned enterprises gradually declined from 65.73 per cent in 1993 to 60.9 per cent in 1995; this showed an urgent need for the reform of SOEs to improve their operating efficiency and competitive strength. Table 3 and 4 below show the upward trend of import and export value of FDIs and the comparative statistical data of national import and export value, population, GDP, and FDIs' output in terms of their portion in the national import and export value by provinces/regions respectively. As revealed by the available data, Guangdong province is most popular for FDIs and the import and export value of FDIs there was also the largest.

TABLE 3
The Upward Trend of Import and Export Value of Foreign-invested Enterprises (FDIs) for the Period from 1993 to 1995 (US$ Billion)

	1993			1994			1995		
	Total	Exports	Imports	Total	Exports	Imports	Total	Exports	Imports
National	195.70	91.74	103.96	236.62	121.01	115.61	280.85	148.77	132.08
FDI	67.07	25.24	41.83	87.64	34.71	52.93	109.82	46.88	62.94
Portion of FDI	34.27%	27.51%	40.24%	37.04%	28.69%	45.79%	39.10%	31.51%	47.66%

Source : China Statistical Yearbook, 1996 and Various Issues
A Statistical Survey of China, 1996 and Various Issues

The worsening situation of SOEs should partly be attributable to the PRC's previous preferential investment policies for FDIs and partly to the overall problems of SOEs arising from the transition from a "planned economy" to a "socialist market economy". As explained by the theory of product and factor market imperfections, the PRC's preferential investment policies for FDIs created a number of competitive advantages for FMNCs. Thus, the strategies for the utilization of foreign capital and the reform of SOEs as proposed by the PRC's Ninth Five-Year Plan (1996-2000) and Long-Term Targets for the year 2010 will modify previous policies for providing FMNCs and SOEs with a business environment which facilitates their competition on an equal footing. To a certain extent, the implication of these strategies will determine the applicability of the FDI theories. Discussed below are the development of the PRC's policies and strategies for FDIs which make the PRC alluring.

TABLE 4
Comparative Statistics of Foreign Direct Investment, Imports and Exports, Gross Domestic Product, and Population of Mainland China Provinces for the Year 1995

Province /Regions	Population (Million)	Gross Domestic Product (RMB Billion)	National Exports (US$ Billion)	National Imports (US$ Billion)	Total National Imports & Exports (US$ Billion)	Contracted Foreign Direct Investment (FDI) (US$ Million)	FDI's Portion of National Imports & Exports (%)
Greater Pearl River Delta							
Fujian	32.4	216.1	8.1	7.0	15.1	8,906.7	7.49
Guangdong	68.7	538.2	59.0	49.5	108.5	24,832.4	48.45
Yangtze River Delta							
Shanghai	14.2	246.3	13.1	12.8	25.9	10,296.6	10.22
Jiangsu	70.7	515.5	10.1	8.0	18.1	12,374.7	7.11
Zhejiang	43.2	352.5	8.3	4.5	12.8	3,248.9	2.78
Bohai Bay							
Beijing	12.5	139.5	6.0	10.8	16.8	2,735.1	2.35
Tianjin	9.4	92.0	4.4	4.5	8.9	3,850.1	4.54
Hebei	64.4	285.0	2.5	2.0	4.5	2,250.7	0.91
Liaoning	40.9	279.3	7.1	6.1	13.2	3,974.5	4.55
Shandong	87.1	500.2	9.0	7.6	16.6	4,625.2	5.61
Shanxi	30.8	109.2	1.8	0.5	2.3	228.4	0.15
Others							
Anhui	60.1	200.4	1.3	0.8	2.1	1,206.4	0.34
Gansu	24.4	55.3	0.3	0.4	0.7	109.8	0.05
Guizhou	35.1	63.0	0.4	0.3	0.7	86.3	0.08
Hainan	7.2	36.4	0.5	1.4	1.9	2,780.8	0.52
Heilongjiang	37.0	201.5	3.0	1.6	4.6	1,105.7	0.48
Henan	91.0	300.3	1.5	1.4	2.9	915.7	0.46
Hubei	57.7	239.1	1.8	1.9	3.7	1,088.5	0.83
Hunan	63.9	219.6	1.4	1.0	2.4	1,354.6	0.25
Jiangxi	40.6	120.5	0.8	0.6	1.4	539.7	0.18
Jilin	25.9	112.3	1.1	1.8	2.9	847.4	0.77
Qinghai	4.8	16.5	0.1	0.04	0.14	24.2	0.005
Shaanxi	35.1	100.0	1.0	0.9	1.9	403.3	0.18
Sichuan	113.3	353.4	2.0	1.9	3.9	1,206.9	0.47
Yunnan	39.9	120.7	1.2	1.1	2.3	374.0	0.18
Guangxi	45.4	160.6	1.6	1.7	3.3	1,041.8	0.75
Inner Mongolia	22.8	83.3	0.5	0.8	1.3	98.9	0.14
Ningxia	5.1	17.0	0.2	0.07	0.27	28.8	0.014
Tibet	2.4	5.6	0.01	0.2	0.21	-	0.023
Xinjiang	16.6	83.5	0.5	0.9	1.4	91.3	0.095
Total	1,211.2	5,862.1	148.6	132.1	.280.72	91,281.5	100%

Source : China Statistical Yearbook, 1996 and Various Issues
A Statistical Survey of China, 1996 and Various Issues

THE CONTRIBUTION OF FOREIGN DIRECT INVESTMENT TO THE PRC'S ECONOMIC REFORMS AND GROWTH

As a result of its low wage level, low land cost, the prospects of a vast domestic market of relatively untapped consumers, and its endeavors in modernizing its industries and infrastructure, the PRC has become one of the most competitive production bases for FMNCs in the world. By the end of 1995, more than 16 million workers had been employed by more than 150,000 foreign-invested enterprises (FIEs), whose economic contribution accounted for 39.1 per cent of the PRC's total foreign trade and 13.8 per cent of the total industrial output. As at 31 December 1995, the accumulated number of approved FDI contracts and the actual value of FDI were 258,788 and US$133.16 billion respectively. Since 1983, the share of FDI in total fixed assets investment in the PRC grew by 18.52 times, from 0.87 per cent to 16.11 per cent in 1995.

In the past 17 years since the beginning of economic reforms and the open door policy in late 1978, the PRC's GDP reached RMB5,773 billion or US$691 billion in 1995 with an average annual growth rate of 9.8%. In 1995 the ranking of the PRC in the largest trading nation of the world rose to 11th from the 28th place in 1978. All of the above-mentioned is evidence proving FDI's extensive contribution to the PRC's economic reforms and growth. Table 5 below shows the details of the distributions of actually used FDIs and foreign loans in the coastal regions for the period from 1994 to 1995.

TABLE 5
The Distribution of Actually Used Foreign Direct Investment and Foreign Loan for the Period from 1994 to 1995

(US$ 10,000)

Provinces/ Regions & Ministry	1994				1995			
	Percentage	Total	Foreign Loans	FDI & Other Foreign Investment	Percentage	Total	Foreign Loans	FDI & Other Foreign Investment
Guangdong	25.29%	1092758	146415	946343	22.17%	1066967	40956	1026011
Jiangsu	8.76	378568	2253	376315	11.06	532577	13495	519082
Fujian	8.62	372328	1010	371318	8.62	414908	10518	404390
Shanghai	5.96	258217	10908	247309	6.24	300543	11282	289261
Shandong	6.02	260143	4901	255242	5.74	276497	7599	268898
Tianjin	2.69	116176	14677	101499	3.30	158686	6593	152093
Liaoning	3.51	151471	7457	144014	3.26	156838	14377	142461
Zhejiang	2.68	115650	624	115026	2.68	128968	3162	125806
Beijing	3.19	137911	754	137157	2.30	110648	2649	107999
Other Provinces/ Regions & Ministry	33.28	1438062	737701	700361	34.63	1666637	922069	744568
Total	100%	4321284	926700	3394584	100%	4813269	1032700	3780569

Source : China Statistical Yearbook, 1996

UTILIZATION OF FOREIGN LOAN AND FOREIGN DIRECT INVESTMENT

In the 1950s, the PRC began to make use of foreign funds provided by government loans from foreign countries. In the 1970s, she also utilized export credit facilities extended by foreign commercial banks for the international trade transactions. Prior to 1 July 1979, there were no FDIs because they were not permitted in the PRC; and compensation trade and processing materials supplied by foreign clients were the only economic cooperative activities undertaken by SOEs with foreign firms as well as banks. FDIs have been brought in since 1 July 1979 when the enactment of the "Law of the People's Republic of China on Joint Ventures Using Chinese and Foreign Investment" came into effect. Thereafter, a number of foreign investment legislations relating to various aspects of foreign investment have been promulgated to encourage FDIs and for biding to join the World Trade Organization (WTO), successor to the GATT. The most popular forms of FDI are wholly foreign-owned enterprises, cooperative joint ventures, joint-stock limited companies and Chinese-foreign equity joint ventures. The typical FDI legislations include :

(i) *"Law of the People's Republic of China on Chinese-Foreign Equity Joint Ventures"* - effective as of 8 July 1979;

(ii) *"Law of the People's Republic of China on Wholly Foreign-Owned Enterprises"* - effective as of 12 April 1986, and the *"Detailed Implementing Regulations for the Law of the People's Republic of China on Wholly Foreign-Owned Enterprises"* - effective as of 12 December 1990;

(iii) *"Law of the People's Republic of China on Chinese-Foreign Cooperative Joint Ventures"* - effective as of 13 April 1988;

(iv) *"Company Law of the People's Republic of China"* - effective as of 1 July 1994, and *"Guangdong Company Law"* - effective as of 1 August 1993;

(v) *"Provisional Regulations of Shanghai Municipality Concerning Joint-Stock Limited Companies"* - effective as of 1 June 1992, and *"Regulations of the Shenzhen Special Economic Zone Concerning Joint-Stock Limited Companies"* - effective as of 1 October 1993;

(vi) *" Provisions of the State Council for the Encouragement of Foreign Investment"* - effective as of 11 October, 1986, and *"Regulations of the People's Republic of China Concerning Financial Administration of Foreign-Investment Enterprises"* - effective as of 24 June 1992.

In addition to making great progress in establishing up to date legal frameworks governing and protecting foreign FDIs as a means to further utilize foreign capital, the PRC has also utilized huge amounts of foreign loans for her economic development. Table 6 below shows details of the PRC's utilization of foreign loans, FDIs and other foreign investments.

TABLE 6
PRC's Utilization of Foreign Loans, Foreign Direct Investments and Other Foreign Investment for the Period 1979 – 1996

(US$100,000,000)

Year	Total		Foreign Loan		Foreign Direct Investment		*Other Foreign Investment
	Number of Contract	Value	Number of Contract	Value	Number of Contract	Value	Value
Total Value of Foreign Loans and FDI Through Signed Contracts Agreements							
1979-1983	1471	239.78	79	150.62	1392	77.42	11.74
1984	1894	47.91	38	19.16	1856	26.51	2.24
1985	3145	98.67	72	35.34	3073	59.32	4.01
1986	1551	117.37	53	84.07	1498	28.34	4.96
1987	2289	121.36	56	78.17	2233	37.09	6.10
1988	6063	160.04	118	98.13	5945	52.97	8.94
1989	5909	114.79	130	51.85	5779	56.00	6.94
1990	7371	120.86	98	50.99	7273	65.96	3.91
1991	13086	195.83	108	71.61	12978	119.77	4.45
1992	48858	694.39	94	107.03	48764	581.24	6.12
1993	83595	1232.73	158	113.06	83437	1114.36	5.31
1994	47646	937.56	97	106.68	47549	826.80	4.08
1995	37184	1032.05	173	112.88	37011	912.82	6.35
1996	24673	816.09	117	79.62	24556	732.76	3.71
Total Value of Foreign Loan and FDI Actually Used							
1979-1983		144.38		117.55		18.02	8.81
1984		27.05		12.86		12.58	1.61
1985		46.47		26.88		16.61	2.98
1986		72.58		50.14		18.74	3.70
1987		84.52		58.05		23.14	3.33
1988		102.26		64.87		31.94	5.45
1989		100.59		62.86		33.92	3.81
1990		102.89		65.34		34.87	2.68
1991		115.54		68.88		43.66	3.00
1992		192.02		79.11		110.07	2.84
1993		389.60		111.89		275.15	2.56
1994		432.13		92.67		337.67	1.79
1995		481.33		103.27		375.21	2.85
1996		548.04		126.69		417.26	4.09

*Note: Other Foreign Investments consist of (i) Financial Leasing, (ii) Compensation Trade, and (iii) Processing and Assembly.

Source: Statistical Yearbook of China, 1997 and various issues

THE POLICIES WHICH EXTENSIVELY CONTRIBUTED TO PRC'S RAPID ABSORPTION OF FOREIGN INVESTMENTS

The following are the major policies which have greatly encouraged foreign investment and created an increasingly congenial environment for foreign business operations since the adoption of the open door economic policy in 1979.

1. THE CONTINUOUS OPEN DOOR POLICY AND POLITICAL STABILITY

At the Third Plenary Session of the Eleventh Central Committee of the Communist Party of China in December 1978, the economic reform policy for opening the PRC to the outside world and measures for stimulating the domestic economy were decided upon. In order to lay great stress on the continuation of the policy, it has been reaffirmed frequently at important conferences of the National People's Congress and the Communist Party, in speeches made by State and Party leaders and in directives issued by the State and the Party thereafter.

On 15 May 1984, Mr. Zhao Ziyang, Premier of the State Council, reported on the 'Work of the Government' to the Second Session of the Sixth National People's Congress. He pointed out the following development plan for the economic reform :

(i) The open door policy will be unswervingly implemented in such a way that it will effectively conform to the actual conditions in the PRC;
(ii) The State Council has decided that a number of coastal cities will be opened as special economic zones to foreign investment;
(iii) Under the unified guidance of the open door policy, all local authorities and departments should adopt an enthusiastic attitude to develop economic and trade relations with foreign countries and actively utilize foreign funds and advanced foreign technology.

Soon after this congress, the PRC opened the Hainan Administrative Region as well as fourteen coastal cities as special economic zones (SEZs) in 1984: namely, Zhanjiang, Guangzhou, Shanghai, Fuzhou, Wenzhou, Ningbo, Nantong, Lianyungang, Qingdao, Yantai, Tianjin, Qinhuangdao, Dalian and Beihai.

In these coastal cities and administrative regions, the economic-technological development zones (ETDZs) were designated for greater encouragement of advanced technology transfer. In addition to the common respects between SEZs and ETDZs, FDIs in ETDZs would enjoy more preferential treatment in taxation. Higher autonomy was given to local authorities for them to approve the FDIs with advanced technology. The setting up of wholly foreign-owned enterprises was allowed. The equity joint ventures and cooperative joint ventures were allowed to extend their terms of operation when necessary. A bigger sales ratio in the domestic market in the PRC was granted to products of advanced technology manufactured by FDIs.

TABLE 7
Comparative Statistics of Urban Per Capita Income, Retail Market Size, Added Value Output of Secondary Industry for the Year 1995

Province/Regions	Urban Per Capita Income (RMB)	Retail Market Size Retail Sales		Added Value Output of Secondary Industry (RMB Billion)
		Amount (RMB Billion)	Percentage %	
Greater Pearl River Delta				
Fujian	4,326	58.7	2.85	98.0
Guangdong	6,849	230.4	11.18	276.0
Yangtze River Delta				
Shanghai	6,822	97.0	4.71	141.6
Jiangsu	4,209	165.0	8.01	250.0
Zhejiang	5,718	139.6	6.78	183.2
Bohai Bay				
Beijing	5,868	82.7	4.02	64.4
Tianjin	4,626	37.6	1.83	N/A.
Hebei	3,960	84.9	4.12	132.5
Liaoning	3,307	112.6	5.47	157.7
Shandong	3,953	144.3	7.00	238.4
Shanxi	2,927	37.6	1.83	56.4
Others				
Anhui	3,406	60.0	2.91	94.9
Gansu	2,855	23.0	1.11	25.7
Guizhou	3,427	19.8	0.96	24.3
Hainan	4,344	10.9	0.53	14.0
Heilongjiang	2,968	68.3	3.32	96.1
Henan	3,029	90.7	4.40	142.5
Hubei	3,606	93.2	4.52	103.0
Hunan	4,069	83.7	4.06	81.8
Jiangxi	3,046	41.1	1.99	60.3
Jilin	2,914	48.2	2.34	51.5
Qinghai	3,051	5.8	0.28	6.5
Shaanxi	3,046	37.0	1.80	42.8
Sichuan	3,586	130.1	6.32	148.6
Yunnan	3,684	37.0	1.80	47.5
Guangxi	4,289	53.3	2.59	65.7
Inner Mongolia	2,600	29.5	1.43	32.0
Ningxia	3,026	5.7	0.28	7.5
Tibet	4,000	2.5	0.12	1.0
Xinjiang	3,800	25.4	1.24	34.6
Total	-	2,060.0	100%	2,827.0

Source: China Statistical Yearbook, 1996 and various issues
A Statistical Survey of China, 1996 and various issues

In order to completely open coastal regions from north to south, the Changjiang (Yangtze) River Delta, the Zhujiang (Pearl) River Delta and the triangular zone in southern Fujian Province comprising Xianmen (Amoy), Zhangzhou and Quanzhou were opened in 1995. This makes the complete opening of coastal region, starting from Dalian in the north, extending all the way down to Beihai City in the south. Political stability is one of the chief goals of the PRC in her four phases of modernization. Table 7 above shows thorough details of the distribution of FDI, market size, urban per capita income and added value output of secondary industry in the coastal province / regions.

As advocated by Mr. Deng Xiaoping, Chairman of the Central Advisory Commission of the Chinese Communist Party, the open door policy and other economic reform measures can greatly contribute to the stimulation of the domestic economy, and then the goals of political stability can be realized. With the full opening of coastal regions from north to south, the economic development of the interior regions from east to west can in turn be given a great impetus by funds, technological know-how, management expertise, marketing skill, well-trained personnel and international economic information provided by FDIs. By the end of 1995, an overwhelming amount of FDI was established in the coastal region. In total it accounted for about 84% of PRC's cumulative utilized FDI. Among the coastal regions, Guangdong was the largest recipient of FDI, it received for 27.13 per cent and the second largest was Jiangsu which received for 13.73 per cent. Table 5 above shows the details of the distribution of actually used FDIs and foreign loans in the coastal regions for the period from 1994 to 1995.

2. THE POLICY OF OFFERING ATTRACTIVE PREFERENTIAL TREATMENTS TO FDI

To further encourage FDI , numerous preferences as discussed below have been offered to FDI :

(I) THE OPENING OF THE DOMESTIC MARKET

Those FDIs which can introduce advanced and new technology to the PRC and manufacture products that are superior to those produced by domestic industries, both in quality and variety, are permitted to sell a larger portion of their products in the domestic market. Furthermore, FDIs can set payment terms to be denominated in foreign currencies to their domestic buyers for their products which could be classified as import substitutes by the Chinese government.

(II) THE RELAXATION OF IMMIGRATION CONTROL ON FOREIGN BUSINESSMEN

To enable foreign businessmen to better fulfill contracts and run the foreign-owned enterprises, Chinese foreign joint ventures, contractual joint ventures, joint exploration and exploitation of offshore petroleum and compensation trade, they and their families and dependents will be granted visas or resident permits issued by the Public Security Bureau of the province, autonomous region, or the municipality directly under the central government. The regulations governing this operation promulgated by the Ministry of Public Security came into effect in June, 1983.

(III) THE EXTENSION OF INCOME TAX REDUCTION AND EXEMPTION PERIODS TO CHINESE FOREIGN JOINT VENTURES

According to Article 5 of the "Income Tax Law of the People's Republic of China Concerning Joint Ventures Using Chinese and Foreign Investment", promulgated in September 1980, a newly established joint venture scheduled to operate for a period of ten years or more will be entitled to submit an application to the tax authorities for income tax exemption in the first profit-making years and for 50 per cent reduction in the second and third years.

To further encourage foreign investment, in June 1983 the Ministry of Finance amended this regulation with more preferential treatments which allowed the newly established joint venture to be exempted from income tax in the first two profit-making years and be allowed a 50 per cent tax reduction in the third, fourth and fifth years. This preferential treatment could also be granted to those joint ventures approved before 1 April 1983 which have not yet made any profits. For those joint ventures which are presently in their first profit-making year, their periods of tax exemption and reduction will be extended by one year respectively. In case where they are presently in their second or third year of profit-making, their tax reduction period will be extended by one year.

(IV) PREFERENTIAL TAX RATES FOR FDIS IN THE ECONOMIC-TECHNOLOGICAL DEVELOPMENT ZONES (ETDZ) IN THE COASTAL CITIES

Since May 1985, Economic-Technological Development Zones have gradually been set up in the coastal cities of economic zones in order to facilitate technology transfer from FDIs. In December 1984, the Standing Committee of the National People's Congress decided on a series of income tax regulations with preferential tax rates for FDI in ETDZs. These tax preferential treatments include : (a) the preferential income tax rate for FDIs in ETDZs will only be half of that for those outside the zone, i.e. 15 per cent (50 per cent of 30 per cent). Furthermore, they will also be exempted from the local surcharge. (b) Outward remittance of FDIs for their profits earned from investment in SEZs and FTDZs will be exempted from 10 per cent outward remittance tax. (c) FDIs' incomes accrued in SEZs and ETDZs in the forms of technology transfer charges, interest on loans, royalties and technical service fees will be exempted from a 20 per cent income tax.

(V) PREFERENTIAL TREATMENT TO FOREIGN INVESTMENT IN THE OLD AREAS OF THE COASTAL CITIES

To channel FDIs to old areas of the coastal cities, the State Council promulgated in December 1984 the following two preferential treatments : (a) FDIs will pay only 80 per cent of the income tax as levied by the "Income Tax Law Concerning Foreign Enterprises" and the "Income Tax Law Concerning Joint Ventures Using Chinese and

Foreign Investment"; (b) FDIs' investment projects which have not less than US$30 million and a long playback period and which are engaged in producing import substitutes, applying advanced technologies, communications, harbor construction and energy infrastructures will be subject to a preferential income tax rate of 15 per cent.

(VI) THE REMOVAL OF REMITTANCE RESTRICTIONS ON PERSONAL INCOME OF FOREIGN EMPLOYEE

In 1983, article 25 of the Provisional Regulations on Foreign Exchange Control of the People's Republic of China was amended. It removed the restrictions on outward remittance which only allowed 50 per cent of the after-tax total of wages and other legitimate net earnings of foreign employees to be remitted or taken out of the PRC. With the amendment, they are allowed to remit abroad or take out the full amount of their after-tax wages and legitimate earnings.

(VII) OPENING MORE INDUSTRIAL SECTORS TO FOREIGN INVESTMENT

As of 1985, FDIs are allowed to invest in the industrial sectors of finance and commerce in the Special Economic Zones. FDIs are encouraged to invest in the mining, melting and processing of ferrous metals, coal mining, quarrying and processing of marble and granite, the mining and processing of phosphate and potassium, etc.

(VIII) ALLOWING MORE FORMS OF FOREIGN INVESTMENT

At the outset of the open door policy, the foreign investment brought into the PRC was confined to contractual joint ventures, Chinese-foreign equity joint ventures and compensation trading. Later on, other forms of FDIs were permitted to established, including wholly foreign-owned enterprises, branches, representative offices, processing and assembly contracts, management contracts, service centres, and a variety of other forms of operations.

3. THE IMPROVEMENTS IN LEGISLATION AND LEGAL FRAMEWORK

For the protection of foreign investment and the creation of an increasingly hospitable operation environment for foreign businesses, the PRC has made great progress in improving the legal system governing foreign investments and international trade, in generalizing the basic principles of commercial law, and in strengthening and specializing the court system. To keep the continuing fast pace of change with the business environment, new business laws are being promulgated every few months. During 1993 and 1994, a variety of new business laws with an international standard have been introduced, including national company laws, unfair competition laws, national securities regulations, national foreign trade laws, laws on foreign financial institutions, adoption of a new foreign exchange regime, national labor laws, urban real estate laws, new set of rules for international arbitrations conducted in China, new arbitration laws, company registration laws, new laws on foreign investment in the mining sector and so forth. Various laws, regulations, decrees and administrative rules for encouraging foreign investments fell into the following categories :

(I) THE "IMPLEMENTING REGULATIONS FOR THE LAW OF THE PRC ON JOINT VENTURES USING CHINESE AND FOREIGN INVESTMENT."

These regulations lay down specific provisions in the face of potential problems arising in the implementation of the "Law on Joint Ventures" which was promulgated by the State Council on 20th September 1983. The provisions concern mainly the following areas :

(a) Sectors of industry in which foreign investment is encouraged or prohibited;
(b) Requirements for the approval of joint ventures;

The Ministry of Foreign Economic Relations and Trade (MOFERT) will approve or may authorize the local government of a province, an autonomous region or a municipality directly under the State Council to examine and approve a joint venture if it satisfies the following requirements :

- the total amount of investment for the joint venture is within the prescribed amount specified by the State Council and the investment from the Chinese side has been ascertained;
- the joint venture will not require any assistance from the State for allocation of raw materials and processed materials and will not burden the country with adverse effects on such economic sectors as export quotas, transportation, communications, fuel and power.

(c) The regulations of the foreign exchange are defined;
(d) The regulations governing technology transfer has been clearly stated;
(e) The regulations governing the application for the right to use the land and business site and the principle for charging fees for using the land and business site have been clearly stated;
(f) Preferential treatment to the joint venture for its purchases of raw materials from the China market have been stipulated;

The joint venture will enjoy the same prices or fees as those to be charged to SOEs when they buy raw materials for which distribution is planned and handled by commercial departments of the local government, such as electricity, supplies of water, gas and heat, transportation service, project design service, consultancy service, labor service, as well as product advertisements;

> (g) Various terms for joint venture according the particular conditions of the business and project are set;

(II) THE ENACTMENT OF THE PATENT LAW

The Patent Law was resolved and promulgated at the Fourth Session of the Standing Committee of the Sixth National People's Congress on 12th March, 1984 and came into effect on 1st April, 1995. The Patent Law consists of eight chapters with 188 articles which mainly stipulate five provisions of regulatory frameworks for patents : (a) the protection of patents; (b) items to which no patents shall be granted; (c) the principle of priority for dealing with the patent application; (d) the duration, expiration and invalidation of patents; (e) the regulations for the compulsory utilization of patents and the compulsory license issued to a third party.

(III) THE ENACTMENT OF THE TRADE MARK LAW

The Trade Mark Law was resolved and enacted by the Twenty Fourth Session of the Standing Committee of the Fifth National People's Congress on August, 1982. The Trade Mark Law mainly stipulates the following four provisions : (a) the compulsory product registration of trade marks to ensure the quality of the products; (b) the application procedure for trade mark registration and the trade mark administration; (c) the protection of the exclusive right to use a registered trade mark; (d) the licensing, assignment and renewal of registered trade marks.

4. THE ENACTMENT OF THE "ECONOMIC CONTRACT LAW" OF THE PEOPLE'S REPUBLIC OF CHINA CONCERNING OVERSEAS INTERESTS

At the Tenth Session of the Standing Committee of the Sixth National People's Congress, the "Economic Contract Law" was resolved. The Presidential Decree no. 21 in connection with the law was issued on 21st March, 1985. The "Economic Law" consisting of seven chapters with 43 articles came into effect on 1st July, 1985. The provisions of the Law mainly fall into the following categories :

> (i) definition of the application scope of the law and the indications
> of appropriate
> laws for settlement of contractual disputes;
> (ii) conclusion and validity of a contract;
> (iii) obligation of contract execution;
> (iv) termination, assignment and alternation of a contract;
> (v) method of arbitration.

THE PERSISTENT OPERATING PROBLEMS OF STATE-OWNED ENTERPRISES AND ITS IMPACT ON THE PRC'S ECONOMY

With reference to the World Bank's report on "The Assets of Enterprises Managed by the PRC", there are approximately 7.61 million industrial enterprises in the PRC which can broadly be classified into three groups, namely, private enterprises, Town-and-Village owned enterprises and State-owned enterprises. They are distributed in this manner: (i) 5.76 million private enterprises of which 5.7 million are small-sized (with 7 employees on an average) and 60,000 are medium to large-sized (most of the medium to large-sized enterprises are in the forms of wholly foreign-owned enterprises, Chinese-foreign equity joint ventures, and cooperative joint ventures); (ii) 1.5 million Town-and-Village owned enterprises; and (iii) 350,000 State-owned enterprises.

Ever since the economic reform of the PRC began in late 1978, the State-owned enterprises have always been one of the main hindrances to the reform progress. With reference to the official statistical data of the PRC, the overall net profit after tax of SOEs for the financial year ended 31st December, 1996 deteriorated further by a decline of 37.1 per cent in contrast to the decline of 19.7 per cent for 1995. Among SOEs, those which showed a net loss accounted for 37.7 per cent and 39 per cent of the total in 1996 and 1995 respectively.

The reform measures set forth by the Eighth Five-Year Plan (1990-1995) clearly failed to deal with the problems during the implementation of the SOEs reform measures. The main problems include the preferential treatment given to FMNCs, such as taxation, trade policy and investment policy, resulting in (i) their overwhelming competitive advantages; (ii) unclearly-defined property rights, powers and responsibilities of SOEs; (iii) ambiguous separation of government administration from SOEs' management; (iv) unrealistic transfer pricing practices, reciprocal business contracts, and backlog of long overdue accounts receivable and payable among SOEs; (v) management ethical problems; (vi) excessive reliance on national industrial protections through a preferential policy, a industrial subsidy and a commodity price subsidy; (vii) excessive tax imposition by provincial/local government on SOEs, etc. The following are the main adverse impacts of the SOEs' poor performance on the PRC's economy :

1. HEAVY BURDEN ON THE BANKING SYSTEM

Mr. Dai Xianglong, the president of the People's Bank of China (PBC), announced on 14th August, 1997 that the debt ratio of SOEs was too high and this resulted in the Bank having to bear a huge amount of bad and doubtful debt. The overdue loan interest as at 31st July, 1997 amounted to the considerable sum of RMB 140 billion; this was already two years overdue on an average. Mr. Zhu Rongji, the Vice Premier of the State Council, announced on 24th July, 1997 that for the sake of improving SOEs' solvency and reducing their liabilities, RMB 30 billion will be especially allocated in the 1997, along with a series of actions taken for assisting those SOEs with persistent losses to get rid of their awkward dilemma within a targeted time frame of three years.

2. THE STATE FINANCIAL DISEQUILIBRIUM AS A CONSEQUENCE OF HUGE AMOUNT OF SUBSIDIES TO SOES

As a result of SOEs' inefficiency and uncompetitiveness, one-third of them are currently running operating losses which require a substantial amount of subsidy for their deficit and a commodity price subsidy from Chinese government to keep their business running. With the exceptions of 1978 and 1985, the PRC has always been in financial disequilibrium since the introduction of economic reform in 1978. Statistical data shows that ever since 1980 there has been a continuous increase in the state financial deficit. The deficit has accelerated from RMB 12.75 billion in 1980 to RMB 62.14 billion in 1995. The Table 8 below shows the details.

TABLE 8
State Revenue, Expenditure and Persistent Deficit
for the Period from 1978 to 1995

Year	Total Revenue (100 Million)	Total Expenditure (100 Million)	Net Surplus / (Deficit) (100 Million)	Indices (Preceding Year = 100) Total Revenue %	Total Expenditure %
1978	1121.1	1111.0	*10.1*	128.2	131.7
1979	1103.3	1273.9	(170.6)	98.4	114.7
1980	1085.2	1212.7	(127.5)	98.4	95.2
1981	1089.5	1115.0	(25.5)	100.4	91.9
1982	1124.0	1153.3	(29.3)	103.2	103.4
1983	1249.0	1292.5	(43.5)	111.1	112.1
1984	1501.9	1546.4	(44.5)	120.2	119.6
1985	1866.4	1844.8	*21.6*	124.3	119.3
1986	2260.3	2330.8	(70.5)	121.1	126.3
1987	2368.9	2448.5	(79.6)	104.8	105.0
1988	2628.0	2706.6	(78.6)	110.9	110.5
1989	2947.9	3040.2	(92.3)	112.2	112.3
1990	3312.6	3452.2	(139.6)	112.4	113.6
1991	3610.9	3813.6	(202.7)	109.0	110.5
1992	4153.1	4389.7	(236.6)	115.0	115.1
1993	5088.2	5287.4	(199.2)	122.5	120.5
1994	5218.1	5792.6	(574.5)	120.0	124.8
1995	6242.2	6823.7	(581.5)	119.6	117.8
1996	7366.6	7914.4	(547.8)	118.0	116.0

Source : A Statistical Survey of China, 1997 and various issues

The notable items which constituted the persistent state financial deficit are the 'Subsidy to State-owned Enterprises' and the 'Commodity Price Subsidy' (for agricultural products, meat, coal and petroleum products and so on), accounting for 10.53 per cent (5.18 per cent + 5.35 per cent) of the total expenditure in 1995 and 31.99 per cent (19.7 per cent + 12.29 per cent) in 1989. Table 9 below shows the thorough details.

TABLE 9
Subsidy to State-owned Enterprise and Commodity Price Subsidy
for the Period 1986 to 1996

Year	Subsidy to State-owned Enterprise for their Deficit		Commodity Price Subsidy	
	RMB Billion	Percentage of State Total Expenditure	RMB Yuan Billion	Percentage of State Total Expenditure
1986	32.478	13.94	25.748	11.05
1987	37.643	15.37	29.460	12.03
1988	44.646	16.5	31.682	11.71
1989	59.888	19.7	37.355	12.29
1990	57.888	16.77	38.080	11.03
1991	51.024	13.38	37.377	9.80
1992	44.496	10.14	32.164	7.33
1993	41.129	7.78	29.930	5.66
1994	36.620	6.32	31.450	5.43
1995	32.780	4.80	36.490	5.35
1996	32.550	4.11	45.390	5.74

Source : Statistical Yearbook of China, 1997 and various issues

3. HINDRANCE TO THE PROGRESS OF COMPLETE OPENING OF THE DOMESTIC MARKET AND JOINING THE WORLD TRADE ORGANIZATION (WTO)

As most SOEs are only sustainable through subsidies and protectionist policies such as the establishment of trade barriers by means of import tariffs, import quota, the trade restriction for the domestic market, etc., it constrains the PRC's faster progress in completely opening the domestic market and joining the WTO. As part of its strategy to join the WTO, which is the successor to the GATT, the PRC has been gradually reducing import tariffs since 1991 to a targeted level of 15 per cent before 2000. On 19th November 1995, Chairman Jiang Zemin of the PRC announced at the Asian Pacific Economic Cooperation Association ('APEC') conference held in Osaka, Japan that the PRC will reduce import tariff rates by no less than 30 per cent in 1996. Subsequent to Chairman Jiang Zemin's announcement, the State Council of the PRC promulgated new tax and trade reforms which took effect on 1st April 1996. Under these reforms, the average customs tariff rate will be reduced by 36 per cent (down from 35.9 per cent to 23 per cent) for 4,962 trade items.

Obviously, the protection for SOEs will be the main constraint for the PRC's further elimination of trade barriers with major trading partners by aligning rates of import tariffs in a faster manner which will permit further expansion of international trade. Prior to a series of tax reductions, the PRC's average import tariff rate was as high as 35.9 per cent, more than double the 15 per cent generally adopted in developing countries around the world.

4. UNHEALTHY BUSINESS ENVIRONMENT

As part of the industrial protection strategy for SOEs, Chinese government acquires most supplies from SOEs. To solve the cash flow problem and follow the directive of the local government, SOEs always undertake intra-group acquisition of materials and goods through which the backlog of accounts receivable and accounts payable could be offset by bilateral and multilateral netting. This business phenomenon not only distorts market efficiency but also hinders the complete opening of domestic market and in turn the joining of the World Trade Organization. In the long run, it is disadvantageous to the healthy development of the economy.

THE REFORM OF STATE-OWNED ENTERPRISES

THE STRUCTURE OF STATE-OWNED ENTERPRISES

Most of the SOEs are in a difficult situation as a result of their inefficiency and uncompetitiveness. Currently, their employees account for 67 per cent of the total worker of the cities. They absorb 54.4 per cent of the total investment of the state. The total assets of the state as at 31st December, 1996 was RMB 6,589 billion. There was a 15.4 per cent growth in contrast to that of 1995. Yet, the SOE's amount of output only accounted for 32 per cent in the whole country. 33 per cent of SOE's are currently suffering operating losses.

To classify SOEs according to the size of their business operation in terms of the amount of assets, the total asset value of medium to large-sized SOEs and small-sized SOEs as at 31st December, 1996 were RMB 8,923 billion and RMB 2,976 billion, accounting for 75% and 25% of the total asset value of SOEs respectively. As some of the SOEs are listed on local and overseas stock markets, the aforesaid figures consisted of the majority share capital contributed by the State and the minority share capital contributed by local and overseas investors. In terms of number, the proportion of medium to large-sized SOEs was 19.9%, and of small-sized SOEs was 80.1%. [19]

THE OPERATING LOSS AND BANKRUPTCY OF SOES

According to official statistical data, the total amount of operating loss of SOEs for the period from January to July 1997 was RMB 39 billion. There was an increase of RMB 4.6 billion in contrast to that for the same period in 1996. There is evidence which can prove the loss of small-sized SOEs to be worsening; for example, the loss of small-sized SOEs for the period from January to February 1997 was RMB 2.4 billion. But, up to April 1997, the amount of loss rose to RMB 4.75 billion with 3 per cent increase in contrast to that of the same period of 1996. As revealed by the statistical data of Supreme People's Court, 4,900 enterprises went bankrupt in 1996, of which 2,348 were SOE's, accounting for 47.92 per cent of the total. On the other hand, 1,190 SOEs were merged or acquired in 1996, which caused 1.23 million employees to be dismissed or transferred to new jobs.

Since 1993, SOE's applications for bankruptcy are fast growing. The trend of the SOE's application for bankruptcy in the past four years was rose sharply. The statistical data show that in 1993, 1994, 1995 and 1996 the numbers of bankruptcy application were 710, 1,625, 2,385, 6,232 respectively. In this regard, the reform of SOEs will intensify the bankruptcy, acquisition and merger of uncompetitive and inefficient SOEs. This will facilitate the PRC's economic reforms but will cause serious social problems of unemployment. [20]

THE NEW POLICY AND STRATEGY OF STATE-OWNED ENTERPRISES REFORM

On 13th September 1997, during the 15th Chinese Communist Party (CCP) Congress, Mr. Jiang Zemin, the Chairman of the State, delivered a notable report on the economic reform entitled "Hold High the Big Banner of Deng Xiaoping Theory for the All-Round Advancement of the Cause of Building Socialism with Chinese Characteristics to 21st Century". The report explained that the PRC will be poised to make a breakthrough in economic restructuring through the policy of intensifying the reform of state-owned enterprises. The proposed strategies of the reform include :

(1) turning the State-owned enterprises into joint-stock companies

---

[19]Lee, Sau Hang. 1997. "The Structure of State-owned Assets and Its Distribution," *Hong Kong Economic Journal*, September 10, p. 21. (in Chinese).

[20]Lee, Shau Hang, 1997. "The Utilization of Foreign Investment to Solve the Unemployment Problem", *Hong Kong Economic Journal*, September 11, p. 28. (in Chinese).

It is expected that there will be an upsurge of enterprise reform in the wake of the Congress.

(2) *strengthening the competent of State-owned enterprises through merger, reorganization, union and leasing*

With the form of joint-stock companies and using capital as a link, State-owned enterprises in all parts of the country will form competitive multi-regional, multi-ownership, multi-national and multi-industrial conglomerates.

(3) *allowing greater autonomy to state-owned enterprises.*

As the State-owned enterprises have been turned into joint-stock companies and some of them can even become listed companies, they will be allowed to be independent of the government. The management of such a conglomerate will run its operations on its own, answer to the shareholders by maximizing their wealth and assume sole responsibility for its profits or losses.

THE EFFECTIVENESS OF JOINT-STOCK COMPANY SYSTEM FOR THE STATE-OWNED ENTERPRISES REFORM

As a consequence of the ownership problem of the SOEs, the PRC has for long remained unable to make much progress in reforming SOEs. The root of the problem is their ill-defined scope of responsibilities and authority and less than clear ownership which lead most of them to be inefficient and uncompetitive. Theoretically, the joint-stock company system could solve the ownership, responsibility and authority problems. Furthermore, its effectiveness has been proved to hold good by the improved profitability, return on total assets ratio and solvency ratio of those SOEs listed on the Shenzhen Stock Exchange and the Shanghai Stock Exchange.[21] The upward trend in the number of listed companies and in transaction volumes of both the Shenzhen Stock Exchange and the Shanghai Stock Exchange as revealed by those statistical data in Table 10, 11 and 12 below provide the obvious evidence to prove the beneficial effects of the joint-stock company system.

---

[21]Chen, Shoudong, 1997. "The Development and Problems of Stock Exchange in China", *Hong Kong Economic Journal Monthly*, Volume 21, Issue 246, September, pp. 17 - 21. (in Chinese).

TABLE 10
Total Number of Listed Companies and Transaction Volume of the Shenzhen Stock Exchange and the Shanghai Stock Exchange for the period from 1990 to 1996

Items /Years	1990	1991	1992	1993	1994	1995	1996
Total Number of Listed Companies in Shenzhen S. E. & Shanghai S. E.	8	13	58	182	289	311	530
Total Transaction Volume of Shenzhen S. E. & Shanghai S. E. (RMB Billion)	1.8	5.155	6.93	418.7	812.7	401.8	2,133.2

Source : Almanac of China's Stock Markets 1997 and various issues
Almanac of China's Finance and Banking, 1997.

As shown by Table 11 and 12 below, from 1993 onward there was a big jump in transaction volume, number of listed companies, issued share capital and share market value. It revealed the positive recognition of the advantages of the joint-stock system by both the central and local governments. These developments afterward served as the groundwork for the new SOE reform policy on the joint-stock system as promulgated at the 15th Chinese Communist Party Congress in September 1997.

TABLE 11
The Size of the Shenzhen Stock Exchange for the period from 1991 to 1995

(RMB Billion)

Year / Items	Par Value of Issued Share Capital	Market Value of Share Capital	Number of Listed "A" Shares and "B" Shares*		Total Amount of Transactions
			"A" Share	"B" Share	
1991	0.56	8.078	6	0	3.557
1992	2.614	48.977	24	90	42.40
1993	12.206	132.677	76	16	128.667
1994	22.059	113.533	113	19	239.20
1995	26.739	105.935	127	34	91.50
1996	43.953	436.46	227	43	1221.74

*Note : "A" shares can only be traded by the PRC nationals;
"B" shares are the only class of shares for foreign investors.
Source : Almanac of China's Stock Markets 1996 and various issues
Almanac of China's Finance and Banking, 1997.

TABLE 12

The Size of the Shanghai Stock Exchange for the Period from 1990 to 1996

(RMB Billion)

Year / Items	Par Value of Issued Share Capital	Market Value of Share Capital	Number of Listed "A" Shares and "B" Shares		Total Amount of Transactions
			"A" Share	*"B" Share*	
1990	0.26118	1.23433	8	0	0.00094
1991	0.27223	2.94271	8	0	0.80714
1992	4.96429	55.84036	30	90	24.71854
1993	23.55353	220.61962	101	22	246.76881
1994	41.88797	260.01298	169	34	573.50739
1995	49.825	252.566	184	36	310.30
1996	111.04	984.24	287	42	2,133.22

*Note : "A" shares can only be traded by the PRC nationals;
"B" shares are the only class of shares for foreign investors.
*Source : Almanac of China's Stock Markets 1996 and various issues
Almanac of China's Finance and Banking, 1997.*

In comparison with previously, SOEs' financial and operating difficulties have gradually been mitigated since May 1997. In particular, the improvements of listed companies were quite obvious. By the end of October, 1997, nearly seven hundred listed SOEs (joint-stock SOEs) have shown gradual improvement in profitability and return on total assets as a result of the improved management system, higher level of technology, re-structuring of optimal assets, greater operating autonomy, better economy of scale through merger and acquisition, etc.

According to the "Profit After Tax Per Share" for the interim result in 1997 of those SOEs listed in the two principal stock exchanges located in Shenzhen and Shanghai, there was a satisfactory average increase of 8.5 per cent. The average Profit After Tax Per Share for the period ended 30th June 1997 was RMB 0.1514. The conservatively estimated amount for the whole year would be RMB 0.3244, accounting for a 8.5 per cent increase as compared with RMB 0.299 of last year for the period ended 31st December 1996. In the case of the Shenzhen Stock Exchange, the interim result of listed SOEs for the period ended 30th June 1997 was greatly improved: which the "Return On Total Assets" was 5.66 per cent, accounting for an increase by 11.1 per cent as compared with 5.095 per cent for the same period last year. As for the "Profit After Tax per Share", there was an increase of 9.1 per cent, from RMB 0.1458 for the period ended 30th June 1996 to RMB 0.159 for the period ended 30th June 1997.[22]

THE STRATEGIES FOR SOE REFORM SET IN THE NINTH FIVE-YEAR PLAN (1996-2000) AND LONG-TERM TARGETS FOR THE YEAR 2010

(1) THE STRATEGY FOR THE SOE REFORM SET IN THE EIGHTH FIVE-YEAR PLAN (1991-1995) PERIOD

Even when the PRC began the SOE reform in the 1980s, SOEs were still beset with such problems as mounting chain debts, inefficiency, low profitability, uncompetitiveness, increasing dependence on government subsidies, etc. Thus, among reform areas such as the fiscal system, banking, trade, market and price system, SOE reform becomes the main theme of PRC's economic reforms and it is the most important area for the success in making the transition from planned economy to market economy. The following are the key points of SOE reform strategies set in the Eighth Five-Year Plan (1991-1995) period which failed in truly integrating SOEs into the market economic system :

> (i) to explore effective means to building up the State-owned economy;
> (ii) to improve the operation of SOEs through the establishment of modern management systems, efficient operating mechanisms and effective self- regulatory mechanisms;
> (iii) to vitalize enterprises, particularly for medium and large-scale SOEs.

The result of the reform in this period was not satisfactory, largely because the resistance to the SOE reform remains strong, and most SOEs' business operations were overwhelmed by the competitive advantages of foreign-invested enterprises.

(2) THE STRATEGY FOR THE REFORM OF SOE SET IN THE NINTH FIVE-YEAR PLAN (1996-2000) AND LONG-TERM TARGETS FOR THE YEAR 2010

The "Joint-Stock Company System" has not been proposed in the Ninth Five-Year Plan (1996-2000) and Long-Term Targets for the Year 2010 as a result of the objection of the left wing of the Chinese Communist Party. They strongly advocated the ultra-leftist dogma that the joint-stock company system will shake the foundation of socialism so that such enterprises should be other than public-owned. Ultimately, this trammel of dogma has been smashed by the proposed strategy of the joint-stock company system in the 15th Chinese Communist Party congress in September, 1997. Such a ground-breaking reform

---

[22]Chen, Dongqi, 1997. "The Economy of China Could Be Maintained With High Growth Rate and Low Inflation Rate in 1998," *Hong Kong Economic Journal*, November 11, p. 39 (in Chinese).

is based on the rationale that there should be a wide variety of forms of public ownership and it is quite acceptable to adopt socialist as well as capitalist joint-stock company systems.

The following are the key points of the strategy of SOE reform set in the Ninth Five-Year Plans and Long-Term Targets for the year 2010 :

(I) THE GOAL OF SOE REFORM

To set the goal for reforming SOEs with the modern enterprise system in order to optimize the industrial structure and then establish a micro-economic foundation for a highly efficient economy. In pursuit of this goal, SOE will be reorganized with the transformation of management.

- The basic features of the modern enterprises system should include :

~ The Clearly Defined Property Right;
~ The Clear Authorities and Responsibilities;
~ The Separation Government Administration from the Management of Enterprise;
~ The Establishment of Scientific Management.

- The achievement time span for the aforesaid goals during the Ninth Five-Year Plan period are as follows :

~ **Phase One** : for Pilot Run from 1995 to 1996 :

The selected pilot projects will run with the defined features of the modern enterprises system with a view to achieving breakthroughs.

~ **Phase Two :** for Full Implementation from 1997 to 2000 :

To legislate a complete set of laws, regulations and regulatory frames with reference to the experiences gained in phase one, and then implement the SOE reform in the whole country.

(II) THE IMPLEMENTATION OF THE REFORM

The Reform will go through a series of reforms in structural re-organization, replacement of operational mechanism, technological transformation, internal management, enterprise leadership and the separation of government administration from enterprise management. The details are as follows :

(a) The Launch of Four Pilot Run Projects

To gain experience, explore potential problems and search for a most suitable path for SOE reform, four pilot run projects of the following reform means have been launched since 1994 to explore the outcomes :

- The "Modern Enterprise System" was run in 100 selected SOEs;
- The Establishment of three "Joint-stock Companies";
- The formation of "Conglomerates" by 56 selected SOEs;
- The experiment of the optimization of the capital structure of SOEs in 18 selected cities.

(b) The Structural Re-Organization for State-Owned Economy

The State-owned economy will be modified by structural re-organization. It includes the mergers, leasing, contracting, bankruptcy of SOEs and other kind of State-owned assets. Benefit accrued from State-owned assets could be optimized and the quality and efficiency of SOEs could be improved.

(c) To Put the Policy of "Restructuring, Transformation and Reforming" into Practice

SOEs will undertake structural reorganization and do the utmost to intensify technological transformation in its production. Reforming refers to the replacement of the inefficient operational system with the modern enterprise system.

(d) The Separation of Government Administration from Enterprise Management

In order to give greater autonomy to SOEs' management and thereby to improve their efficiency and competitiveness, the government administration and directives will be separated from the management of the SOEs.

(e) The Formation of Conglomerates

Some key and sizable SOEs will be selected to implement the strategy of forming conglomerates as a means to improve their efficiency, competitiveness and monopoly on the domestic market,.

THE ECONOMIC REFORM MEASURES FOR IMPROVING SOE'S OPERATING EFFICIENCY AS WELL AS PROFITABILITY AND ITS IMPACTS ON FDI

Since the implementation of the Ninth Five-Year Plan (1996-2000) and Long-Term Targets for the Year 2010, which is aimed at achieving the transition from a "Planned Economy" to a "Socialist Market Economy" and reaffirming a market opening policy, there have been a series of economic reform measures in taxation, trade policy, banking, SOEs, financial systems, etc. They seem to improve SOEs' operating efficiency and profitability; at the same time they will weaken FMNCs' competitive advantages and make the FDI decision process more complex. The implication of the reform measures will in turn affect the FDI motives as asserted by various foreign direct investment theories.

The Ministry of Foreign Trade and Economic Co-operation of the PRC (MOFTEC) announced the first half-yearly statistical data of FDI on 30th July, 1997: the number of newly established foreign-invested enterprises was 9,763, and the approved investment project amount was US$22.9 billion. This revealed a decrease of 30 per cent and 50 per cent respectively as compared with those of the same period in 1996.

The MOFTEC's explanations for such a shocking decrease in FDIs were : (1) to establish the preconditions for joining the World Trade Organization, there have been a series of taxation reform measures in order to align PRC's tariff and taxation practices with international norms, such as the gradual cancellation of numerous preferential import tariff exemptions and reductions for FDI enterprises' exports, the reduction of refunds for VAT for exports, etc.; (2) the implication of the macroeconomics reforms in the last three years suppressed the overheated economic growth. Quite obviously, MOFTEC's explanation was an oversimplification to the puzzling problems of SOEs and the implication of the reforms measures. This research paper attempts to assess the important implication of the SOE reform and other supplementary reforms for FDIs such as the impact on FDIs' competitive advantages, investment motives, responsive organizational changes, performance evaluation and control practices, strategy for added business risk, etc..

THE IMPLICATIONS OF THE SOE REFORM FOR FDI

The success in SOE reform can restore the State's financial disequilibrium caused by the huge amount of subsidy to SOEs and thereby can turn SOEs into contributive to the economic growth. The leaders of the Chinese Communist Party and most economists believe that the PRC will usher in a new era of economic growth and prosperity through successfully reforming SOEs. To achieve the transition from a planned economy to a market economy, the PRC will focus on six major areas of reforms: the SOE, the fiscal system, banking, trade, the market and pricing system. According to the marvelous speech of Mr. Zhu Rongji, Chinese Vice Premier, at a group seminar on the PRC's economic development at the 15th Chinese Communist Party Congress in September, 97, the SOE reform will be crucial among these six major reforms. Mr. Zhu overtly expressed in the speech that we will strive to extricate most loss-making SOEs from their difficulty in three years.

As alleged by Mr. Zhu Rongji, three actions will be taken to extricate SOEs from their difficulty. The first is the investment system reform which will set up an investment system under which the government is separated from SOEs. Under the new investment system, profitability would be the sole consideration in investment and governments will refrain from administrative interference. Under the old investment system, local governments used to invest in all industrial sectors in their localities for craving great achievements regardless of cost effectiveness and feasibility under the actual circumstances. As a consequence, there are too many SOEs making similar products over the country, which causes serious oversupply and too many production plans lie idle. The second will be the reform of the financial system under which government policy-based funding would be separated from commercial lending, and SOEs would no longer be unconditionally subsidized by banks. In such a business environment, SOEs will only do what they can to expand their operations. To improve the liquidity and reduce debts, they will prevent an imbalance between production and sales turnover. Finally, a social security system must be set up urgently in order to enable SOEs to lay off redundant workers. In doing so, unemployed and semi-employed workers will manage to survive and then the threat of social unrest can be mitigated.

Mr. Zhu Rongji's speech sent a clear message that the interplay of other economic reforms such as those of the fiscal system, banking, trade, market, and the pricing system are very important for SOE reforms. The success in SOE reforms will relieve the state of a heavy financial burden and pave the way for the PRC's rapid economic growth. To investigate the implication of SOE reforms for FDI and the applicability for FDI theories, it is necessary for us to have an in-depth perspective on the blueprint for economic development and reform as drawn up in the Ninth Five-Year Plan (1996-2000) and Long-Term Targets for the year 2010. The following are detailed analyses of the implications.

THE JOINT STOCK COMPANY SYSTEM PROVIDES FDI WITH ATTRACTIVE FINANCING OPTION

With the adoption of the " Joint-Stock Company System" for SOE reform, significant reforms will take place in the PRC's securities markets. It is anticipated that the size of the equity and bond market will growth tremendously in the next few years. Foreign-invested enterprises can utilize this attractive financing option by means of running joint venture with SOEs and then go public to pursue this source of potential financing. The current credibility weaknesses of the PRC's stock markets will be removed with the maturity of the market and the standardization and streamlining of the public companies. At present, the credibility weakness of the markets include inadequate disclosure mechanisms, poor liquidity, overt inside trading, lack of standardization in the presentation of financial information, periods of extreme volatility, and uncertainties concerning shareholders' rights and other fundamental principles of international corporate and securities law.[23]

The financial strength is typically one of the competitive advantages for FMNC to invest in the PRC. This includes not only economies of scale but also the ability to reduce risks through diversification of borrowing sources and operations. The joint-stock company system can provide FMNCs with both lower costs and more easily available capital through going public in the Hong Kong Stock Exchange, the Shenzhen Stock Exchange and the Shanghai Stock Exchange.

THE GOLDEN OPPORTUNITY FOR FMNCS TO ESTABLISH AN OPERATING PRESENCE IN THE PRC THROUGH ACQUISITIONS OF SMALL SOES

In the PRC, 80 per cent of SOEs are small-sized ones. As the breakthrough of the SOE reform lies in the transfer of State-owned property, the main policy of the reform is to "focus the efforts on medium to large-sized SOEs rather than small ones". There will be the organization and assets restructuring through merging medium and large-sized SOEs into multi-industrial, multi-ownership, multi-regional and multi-national conglomerates for the sake of strengthening their competitiveness in economies of scale and scope arising from large size and financial strength through pooling of cash and assets, etc. The reform policy for the small-sized SOEs will be to reorganize them through merger, selling, formation of joint-stock companies, contracting out and leasing.

The reform of small-sized SOEs offers a rare acquisition opportunity to FMNCs to establish an operating presence or a geographic market in the PRC in a much quicker way. It may also be a more cost-effective way for FMNCs to capture valuable technology rather than developing it internally.

As a matter of fact, a considerable proportion of small-sized SOEs are ill-managed as a result of their less than clear ownership and ill-defined scope of authority and responsibilities. But, their valuable tangible and intangible assets, such as imported world-class equipment, land, building, production plants, technical experts and skilled workers, can provide excellent potential for better performance and development. Such a rare acquisition opportunity can satisfy FMNCs' strategic, behavioral, and economic motives of FDI to invest in the PRC, such as production efficiency seekers, market seekers, raw material seekers and political safety seekers. With competitive advantages in financial strength, expertise and experience in advanced technology and modern business management, FDIs can achieve twice the result with half the effort by rationally re-deploying the acquired small-sized SOEs' means of operation or production.[24]

[23]Guo, Saiping, 1995. "The Growth of Chinese Sock Markets", *The Economic Trends of China-1995*. Hong Kong: Commercial Press, Chapter 5.6, pp. 208-215. (in Chinese).

[24]Zhou, Wendao, 1996. "Focus the Efforts on Big State-owned Enterprises Rather Than Small Ones - A Way to Change State-owned Assets to Private-owned Assets," *Hong Kong Economic Journal*, January 22, p. 32 (in Chinese).

THE BANKING SYSTEM REFORM AND THE INJECTION OF GOVERNMENT SUBSIDY FOR RMB 1,000 BILLION TO SOES IN THE FORTHCOMING THREE YEARS

In addition to Mr. Zhu Rongji's pledge to extricate most loss-making SOEs from their difficulties in three years at the World Bank / IMF annual meeting on 22nd September 1997, Mr. Dai Xianglong, the China's Central Bank Governor, also expressly announced that the loan interest receivable overdue within two years as at 31st July 1997 due from SOEs was RMB 143.1 billion, accounting for a 20 per cent growth since 1st January 1997. Mr. Dai also said that the State will subsidize SOEs in the form of writing off annual bank bad debts in the forthcoming years; this will amount to RMB 30 to 40 billion per annum. According to financial professionals' estimation, this strategy will last for ten years at the least. On 23rd April 1996, Mr. Dai noted that the Bank of China will plan to set up a new banking system for dealing with bank loans to insolvent SOEs; this will be segregated from normal bank loans to solvent SOEs with good bank credit stating.[25]

The SOE reform policy as promulgated at the 15th Chinese Communist Party Congress aims to turn the medium to large-sized SOEs into joint-stock conglomerates. However, they are currently heavily in debt and in urgent need of money to undertake organizational restructuring and technological renewal. As a means of putting them in a satisfactory financial position by going public on the Shenzhen Stock Exchange and the Shanghai Stock Exchange in the shortest time, Mr. Dai Xianglong, estimates that it is necessary to inject RMB 1,000 billion into them in three years in order to increase their assets and reduce their liabilities. It is anticipated that except for those moneys injected into such SOEs at the early stage, the money will be raised mainly by having SOEs listed on local stock markets, the Hong Kong stock market and overseas stock markets.

Under such an arrangement, the business environment will be greatly improved. However, the competitive advantages of FDI, such as financial strength, economies of scale and scope, superior technology, managerial and marketing expertise and differentiated products, will be relatively weakened due to SOEs' improvement in the clearly defined ownership and scope of authority and responsibilities after turning into joint-stock companies, and their restructuring as multi-ownership, multi-industrial, multi-regional, and multi-national conglomerates through merger, reorganization and leasing.

---

[25]Shi, Jianping. 1995. "Finance Legislation and the Banking System Reform", *The Economic Trend of China-1995*. Hong Kong : Commercial Press, Chapter 5.2, pp. 160-163 (in Chinese).

THE INDUSTRIAL PROTECTION FOR SOEs BY THE TAX REFORM

To attract FDI, the PRC has offered numerous preferential treatments in import tariff exemptions and concessions to FIEs for their imported raw materials and production equipment. The PRC's current policies laid down in the Ninth Five-Year Plan (1996-2000) and Long-Term Targets for the Year 2010 are intended to remove gradually these exemptions so as to undertake industrial protection for SOEs and offset potential declines in tax revenue due to a reduction of import tariffs. It is also aimed at establishing a tax system with a broader tax base and lower tariff rates within the framework of a standardized and fair tariff policy. In the forthcoming years, the extension of national treatment will replace the previous strategy of mainly relying on preferential policies to attract FDIs. This policy will provide SOEs and FMNCs with a business environment where they can compete on an equal footing under a sound regulatory framework and legal system.

In 1995 and 1996, the PRC undertook intensive reforms in two areas of the tax system, namely, the "Reduction of Import Tariffs" and the "Reduction of Refund for Value-Added Tax Paid on Inputs for Export". It is anticipated that the benefits of these reforms will outweigh the adverse impacts in the long run. In the short run, the implications of these reforms will cause considerable concern to foreign investors.[26]

Overall, the positive effects of the reforms include: (i) aligning PRC tariff practices with international norms; (ii) establishing the preconditions for joining the WTO; (iii) establishing a fairer domestic business environment and trading mechanisms which favor fair market competition, optimal allocation of resources and the healthy and rapid development of the economy; (iv) placing domestic enterprises and foreign-invested enterprises on the same level playing field; (v) channeling foreign investments to such priority industrial sectors as energy, infrastructure facilities, transport, advanced technologies, raw materials, etc.

On the other hand, there are a number of adverse implications for FDI. As far as the Reduction of Import Tariffs is concerned, the adverse effects are: (i) the preferential import tariff exemptions and reductions for FIEs' exports will be gradually canceled; (ii) the refunds for VAT for exports will be reduced; (iii) import tariff exemptions for production equipment used in export processing will be canceled; (iv) FIEs' extra capital investments, added business risk and longer pay back periods for participation in domestic industrial sectors will be favored by the PRC's industrial policy, and, (v) added business risks will arise from the domestic sales of their products such as : a higher rate of doubtful debt under current macroeconomics modification, unfamiliar business custom and practices, lengthy legal proceedings for business disputes, extra capital investments, ever changing regulatory frameworks and practices of accounting and taxation, insufficient professional and legal advice.

---

[26]Li, Daniel and Gordon Walker. 1996. "Tax and Trade Reform in the People's Republic of China : Implications for Foreign Direct Investment," *Journal of Asian Commercial Law Review*, December, pp. 241 - 253.

The adverse impacts on FDI in respect of the Reduction of Refund for Value-Added Tax Paid on Inputs for Export are mainly on the financial side, namely: (i) lower profit margins and rise of product costs; (ii) cash flow problems due to the delay in refunding the VAT - Exports from the State Tax Bureau, and, (iii) the potential detriment of bank credit stating as a result of the squeezed profitability and cash flow.

This is the typical instance of the firm-specific, or micro political risks of FDI as classified by Stephen J. Kobrin [1982][27] which arises from a conflict between bona fide objectives of host governments and foreign private firms. In the case of FDI in the PRC, it can be classified as the economic goal conflicts between FMNCs and the Chinese government. The goal conflicts in general relate to the Chinese government's policies for economic protectionism and economic development.

IMPLICATION OF THE ASIAN FINANCIAL CRISIS FOR FDI AND THE REFORM OF SOE

THE DEVALUATION TREND OF RENMINBI AND THE CHINESE GOVERNMENT'S IDEOLOGY TOWARD IT

During the last 49 years, the exchange rate of RMB has changed with the Chinese government's ideology for economic reform which can be broadly related to three phases of economic developments. In the first phase, under the "Socialism Planned Economic System", the official exchange rate of RMB remained stable at RMB Yuan 1.5/US$1 for 30 years from 1949 to 1978. In the second phase, the "Economic Open Door Policy" has been implemented, the RMB was devaluated from RMB Yuan 1.5/US$1 to RMB Yuan 5.78/US$1 through six stages from 1st January, 1979 to 1st April 1991 in order to facilitate exports and the foreign exchange rate system reforms. During this period, the Foreign Exchange Adjustment Centre was established in early 1986 in the Shenzhen Special Economic Zone for handling fast-growing transactions of foreign investments. In the third phase, since 1st January 1994, the "Managed Floating Exchange Rate System" has been established as one of the PRC's preconditions for joining the World Trade Organization under which the RMB was devaluated from RMB Yuan 5.78/US$1 to RMB Yuan 8.68/US$1 on 1st January 1994. Thereafter, the RMB floats around RMB Yuan 8.68/US$1 within a narrow range of fluctuation. Table 13 below shows details of the devaluation and appreciation trend of the RMB.

---

[27]Kobrin, Stephen J. 1982. *Managing Political Risk Assessment: Strategic Response to Environmental Change*, Berkeley: University of California Press, p. 35.

TABLE 13
The Devaluation and Appreciation Trend of the RMB
for the Period from 1.1.1949 to 30.6.1998

Phase	Time/ Period	RMB Yuan/US$1	Percentage - (Devaluation) / Appreciation
First	1.1.1949 to 31.12.1978 (30 Years)	**RMB Yuan 1.5/US$1** (*Official Fixed Rate*)	Under the Socialism Planned Economic System, the official exchange rate of RMB remains stable for 30 Years.
Second	1.1.1979	**RMB Yuan 2.0/US$1** (*Official Fixed Rate*)	- Devaluation by 33.3% for the Implementation of Economic Open Door Policy.
	1.1.1981	**RMB Yuan 2.8/US$1** (*Official Fixed Rate for Trading Transactions*)	1. Devaluation by 40% for trading transactions in order to gain competitive advantages for the export; 2. The old official rate for non-trading transactions remained unchanged.
	1.1.1985	**RMB Yuan 3.2/US$1** (*Official Fixed Rate for both trading and non-trading transactions*)	1. Devaluation by 14.29% to facilitating export; 2. Unifying the official rate for trading and non-trading transactions in order to simplify the fast growing foreign exchange transactions; 3. The foreign exchange transactions must be undertaken through the People's Bank of China or The State General Administration of Exchange Control ('SGAEC')
	1.10.1986	**RMB Yuan 3.72/US$1** (*Official Fixed Rate other than the Rate of FEAC*)	1. Devaluation by 16.25% to facilitate export; 2. A Foreign Exchange Adjustment Centre ('FEAC') was established in early 1986 in the Shenzhen Special Economic Zone in order to handle fast growing transactions of foreign investments. 3. The rate of FEAC rate reflected the black market rate which significantly differed from the official rate due to the high inflation rate of the PRC which made the theory of Purchasing Power Parity (PPP) being hold good.

	16.12.1989	**RMB Yuan 4.72/US$1** *(Official Fixed Rate)*	1. Devaluation by 26.88% due to strong demand for foreign exchange and high inflation of the PRC. 2. The transaction amount of FEAC grew sharply by 36.96 per cent from US$ 6.25 billion in 1988 to US$ 8.56 billion in 1989.
	1.4.1991	**RMB Yuan 5.78/US$1** *(Official Fixed Rate)*	1. Devaluation by 22.46% for adjustment to reflect the demand and supply situation in FEAC and the inflation-adjusted value. 2. In 1988 FEACs were set up in most large cities of the coastal areas as a foundation for the introduction of floating-rate system on 1.1.1994.
Third	1.1.1994	**RMB Yuan 8.68/US$1** *(Managed Floating Exchange Rate)*	1. Devaluation by 50.17% due to the overheated economy. RMB's exchange rate was stabilized at RMB8.68/US$1 as a result of the implementation of 'Macro-economic Adjustment' policy as from July 1993 as well as the huge amount of supply of foreign currencies in the market by Chinese government during July and August 1993. 2. Introduction of the Floating Exchange Rate System with the implementation of the following main exchange control procedures : a. Abolition of both the fixed exchange rate system and the Foreign Exchange Adjustment Centre rate system; b. Abolition of direct intervention in the foreign exchange market; c. The operation of foreign exchange services by commercial and professional banks.
	13.6.1998	**RMB Yuan 8.51/US$1** *(Managed Floating Exchange Rate)*	Slight appreciation by 1.96% as a result of: 1. The greatly improved inflation rate. The inflation rate declined from 27.2%, the peak in 1994, to 3.3% in January 1997 under the Macro-economic

			Adjustment Policy.
			2. The fast-growing foreign exchange reserve.
			The amount of foreign exchange reserve grew by 5.63 times from US$21.20 billion as at 1.1.94 to US$ 140.6 billion as at 28.2.1998.
			3. The huge amount of net capital inflow (surplus of Capital Account Balance, e.g. US$38.674 billion and US$39.967 billion in 1995 and 1996 respectively), and surplus of Current Account balance, i.e. foreign trade balance, of the Balance-of -Payment.

THE POLICY OF CHINESE GOVERNMENT FOR NON-DEVALUATION OF THE RMB

During the Asian financial crisis starting with the serious devaluation of Thailand Baht since July 1997, the US dollar, the RMB and the Hong Kong dollar are the strongest currencies not devaluated. The stabilization of the US dollar, the RMB and the Hong Kong dollar are of vital important to prevent the further worsening of the Asian financial situation. Particularly, it is important for some 20 countries out of the 167 members of the International Monetary Fund which peg their currencies to the U. S. dollar, including Hong Kong.

THE RELATION OF HONG KONG DOLLAR AND RENMINBI (RMB)

The linked exchange rate system of Hong Kong, in the form of pegging to the U. S. dollar, is a "Currency Board System". Such a system can undertake three lines of defence against the assault on the Hong Kong dollar by international speculators; these are (i) ample foreign exchange reserves, (ii) prudent fiscal policies, and (iii) a sound banking system. Hong Kong's strongest line of defence is found the ample foreign exchange reserves which are several times the Hong Kong dollars in circulation. As the Hong Kong dollar has interlinking effects to the RMB due to the close economic relation in the sectors of FDI, financial and banking services, international trade and technology transfer, etc., the stabilization of the Hong Kong dollar can significantly contribute to the non-devaluation of RMB.

THE RATIONALITY OF RENMINBI'S (RMB) NON-DEVALUATION

As soon as Mr. Zhu Rongji was elected Premier of the State Council of the PRC in March 1998, he expressly pledged three economic achievements in the forthcoming three years: (i) the non-devaluation of RMB, (ii) the growth of China's economy by 8 per cent, with state-owned enterprises to go out of difficulty in three years, and (iii) the inflation rate to be kept below 3 per cent. Premier Zu Rongji explained the reasons for the non-devaluation of RMB: (a) the devaluation will cause a new round of devaluations of Asian currencies and the further worsening of the economies of the affected countries, (b) the non-devaluation of RMB can alleviate the high devaluation pressure on the Hong Kong dollar, and (c) the devaluation of RMB will facilitate export and bring with it the larger surplus of trade account balance with U. S. A. It means trade relation with the U. S. A. will deteriorate.

In addition to Premier Zu Rongji's explanation, another underlying reason for the non-devaluation of RMB would be the economic diplomacy for joining the World Trade Organization ('WTO'). Previously, as part of its strategy to join the WTO, the PRC has initiated an array of reforms in the foreign exchange rate system, the tax system and the trade system. To assist Asian countries such as Thailand, South Korea, Indonesia, Malaysia to tackle with their economic crisis, the PRC has lent huge loans to them through the International Monetary Fund. As a matter of fact, such a loan for US dollar four billions would be large enough for the PRC to stimulate a faster economic growth through infrastructural investments. In view of the PRC's huge amount of external liabilities and its domestic economic constraints, its contribution to the Asian financial crisis would be commendable in comparison with those of Japan. For example, the Japanese Yen was devaluated by 27.78 per cent (down from Yen114.73/US$1 on 13.6.1997 to Yen 146.6/US$1 on 15.6.1998) and the much smaller amount of loan the Japanese lent to the affected Asian countries. Quite obviously, Zhu Rongji and other Chinese governors' pledge not to devaluate the RMB in March 1998 was mentioned when they had not taken into account the 27.78 per cent devaluation of Japanese Yen, which really places great pressure on the economy of the PRC and the Hong Kong and in turn will lead to the potential devaluation of the RMB and the Hong Kong dollar.

THE POTENTIALITY OF THE DEVALUATION OF RMB AND HONG KONG DOLLAR

Statistical data show that the PRC's high economic growth has been on a gradual downward trend. For instance, the economic growth of the PRC in 1993, 1994, 1995, 1996, and 1997 were 13.5 per cent, 12.6 per cent, 10.5 per cent, 9.6 per cent and 8.8 per cent respectively. With the impact of the Asian financial crisis and the sharp devaluation of the Japanese Yen against the U. S. dollar by 27.78 per cent (up to 15.6.1998), the PRC's targets in economic growth by 8% in three years and the stability of the RMB pledged by Premier Zhu Rongji will be quite difficult to achieve. Listed below are the recent events which will reveal a clearer picture for us to evaluate the devaluation pressure on the RMB :

1. THE FIRST CONTRACTION OF EXPORT IN MAY 1998 IN 22 MONTHS SINCE AUGUST 1996

In June 1998, Mr. Dai Xianglong, China's central bank governor, noted that the impact of the Asian financial crisis and, in particular, the sharp devaluation of Japanese Yen are causing much pressure on the PRC's export and the absorption of foreign direct investment. According to the statistical data of the PRC's Customs, there were the first contraction of exports and imports in May 1998 in 22 months since August 1996, by 1.5 per cent and 3.8 per cent respectively. Table 14 below shows the situation of the PRC's imports and exports for the period from January to May 1998.

TABLE 14
The Imports and Exports of the PRC for the Period from January to May 1998

Items	Amount (US$ Billion)	Increase / (Decrease) %
Total Amount of Exports for the period from Jan. to May 1998	71.11	8.6
Total Amount of Imports for the period from Jan. to May 1998	52.58	1.5
Total Amount of Exports for the Month of May 1998	14.93	(1.5)
Total Amount of Imports for the Month of May 1998	11.29	(3.8)

Source : The Chinese Customs

The comments of the Chinese Customs indicated that the worsening import and export situations were the consequences of the impact of the Asian financial crisis as well as the devaluation of the Japanese Yen, and the decrease in domestic demand for imports. However, part of the decrease in exports to Asian markets during the period has been offset by the great increase in other overseas markets such as Latin America, Africa, etc., through aggressive market development programmes. For instance, the exports to the Africa and the USA have notable growths - by 44.7 per cent and 18 per cent respectively. It clearly reveals that the PRC's exports are vulnerable to the Asian financial crisis.

2. THE ALARMING SLOW GROWTH IN FOREIGN EXCHANGE RESERVE

In contrast to the tremendous growth in the foreign exchange reserve in previous years, there was an alarmingly slow growth for the period from January to May, 1998. For the period ended 31st May 1998, the foreign exchange reserve grew only by US$1 billion to US$140.9 billion. In 1997, in terms of amount, there was a historical height in the growth of the foreign exchange reserve which amounted to US$34.9 billion. It grew from US$105 billion as at 1st January 1997 to US$ 139.9 billion as at 31st December 1997. Table 15 shows the notable upward trend of the foreign exchange reserve since 1978:

TABLE 15
The Upward Trend of the Foreign Exchange Reserve of the PRC for the Period from 1978 to 1998

Items	1978	1985	1990	1994	1995	1996	1997	1998
Balance of Foreign Exchange Reserve (US$ Billion)	0.17	2.64	11.09	51.62	73.60	105.00	139.90	140.9 Jan. to May 98
Amount Increased (US$ Billion)	-	2.47	8.45	40.53	21.98	31.4	34.9	1.0
Increase in Percentage (For Interval Period)	-	1,453 % 7 Years	320 % 5 Years	365 % 4 Years	42.58 % 1 Year	42.66 % 1 Year	33.24 % 1 Year	0.7 % 5 Months

Source : A Statistical Survey of China, 1996 and 1997 Issues
Various Announcements of the Chinese Customs in 1998

According to the explanation of the Chinese Customs, the main reasons for such a alarming slow growth in foreign exchange reserve are the contraction in export and the continuous decline in the absorption of FDI as a result of the Asian financial crisis.

3. THE DECLINE IN THE UTILIZATION OF FOREIGN CAPITAL

As revealed by the statistical data of the utilization of foreign capital announced in June 1998 by the Ministry of Foreign Trade and Economic Cooperation (MOFTEC) for the period from January to May 1998, there was the decline in the numbers of projects, in the amount of foreign capital actually used and in the amount of share issued in overseas stock exchange markets. However, the total amount of foreign capital to be utilized through the signed agreements and contracts could be maintained with a slight growth by 3.46 per cent. Table 16 below shows the worsening situation of the utilization of foreign capital for the period from January to May, 1998.

TABLE 16
The Utilization of Foreign Capital of The PRC
for the Period from January to May 1998

Items	Units / Amount	Increase / (Decrease) %
Number of Foreign Direct Investment Projects	7,308 Units	(7.33)
Total Amount of Foreign Capital to be Utilized Through the Signed Agreement and Contracts	US$17.511 Billion	3.46
Total Amount of Foreign Capital Actually Used	US$14.885 Billion	(1.49)
Shares of State-Owned Enterprises (SOEs) Issued through Overseas Stock Exchange Markets	US$0.071 Billion	(73.21)

Foreign Capital = Foreign Loans + Foreign Direct Investments + Other Foreign Investments
*** Other Foreign Investments = International Lease + Compensation Trade + Processing and Assembly*
Source : Ministry of Foreign Trade and Economic Cooperation

Quite obviously, the notable decrease in the amount of shares of SOEs issued through overseas stock exchange markets by 73.21 per cent, particularly through the Hong Kong Stock Exchange Market, shows the adverse effect of the Asian financial crisis.

CONCLUSION

Ever since the economic reform of the PRC begun in late 1978, the SOEs have always been one of the main obstacles to the reform progress. As a result of SOE's inefficiency and uncompetitiveness, one-third of them are currently running operating losses. SOEs' poor performance have a number of adverse impacts on the PRC's economy, namely, (i) a heavy burden on the banking system due to their insolvency; (ii) the State financial disequilibrium as a consequence of huge amount of subsidies to SOEs; (iii) hindrance to the progress of completely opening the domestic market and joining the World Trade Organization; (iv) an unhealthy business environment.

On 13th September 1997, during the 15th Chinese Communist Party Congress, Chairman Jiang Zemin, promulgated the new policy and strategy of the SOE reform. The new policy is to *"focus the efforts on medium to large-sized SOEs rather than small ones"*. There will be the organization and assets restructuring through merging medium and large-sized SOEs into multi-industrial, multi-ownership, multi-regional and multi-national conglomerates with a view to strengthening their competitiveness in economies of scale and scope and improving their financial strength through pooling of cash, assets, etc. The reform policy for the small-sized SOEs will be to reorganize them through merger, selling, formation of joint-stock companies, contracting out and leasing.

The new strategy of the SOE reform states three goals: (i) to turn the State-owned enterprises into "Joint-Stock Companies". Thereby, the root of their inefficiency and uncompetitiveness problems, such as the less than clear ownership and ill-defined scope of authorities and responsibilities, can be resolved; (ii) to strengthen the competent of SOEs through merger, selling, reorganization, union and leasing; (iii) to allow greater autonomy to SOEs.

The effectiveness of the joint-stock company system has been proved by the improved profitability, return on total assets ratio and solvency ratio of those SOEs listed on the Shenzhen Stock Exchange and the Shanghai Stock Exchange. The upward trends of numbers of listed companies, transaction volumes and sizes of the two stock markets are obvious proofs of the beneficial effects of a joint-stock company system.

The implications of the SOEs reform for FDI mainly stem from the following four reform developments, namely: (i) "the joint-stock company system to provide FDI with attractive financing option", (ii) "the golden opportunity for FMNCs to establish an operating presence in the PRC through acquisitions of small SOEs", (iii) "the banking system reform and the injection of government subsidy for RMB 1,000 billion to SOEs in the forthcoming three years" , (iv) "the industrial protection for SOEs by the tax reform".

In brief, the ground-breaking SOE reform will relieve the PRC of a heavy financial burden and pave the way for a new era of rapid economic growth and prosperity. Through the SOE reform, the FMNCs can be provided with a more congenial business environment and a golden opportunity to establish their operational presence in the PRC by means of the acquisition of small-sized SOEs. Most of the FDI theories will still hold good even though there are micro-political risks arising from the goal conflicts with the PRC's economic policies such as economic protectionism, economic development policies, balance of payments policy, exchange rate policy,[28][29] fiscal policy and monetary policy. So far as the Asian financial crisis is concerned, it is optimistic to anticipate that there will still be a congenial business environment for FDI with the preconditions of the Japanese Yen being stabilized below Yen 150/US$1 and the successful achievement of three main economic targets pledged by Premier Zhu Rongji,

---

[28] Walker, Gordon and Daniel Li. 1996. "Foreign Exchange Reform in the PRC : Impact on Foreign Direct Investment and State-owned Enterprises," *Journal of International Banking Law*, June, pp. 228 - 234.

[29]. Li, Daniel and Gordon Walker. 1996, "Foreign Direct Investment in the PRC : Foreign Exchange Reform and Business Risk," *Journal of International Company and Commercial Law Review*, July. pp. 254 - 260.

namely, the non-devaluation of RMB, the growth of China's economy by 8 per cent with its SOEs going out of difficulty in three years, and the inflation rate to be kept below 3 per cent.

Chapter 8

BUSINESS, BUREAUCRATIC REFORM, AND THE EU IN TURKMENISTAN

ROBERT C. RICKARDS

The International University in Germany
Bruchsal, Germany
and
Harz University of Applied Sciences
Wernigerode, Germany

All the successor states emerging after the former Soviet Union's collapse want to improve their nationals' living standards. To do so, most of them are trying to move from communist economic and political systems toward more Western ones. A crucial step in the transition process involves modernizing the governmental bureaucracy to meet the requirements of a market economy and a political democracy. The European Union (EU) generally has supported the successor states' efforts at civil service reform.

Problems in their respective macro-environments, of course, hamper these efforts. In perhaps no other successor state are such problems as severe as they are in Turkmenistan. To understand the origins and dimensions of Turkmenistan's problems, this article begins with a brief description of that country's territory, population, and recent history. Next, it analyzes Turkmenian politics, the crisis situation that has emerged, and the constraints international relations place on policy options to deal with the economy's dramatic decline. Following an examination of the role the civil service has played, the article then reports how the EU has tried to promote bureaucratic modernization in Turkmenistan. It closes with a discussion of the considerable risks remaining for the reform process there.

TERRITORY AND POPULATION

Turkmenistan, the fourth largest of the Soviet Union's former republics, has a land area of 488,100 km^2. Accordingly, it is slightly larger than California. The country extends for 1,100 km. from its eastern border with Uzbekistan on the Amy Darya River, to the Caspian Sea in the west, and for 650 km. from the Kazakhstan border in the north to its boundaries with Iran and Afghanistan in the south. Turkmenistan's terrain is mostly flat, with just the Kopet Dag and the Bebit Dag mountain ranges in the south and west, respectively. 90% of the country is part of the Kara Kum desert. The climate is continental, with seasons. In the dry, hot summers temperatures range up to 50° C (122° F). Winters, on the other hand, are cool or cold, with temperatures as low as -6° C (21° F). Only the southern parts of the country are frost-free. Rainfall is low, with March the wettest month, and the period from June through September practically rainless. Consequently, all crops require irrigation water, supplied principally by the 1,200 km. long Karakum Canal. The main export commodities are natural gas, oil, and cotton. Turkmenistan is famous for its carpets and akhalteke horses too.[1]

Total population is about 4.8 million, with some 72% Turkmen, 10% Uzbek, 9% Russian, and 3% Kazakh. It is growing at a rate of more than 2.5% annually. With 500,000 inhabitants, Ashkhabad is the country's biggest city and also its capital. Other large cities include Turkmenbashi (formerly Krasnovodsk), Chardzhou, Tashauz, and Mary. The official language is Turkmen, which is related closely to Turkish and Azeri. Although a decree called for all official communications to be in Turkmen beginning January 1, 1996, Russian remains in wide use in the cities and as a governmental working language. Despite 70 years of sovietization, most Turkmen still are at least nominally Sunni Moslems.[2] Since independence, several new mosques have opened or currently are under construction.

In the early 1990s, more than three-quarters of the population lived below the official poverty level. Due to wage growth that has lagged substantially behind the country's high inflation rate, as well as high under- and unemployment, real incomes subsequently have fallen further.[3] Because 40% of the Turkmenian labor force works in agriculture, the population nevertheless can feed itself.[4] Free distribution of natural gas, electricity, water, salt, and bread likewise contribute to maintaining social peace. Not surprisingly, though, the concomitant waste has led to rationing, together with frequent brownouts and service stoppages.

The post-independence decline in real living standards is most evident in Turkmenistan's poor public health. Cholera, diphtheria, hepatitis A and B, and polio pose real risks. Rabies is endemic. Antibiotics, other Western drugs, and sterile needles are unavailable. Foreign aid agencies recommend avoiding local hospitals altogether.[5] Infant mortality is an astonishing 9.4%, and childhood mortality through age six years is nearly

---

[1]For a good, general overview of Turkmenistan, see Colin Thubron, *The Lost Heart of Asia*, (London: Harper Collins; 1994).

[2]Readers interested in more information on this subject should see Alexander Benningsen and S. Enders Wimbush, *Muslims of the Soviet Empire*, (Bloomington, IN: Indiana University Press; 1986).

[3]Jörg R. Mettke, "Der Statthalter Allahs," *Der Spiegel*, Nr. 19, 1994, p. 172.

[4]Tacis, "Turkmenistan Info Sheet", Nr. 4, October 1, 1996.

[5]Tacis Coordinating Unit - Turkmenistan, "Checklist for Visitors and Contractors," September 1995, p. 8.

as high.[6] All drinking water must be boiled or chemically sterilized, while bottled water at best is unevenly obtainable.

RECENT HISTORY

In the 1870s, Russia began conquering large areas of Central Asia that were inhabited chiefly by Turkic tribes. The process began in Turkestan and spread westward to the Caspian Sea. The Tsarist Empire then annexed much of today's Turkmenistan as its Transcaspian Province. The last bastion of Turkmenian resistance fell in 1881, when Russian troops stormed the Geok-Tepe fortress, slaughtering thousands of its defenders. A railroad from Krasnovodsk (Turkmenbashi) on the Caspian Sea to Tashkent via Ashkhabad, completed in 1899, helped the Russians consolidate their hold on the region. During the Russian Civil War (1918 - 1920), Dschunaid Khan led a Turkmenian army that temporarily won control over the Khanate of Khiva. Ultimately, however, the Bolsheviks were able to impose their rule throughout the entire Central Asian region.[7]

As a consequence of their victory, the Bolsheviks reorganized the territory of Turkestan and the former Kahnates of Bukhara and Khiva into ethnically-defined Soviet republics. Thus, the Turkmen Soviet Socialist Republic was founded on February 14, 1925. The Communists' policies of forcibly collectivizing agriculture and permanently settling the Turkmenian nomads again provoked strong resistance in the period from 1929 to 1932.

Besides Turkmenistan on the Caspian Sea, the Soviet Union's Central Asian empire included four other republics: highly russified Kazakhstan, more traditional Uzbekistan, Kirghizistan with its border on China, and Persian-speaking Tadjikistan (now plagued by a low-intensity civil war). Effectively, all five republics were Russian colonies. Within the former USSR they served as strategic forward bases and vast storehouses of raw materials. Yet, as mentioned above, their 50 million inhabitants remained poor. Typical of Moscow's attitude toward the region's residents was its response to a great natural disaster. In 1948, a powerful earthquake destroyed the Turkmenian capital, Ashkhabad, killing more than 100,000 people. Although slow in mobilizing its own relief measures, the Soviet leadership deliberately kept this catastrophe secret from the rest of the world.[8]

Following the Soviet Union's collapse in 1991, all five former Central Asian republics became Newly Independent States (NIS). From that time, they have been searching for sponsors to uphold the political and economic structures they inherited from

---

[6]Central Intelligence Agency, *The World Factbook 1992*, (Washington, D.C.: U.S. Government Printing Office, 1992), p. 347.

[7]For insights into Central Asians' responses to alien rule, see Edward Allworth (ed.), *Central Asia: 120 Years of Russian Rule*, (Durham, NC: Duke University Press; 1989). See also Peter Hopkirk, *The Great Game*, (London: John Murray, 1990), for a thorough treatment of Great Power rivalry in the region.

[8]"Gemeinschaft unabhängiger Staaten", *Informationen zur politischen Bildung*, Nr. 249, 4. Quartal 1995, pp. 43-44.

the USSR. Neither political democracy nor economic stability exists anywhere in the region.

POLITICS

The country's dominant political figure before independence, Saparmurat Niyazov, became the Turkmenistan Communist Party's first secretary in 1985. At that time, he also held a Politburo seat in Moscow. In October 1990, he had himself elected president. When Turkmenistan declared its independence in December 1991, Niyazov remained in place. In 1992, he had his countrymen adopt a new constitution and, in a presidential referendum, confirm him in his new position (with more than 99% of the votes cast). Ever since he has preferred to be called "Turkmenbashi" or "Leader of all Turkmen". In January 1995, Turkmenbashi again used a referendum to have his term of office extended to 2002.

Officially, President Niyazov has sought to avoid the kind of problems accompanying rapid liberalization elsewhere in the ex-Soviet Union. In practice, that has meant giving lip service to gradual democratization, while maintaining firm control of the government. The former republican Communist Party has become Turkmenistan's Democratic Party (TDP). Abandoning communist ideology, Turkmenbashi has embraced Islam. Combining the TDP's structure and religion with a personality cult, Niyasov cleverly has mobilized the masses behind him. This tactic has enabled him to transform a one-party government into a one-man regime.

Under his administration, Turkmenistan's politics therefore have become increasingly Orwellian. Conjointly with heading the government, Niyasov serves as President of the Council of Elders, Chief of the Cabinet, Commander-in-Chief (in the rank of Army General) of the armed forces, head of the civil defense, Chairman of the State Science Council, and so forth. Portraits and statues of the Leader of all Turkmen (often clad in the robe of a Mecca pilgrim) are omnipresent. Frequent, mass ceremonies organized to praise him rival the celebrations once staged for North Korea's Kim Il Sung. As in Stalin's heyday, collective farms, factories, research institutes, airports, and cities vie with one another for the privilege of appending Turkmenbashi's name to their own. In addition, an ongoing initiative of the country's poets perennially supports Niyasov's candidacy for the next Nobel Peace Prize.

In the bazaars, high piles of calendars show Niyasov in a different pose for every month: with flags, with medals, with children -- always concerned about the welfare of his people. Printed with texts in the recently introduced Turkish-Latin alphabet, such a calendar sells for the price of a week's wages. Meanwhile, Niyasov travels the world in his personal, luxury-model, Boeing jet airliner (cost $37 million). Five years ago, the overweight cult figure flew to Houston for a medical examination. Like Russia's

President Boris Yeltsin, the 59-year-old Niyasov suffers from heart disease. Also like Yeltsin, he then underwent heart-bypass and varicose vein surgery.[9]

Neither criticism of Niyasov nor reports questioning his physical health appear in the local media. Western and Russian publications are unavailable at newsstands. While the resident foreign community can receive foreign television channels via satellite dishes, their cost ($700-$1000) is far beyond the general population's means. So the sole sources of information about President Niyasov are official press releases.

Not only news, but the citizenry, too, is under state control. Almost every Turkmenian family once lost members to Soviet terror. Experienced ex-KGB cadres serving in Ashkhabad's new security police exploit the resultant fear most people continue to feel. These secret police officers pressure potential dissidents by restricting their travel abroad, placing them under house arrest, and engaging them in "constructive conversations". Anyone foolish enough to ignore these warning signals risks dismissal from work, physical attack on public streets, or fatal traffic "accidents". Niyasov's critics either have emigrated to Russia (or further abroad) or fallen silent. No political opposition remains.

Consequently, Niyasov's rule now rests on his ability to play off the country's roughly one hundred tribes against one another. Organized into seven clans, they potentially could pose problems for him. For that reason, the Turkmenian constitution provides enough posts in the government or parliamentary bodies for Turkmenbashi to accommodate all clan leaders and other key supporters. Along with a potent presidial system, the constitution of May 18, 1992 established a 50-member parliament (Medjlis). The highest legislative body, however, is the Cabinet of Ministers/People's Council. Headed by President Niyasov, it includes members of the government, individual parliamentarians, the principal regional governors, and representatives of various local elites, including the clans.

PROSPERITY PROGRAM

Certain of his domestic support, Niyasov has articulated an ambitious national development goal: the creation of a Greater Turkmenian Empire with regional strategic significance. To attain this goal, a "Prosperity Program" aims at tapping the riches beneath Turkmenistan's desert sands and along its Caspian seacoast. With annual natural gas production of 55 billion m^3, the country ranks fifth in the world (behind Russia, the USA, Canada, and the Netherlands). Moreover, its estimated gas reserves are 15.5 trillion m^3, plus 6.3 billion tons of oil (approximately the same as those of Azerbaidjan). Because domestic use accounts for less than 15% of Turkmenistan's yearly output, its energy export potential appears vast indeed.

Accordingly, foreign interests have bid for exploration and exploitation rights in 90 districts. Turkish, Dutch, French, Argentinean, and American bidders have paid up to $1

[9]Mettke, *op. cit.*

million just to obtain basic geologic data. Lobbyists on behalf of American interests have included ex-Secretary of State and retired U.S. Army General Alexander Haig. In April 1995, the late President François Mitterand arrived to represent French firms in negotiating a joint prospecting agreement. The fact that French language instruction thereafter became part of the Turkmenian school curriculum attests to the Mitterand mission's success.

Such Western customers potentially would afford Niyasov the option of indefinitely stopping gas deliveries to former fraternal socialist republics unable to pay promptly with valuta. For example, in 1995, Ukraine desperately offered to barter 60,000 tons of wheat in lieu of the $700 million it owed Turkmenistan. With nothing even to barter against its $70 million bill, Azerbaidjan already has had its deliveries cut off altogether.[10]

Besides dropping problem customers while meeting Europe's and Asia's energy needs, President Niyasov wants to be independent of Russia's pipeline and railroads. That requires constructing alternative infrastructure across Turkey to the Mediterranean Sea or across Iran to the Persian Gulf. Such an undertaking would involve costs between $2 and $20 billion per route.[11] It furthermore would be subject to high risks given the region's civil wars, Islamic fundamentalism, and earthquakes, together with the United States' political objections. For the moment, private investors prepared to ante up these sums and accept the associated risks are nowhere in sight. So, Niyasov is courting both the Iranian and Turkish governments. He argues that financial support for Turkmenistan would advance their own economic interests and simultaneously reduce Moscow's influence in the area.

CORRUPTION AND CRISIS

Through his Prosperity Program, Niyasov has promised his subjects a "second Kuweit" within a decade. In the interim, though, the masses must make do with their small rations of free basic commodities. In addition, individual farmers can work up to 50 hectares of land privately. More privatization than that is not part of Niyasov's plans. Instead, he has preferred to run Turkmenistan as if it were his to plunder at will. In the early 1990s, for example, the country earned billions of dollars with gas and cotton exports. Excluding his ministers from the negotiations, Niyasov used these funds to purchase factories from foreign firms. While many of the factories went unbuilt, the Turkmenian treasury nevertheless disbursed all the money. Presumably, large amounts found their way to Turkmenbashi's bank accounts abroad.[12]

In Ashkhabad, Niyasov resides in an opulent official palace, which local wags call "Taj Mahal II". He also has a luxurious, private rural retreat in the mountain resort town of Firjusa. Turkmenbashi had it designed by an Italian architect, built by Slovakian

---

[10]Mettke, *op. cit.*, p. 173.

[11]Mettke, *op. cit.*

[12]Interview with Abdi Kulijew. Until his falling out with Niyasov and emigration to Russia in 1992, he was the Turkmenian foreign minister.

construction workers, and paid for by the state. Special units of the army, the police, and the security service simultaneously guard this country home.

For their part, Niyasov's ministers live quite well too. As loyal members of the ruling clique, they receive luxurious houses and Western cars, well-paid positions in state-owned firms, and generous commissions on sales of the country's raw materials.

Foreign media largely have ignored Niyasov's personality cult, human rights violations, his personal corruption, and that of his regime. Indeed, most Russian and Western officials seem to regard them as trade-offs necessary to maintain Turkmenistan's national unity and to box through essential reforms. For them, the country is an oasis of ethnic and social peace in a highly unstable region.

Yet a serious situation has emerged. Despite the fact that Niyasov's picture adorns the country's paper currency, inflation has been rampant since the early 1990s. Although the state controls the natural gas industry and hence receives all its revenues directly, Turkmenistan has experienced increasing difficulty obtaining foreign credits (which still amounted to more than $1 billion just in the first half of 1998). Even though Niyasov was the first NIS ruler to offer Russian specialists dual citizenship as an incentive to stay, the currency's collapse gradually has driven many of them back home. With neither foreign experts nor political opponents, the regime has no scapegoats to blame for its evident economic failures.

Besides the omnipresent Turkmenbashi, additional causes of the country's impoverishment are its geographic isolation, the competing interests of foreign powers, and low raw material prices on world markets,[13] as well as bureaucratic dishonesty and incompetence. Before describing business conditions in Ashkhabad and the Turkmenian civil service, it therefore makes sense to analyze these other factors behind the economy's collapse.

INTERNATIONAL RELATIONS

Two issues largely will determine future developments in Turkmenistan. The first is whether that country successfully can assert its independence from Russia and thereby retain control over its resources. The second is whether the government invests export earnings sensibly or wastes them on uncoordinated and largely unproductive prestige projects like Ashkhabad's overly large international airport and two dozen luxury hotels.[14]

With regard to the first issue, Turkmenistan takes a cautious approach. On December 12, 1995, the UN's General Assembly recognized Turkmenistan's neutrality.[15] Since that time, it has been the only NIS that is a member of the Non-Aligned Movement. Both at the Commonwealth of Independent States (CIS) and the Central Asian level,

---

[13]Michael Thumann, "Lächelnd in die Armut", *Die Zeit*, July 9, 1998, p. 10.

[14]Rainer T. Hermann, "Turkmenistan: Wirtschaftstrends zum Jahreswechsel 1994/95", *Länderreport*, No. 3267, February 1995, p. 2.

[15]Tacis, "Turkmenistan Info Sheet", *op. cit.*

Turkmenistan also carefully has avoided multilateral cooperation, preferring instead to develop bilateral relationships with its most important partners: Russia, Turkey, and Iran.

Of the three, only Turkey seems to have a genuine, long-term commitment. Evidence of this commitment dates back to 1994. At that time Ashkhabad fell behind in its payments to foreign firms, including formerly privileged Turkish companies. Turkmenistan owed the latter over $100 million. Firms from many countries including Investor Bridas and Lybra (both Argentina) and Suisstal (Switzerland) suspended their operations. In contrast, all the Turkish projects then underway went on to completion. Furthermore, Ankara is by far Turkmenistan's largest bilateral aid donor, giving between $25 and $30 million annually.[16]

On the other hand, multilateral cooperation takes place with the United Nations, the World Bank, and the European Union (EU). The United Nations Development Program (UNDP) opened an office in Ashkhabad in November 1994. Its main points of emphasis lie in the areas of agriculture, energy, the environment, health, and education. The UNDP has supported workshops on project management, finance, and customer service for midlevel Turkmenian civil servants too. For its part, the World Bank provides consulting services to the Ministry of Economics and Finance, the Ministry of Social Affairs, and the Central Bank.[17]

Within its program of Technical Assistance to the Commonwealth of Independent States (TACIS), the EU gives 500 Million Ecu (about $600 million) annually to the former Soviet Union's successor states. The Turkmenian portion of this aid is about $10 million per year.[18] The focus of the assistance is on development of agriculture outside cotton production, especially milk and meat processing, and the fishing industry. That assistance involves among other things, preparation for the privatization of agricultural enterprises, construction of trade infrastructure, measures to increase the production of wheat, and education. Other projects range from preparatory studies for a Europe-to-Central Asia transportation corridor (Traceca) to advising the Ministries of Agriculture, Oil and Gas, and Telecommunications. Additionally, TACIS aims to strengthen Turkmenistan's training capacity in the fields of economics and management. It also is supporting revision of the country's civil law codes and modernization of the bureaucracy.[19]

The focus of TACIS on training in economics and management, professionalization and restructuring of the bureaucracy results from recognition that economic development and sustained reform rely heavily on enhancing people's skills. Thus, by 1994 TACIS had a 1,8 Mio. Ecu project underway to improve economics instruction in Turkmenistan.[20] In addition, 60 university faculty members and civil servants began training in management,

---

[16]Hermann, *op. cit.*, pp. 3-4, 10.

[17]Katharina Tegeder and Robert C. Rickards, "Public Administration Capacity-Building, Turkmenistan", (Cologne, Germany: ICON-Institut, 1996), Annex B, p. 3.

[18]Hermann, *ibid.*

[19]Thumann, "Lächelnd in die Armut", *op. cit.*; and European Commission, "1995 Technical Assistance Program: Action Programme Turkmenistan", pp. 2-5.

[20]Tacis, "Tacis in Turkmenistan", (Extract of the Tacis Annual Report 1994), p.1.

computer skills, and English at Turkmen State University. Then, in 1994 and 1995, TACIS funded two study tours to the Benelux countries and the UK. The first tour afforded 20 participants practical insights into the structure, management, tasks and reforms of public services in these EU countries. The second tour gave three key Turkmenian decision-makers an overview of the different types of civil service training institutions existing in the EU.[21]

Despite all this activity, the EU's degree of commitment to Turkmenistan is low. Besides two advisers in a central coordinating office, just the four EU representatives assigned to the Agriculture Ministry reside there longer-term. The fact that all other EU experts come to Ashkhabad as short-term consultants accurately reflects the difficult local conditions.[22]

On a bilateral basis, Germany, the EU's "economic locomotive", now provides neither technical nor financial assistance to Turkmenistan directly. However, it is considering creation of a DM 35 million fund for the Caucasus region and Central Asian republics. Indirectly, Germany already provides assistance through its Hermes guarantees for private-sector projects in Turkmenistan. Guarantees are attractive because they cover the full project costs. Hermes issues its approval of guarantee applications after individual project review. Projects involving firms from the former East Germany have the best chances of receiving a guarantee. The five projects with Hermes guarantees at present underway in Turkmenistan have a combined value exceeding DM 100 million. Whereas Turkmenistan to date has made only a 15% down payment on the projects, German taxpayers very well may have to pay the outstanding balance. Excluded from this amount is money still owed German firms from the days when Turkmenistan was a Soviet republic.[23]

ECONOMIC DECLINE: COTTON AND CEREALS

International statistics (EBRD, EIU) indicate that since independence, Turkmenistan's GDP has declined between 5% and 20% annually. Some of the underlying reasons are similar to the problems faced by other NIS: disruption of interrepublican trade flows, a command economy with inefficient production methods, underdeveloped market infrastructure, high inflation, and bureaucratic dishonesty and incompetence.[24]

Four more reasons, though, are specific to Turkmenistan. First, there is Niyasov's aforementioned personal corruption. Second, Turkmenistan's natural gas customers often have been unable to pay for deliveries in hard currency. Despite the dearth of data about natural gas exports in Ashkhabad, it is clear that they have declined drastically.

---

[21]European Commission, *ibid.*, pp. 4-5; and Tacis, "Turkmenistan Projects", (Information Leaflet of the Coordinatiing Unit in Turkmenistan), No. 4, December 1995, p. 1.

[22]Hermann, *op. cit.*, p. 10.

[23]Hermann, *op. cit.*

[24]Tacis, "Turkmenistan Info Sheet", *op. cit.*

Consequently, the state budget has lost one of its major income sources. Ashkhabad likewise has continued selling a portion of its cotton crop in barter exchanges rather than for valuta. The result has been a severe foreign currency shortage. Third, questionable expenditures have narrowed further the government's room for financial maneuver. Over and above the international airport and luxury hotels, they include shopping centers, a convention center, and spacious office buildings for foreign energy companies. Fourth, the government at best has proceeded halfheartedly in reforming the economy.[25]

Within the former Soviet Union, Turkmenistan was mainly a supplier of agricultural products and raw materials. Its processing industry was undeveloped. Since 1991, the agricultural sector's relative importance appears to have declined sharply, from 46% to less than 20% of GDP. Yet, in fact, no real structural change has taken place. Instead, Ashkhabad merely has allowed energy prices to rise to world market levels, while agricultural prices have remained largely fixed at artificially low, centrally determined levels. Moreover, the agricultural sector today continues to employ some 40% of the total labor force.[26]

The government's priorities for this most important sector of the Turkmenian economy involve cotton and cereal production. These priorities are problematic. On one hand, the crop mix suffers from a historical emphasis on cotton production. On the other hand, together with natural gas, cotton is Turkmenistan's chief export commodity. By boosting cereals output, Ashkhabad hopes to reduce the country's dependence on food imports, notably wheat.

In recent years, Turkmenistan has mortgaged future cotton harvests to obtain foreign exchange. For example, of the 1,280 million ton 1994 raw cotton crop, about 400,000 tons were sold as fibre, which fetched between $450 and $600 million in valuta. But the Agriculture Ministry alone required over 650,000 tons just to satisfy its creditors!

In 1992 and 1993 that Ministry had signed construction contracts for more than 250 projects with a value of $1.5 billion. By 1994 deliveries on the contracts already totaled $700 million, but payments were only $500 million due to the foreign exchange shortage. Floods, a frequent problem in Turkmenistan, took 20,000 hectares out of cotton production altogether. So, business transactions increasingly have required foreign credits. Purchases of seeds, fertilizer, and technology abroad have heightened the country's dependence on such credits further. Turkmenistan's obligations from current contracts and payments arrears now are mostly short-term and exceed $2 billion.

Because net receipts from cotton exports have proved unattainable, a severe liquidity crisis has ensued. In fact, Turkmenistan appears likely to be a problem debtor for years to come. As a result, many development projects have encountered delays. For these reasons, the government no doubt will adhere to its policy of forcing the cultivation of cotton as the country's single largest, foreign currency earner. Extracting as much foreign exchange as possible from cotton at the same time means squandering vast quantities of

---

[25]Hermann, *ibid.*, pp. 2-4, 7.
[26]Tacis, "Turkmenistan Info Sheet", *ibid.*

scarce irrigation water, whose free delivery practically invites waste.[27] It involves abuse of the land (*e.g.*, monocultures, overuse of pesticides and fertilizers, and leaching of the soil) as well as exploitation of agricultural labor too. For example, a cotton picker's pay is a mere 6 cents for ten pounds of raw cotton. For 2,500 pounds of cotton picked in a month, a laborer thus earns about $15, paid out largely in fat and vegetables.[28]

Agricultural labor has become increasingly important since independence. In the Soviet period, cotton cultivation was about 50% mechanized. Due to the chronic foreign exchange shortage since the mid-1990s, imports of spare parts for farm machinery have fallen drastically. Even with widespread cannibalization, the remaining machinery is out-of-service between 30% and 40% of the time. Consequently, less than 10% of the cotton production process still is mechanized. Likewise there has been practically no foreign exchange available to purchase spare parts for textile manufacturing machinery. Hence, Turkmenistan's textile factories increasingly have stood idle, while the country's limited potential to add domestic value to its cotton exports has declined correspondingly.

In contrast to cotton, harvests of vegetables, melons, grapes, other fruits, fodder, and most importantly cereals have increased. The latter receives high priority as evidenced by the increase of several hundred thousand hectares of land dedicated to its production. Purchases of the requisite seeds, technology and fertilizer abroad, however, have aggravated the foreign currency shortage further, but brought no breakthrough to self-sufficiency. Instead, cereals harvests have continued to fall short of plan goals, leaving the country to import 40% of the wheat and 10% of the rice consumed.[29]

Increased agricultural demand, together with rapid population growth, makes the question of the water supply in the desert state a particularly acute problem. Today, water already is both scarce and rationed. Worsening the situation is the fact that Turkmenistan wastes about 40% its available water. In addition to the free delivery of water, inefficient irrigation canals are a major cause of this high waste level. Introduction of modern irrigation methods, saving the Aral Sea, and charging for water deliveries are steps urgently needed to ensure adequate future supplies.

ECONOMIC DECLINE: INDUSTRY

---

[27]Seepage and evaporation alone cause considerable water losses. See Hermann, *op. cit.*, pp. 5-6, and "Gemeinschaft unabhängiger Staaten", *op. cit.*, p. 44.

[28]The poor conditions under which Turkmenian cotton pickers live and work closely resemble those in Uzbekistan and Kazakhstan. See Thumann, "Pflücken und Hoffen", *Die Zeit*, July 23, 1998, p. 12.

[29]Hermann, *op. cit.*, pp. 5-6.

A number of major investment projects currently are underway, particularly in the construction, hotel, and textile industries.[30] For example, ABB has completed a feasibility study for the construction of an aluminum plant with an annual capacity of 50.000 tons. The intended market for the plant's output is Japan because prices are higher there than in Europe. Furthermore, Ashkhabad has a plant for the production of light, non-insulated electric cable. For its electricity industry, though, Turkmenistan also needs heavier cable, which it currently must import from Russia. The Turkmenian government therefore plans to expand and modernize its cable works as a joint venture with a foreign partner. The director of the state-owned Kuvvat electric authority meanwhile is pursuing a project for the construction of an iron smelter by a Turkish firm.

Having benefited from construction of luxury hotels, office towers, and the international airport in the mid-1990s, the building industry is looking forward to new projects. High on Ashkhabad's wish list is the construction of a second airport runway. Managing that project is a consortium including John Laing (U.K.) and Alarko (Turkey). Moreover, negotiations are underway with a Turkish firm to modernize the Turkmenbashi harbor facilities.

In the early 1990s, Alcaltel Deutschland led a project to modernize the telephone system with a Hermes-guaranteed contract in the amount of DM 300 million. Subsequently, in November 1994, German Telekom gained observer status as the first non-member in the Regional Commonwealth for Communications (RCC). The RCC coordinates the telecommunications networks of most of the former Soviet Union's successor states, which remain closely linked to one another. Accordingly, a large portion of international calls continue to be routed over Moscow because no foreign country codes are yet in use.

Observer status gives German Telekom an information headstart relative to other international competitors. It wants to use this competitive advantage for projects aimed at educating RCC managers abroad and has made Ashkhabad a proposal in that regard. Another Telekom proposal offers support for the construction of a training site for optical glass fiber technology in Ashkhabad. In the long-run, use of such fiber would allow the region's growing international telecommunications traffic to be re-routed over Germany.

In addition, Turkmenistan has begun an effort to exploit its large potential as a transit country. Of particularly high value is the recently completed connection to the Iranian railroad system. It ensures access to both the Persian-Arabian Gulf and a link to Turkey, and thus enables Ashkhabad to begin breaking out of its physical isolation.

Besides transit projects, the electricity industry has some export potential. Unfortunately, however, the trend since independence has been for electricity production to decline, while domestic consumption increases. This unhappy situation likely will worsen when Turkmenistan's newly constructed cotton, petroleum, and agroindustrial plants start operations. Electricity exports to neighboring states have declined too. Contracts with Kazakhstan had called for it to purchase 4 billion kWh. But due to its own economic difficulties, it has taken just 1.5 billion kWh. Although disappointing, the failure to tap Turkmenistan's electricity export potential more fully is a minor economic

---

[30]Tacis, "Turkmenistan Info Sheet", *op. cit.*

problem. Of the $2 billion in outstanding claims owed Turmenistan, just $30 million arise from unpaid electricity exports.

An agreement signed in the fall of 1994 furthermore calls for Turkmenistan to export 1 billion kWh of electricity to Afghanistan annually. In order to do so, Ashkhabad first must begin manufacturing heavier cable and then lay it. The latter activity is not feasible until the civil war in Afghanistan ends. Ashkhabad also plans electricity deliveries to Armenia, via transmission lines through Iran, and eventually to eastern Turkey. Although Iran, Turkey, and Turkmenistan have concluded appropriate intergovernmental agreements, years no doubt will pass before deliveries actually start.

Exactly how Turkmenistan intends to reverse its declining electricity production to meet increased domestic and foreign demand is a mystery. Kuvvat plans no comprehensive power plant modernization. Major foreign firms such as General Electric and Itocho have held talks in Ashkhabad without signing any agreements. The planned modernization and expansion of the Bismein steam power plant has made no progress. Kuvvat had hoped to equip Bismein with gas turbines and thus to have the first combined gas and diesel power plant in the country. The necessary funding, though, has been unavailable.

ECONOMIC DECLINE: NATURAL GAS AND OIL

With unvaryingly bad news on all other economic fronts, Ashkhabad increasingly has set its sights on natural gas exports. Proceeds from sales abroad were to fill the Turkmenian treasury and make the country a "natural gas Kuweit". Indeed, sufficient foreign cash would have allowed the old management and political nomenklatura to postpone difficult economic reforms indefinitely. Thus, 1994 was a particularly bitter year for Turkmenistan. The country discovered then that its immense natural gas reserves are not much help when major customers like Ukraine are unable to pay their bills.[31]

For the entire year 1994, Turkmenistan had natural gas exports in the amount of 45.5 billion m^3 under contract. However, the country delivered just 23.9 billion m^3. The biggest drop came in exports to Ukraine, which received only 12 billion of the 24.5 billion m^3 it had ordered. There also were major gas export shortfalls to Georgia (2.45 billion instead of 3.6 billion m^3), Azerbaidjan (2.25 billion rather than 3.0 billion m^3), Armenia 0.775 billion instead of 2.0 billion m^3), Kazakhstan (4.5 billion rather than 6.0 billion m^3), and Uzbekistan (1.9 billion instead of 2.9 billion m^3).[32]

Turkmengas explained the lowered deliveries as follows: First, these consumers did not make timely payments for deliveries, which led Turkmenistan to cut them off. Arrearages in payments for Ashkhabad's natural gas exports were $1.6 billion, of which Ukraine alone owed $1.1 billion. Accordingly, Turkmengas negotiated no new contracts

---

[31]This phrase comes from President Niyasov's optimistic post-independence proclamation. See
   Mettke, *op. cit.*, p. 174, and Hermann, *op. cit.*, p. 1.

[32]Hermann, *ibid.*, p. 7.

with these states for 1995. Second, necessary maintenance and repairs closed the pipeline through Uzbekistan, so that temporary delivery stoppages from Turkmenistan occurred. Then Uzbekistan raised its transit fees for natural gas from $1.2 to $2 per 1,000 m^3 for 100 km. When Turkmenistan balked at paying the new fees, Uzbekistan closed the pipeline altogether.

Consequently, instead of the 20% growth in gross domestic product planned for 1994, GDP sank by 20%. Subsequently, ex-Soviet customers' ability to pay for Turkmenian natural gas generally has deteriorated further. Declining world market prices and the lack of alternative pipelines have hindered Ashkhabad's gas exports too.

Unfortunately for Turkmenistan, there is no reason to believe that its ex-Soviet customers' ability to pay will improve soon. Because of a falling out between Ashkhabad and Moscow, sending the gas via Russian pipelines to more dependable customers in Western Europe is not a viable option either. At the beginning of 1997, Turkmenistan was asking $42 for 1000 m^3 of gas, which the giant Russian energy company Gasprom was selling to Western Europe for $83, while offering Turkmengas a mere $32. Gasprom managers defended their practice by pointing to falling world market prices and the necessity to recover transportation costs. In March 1997, Niyasov reacted to this situation by dissolving the Russian-Turkmenian joint delivery corporation. Gasprom promptly shut its pipeline to Ashkhabad's gas. Thereafter, Turkmenian exports fell from 30 billion m^3 in 1996 to just a trickle in 1997 and 1998. Lack of access to international waters thereby prevents the country's ascendancy to a "natural gas Kuweit".[33]

Landlocked in the interior of Central Asia and subject to Russia's pipeline monopoly, Turkmenistan simply has no way to market its natural gas in Western Europe. Yet, all proposals for new pipelines that could solve the country's transportation problem have proved controversial. Turkmenistan sees its independence endangered by any route through Russia, but the United States opposes an alternative route through Iran, even though it would be economically most viable.

Itself a gas exporter, Iran purchases Turkmenian gas for $42 per 1000 m^3. It does so in part, because Teheran wants any pipeline from Turkmenistan to Turkey routed through its territory. In December 1997, Shell won a contract to study that route's feasibility. From Iran's viewpoint, delays in building the pipeline principally hurt Turkmenistan, Turkey, and Shell.

For its part, the United States favors an alternative route through the Caspian Sea to Baku, then across Azerbaidjan and Georgia to the Turkish Mediterranean port of Ceyhan. The U.S. Congress already has contributed $750,000 toward funding a feasibility study. Impediments here include the high costs of undersea construction and political instability in the Caucasus region.

Meanwhile, both the Californian firm Unocal and an Argentine company each have been planning a multibillion dollar pipeline from the Dauletabat gas fields in southeastern Turkmenistan across Afghanistan and Pakistan to the Indian Ocean[34]. This project has been delayed for three years because banks have been reluctant to finance it and the

---

[33]Thumann, "Lächelnd in die Armut", *op. cit.*

[34]Michael Lüders, "Die Herren der Pipeline", *Die Zeit*, 27. August 1998, p. 11.

Saudi Arabian joint partner, Delta, has been unwilling to proceed as long as the Afghan civil war or high tensions with the Taleban continue.[35]

Whatever the future developments in Afghanistan may be, neither the Caspian Sea nor the Afghan alternative possibly could compete successfully with the Iranian pipeline's lower costs. The mellowing American policy toward Khatami's regime enhances the Iranian alternative's attractiveness too.

Yet another projected pipeline foresees transporting Turkmenian gas through Uzbekistan to China. Those plans, however, ignore the difficulties Turkmenistan had with Uzbekistan in 1995. So, any alternative to the existing Russian pipeline, regardless of its eventual route, remains at best a possibility for the distant future.

In contrast to its drastically diminished natural gas exports, Turkmenistan's domestic consumption has been stable at 8-9 billion m^3 per year. Turkmengas nevertheless expects an increase in two to three years when the new industrial enterprises supposedly will come on line. Turkmenistan further consumes between 70.000 and 80.000 tons of propane and butane gas annually. The first propane-butane facility recently began operations in Turkmenbashi. Built by the Finnish firm Urals, it has an annual capacity of 5,000 to 6,000 tons. A second liquefaction plant with a capacity of 1 million m^3 per day now is under construction by an Italian firm in Naip. In addition, plans exist for two more plants with a capacity of 3 million m^3 per day each. Given both sharply decreased exports and GDP, though, this new construction likely will leave Turkmenistan with substantial over capacity relative to its short- and midterm needs.[36]

ECONOMIC DECLINE: IMPORTS AND INFLATION

Until recently, when Turkmenistan's rising prices threatened to explode into hyperinflation, the country had lived for five years with monthly inflation between 20 and 25% (between 1,200% and 1,900% annually). The causes of this galloping inflation were uncontrolled growth of the money supply and shortages of real goods and services. Fearing that social stability could break down, the government fixed prices for 30 basic commodities. It also required state enterprises to apply to the Antimonopoly Commission for permission to change the prices of 2,000 other products.

In contrast, imported consumer goods for the private sector have not been subject to price regulations. Consequently, both domestically produced basic commodities and the products of state enterprises usually are offered first wholesale on the black market and then resold for private consumption at substantially higher retail prices.

The national currency, the Turkmenian Manat (TMM) is not convertible and no neighboring state accepts it as a means of payment. Following its introduction in November 1993, the TMM experienced a breathtaking decline. Officially it went from 1:2 to 1:10 to 1:75 against the US dollar. A year later, on the parallel market, it took 230

[35]Joseph Fitchett, "Worries Rise that Taleban May Try to Export Unrest", *International Herald Tribune*, September 26-27, 1998, pp. 1, 6.

[36]Hermann, *op. cit.*, p. 8.

TMM to purchase one US dollar. Concurrently, the state, the country's largest employer, paid workers at most 2,000 TMM and pensioners 600 TMM per month. As the TMM's value approached zero, the US dollar unofficially replaced it as the means of payment.

Subsequently, Ashkhabad has attempted to re-establish the Turkmenian Manat as the sole currency for domestic transactions. For example, it regularly has decreed that all goods and services payments must be made in the national currency. But Ashkhabad's efforts always have failed when the five star hotels began settling bills only in US dollars. It wounds the national pride of many Turkmen that the US dollar effectively has become the country's real currency. Yet the central bank has no strategy that plausibly could stabilize the TMM.

When granted, interest rates for short-term credits at the commercial banks range between 160% and 180%. Savings banks offer the deposits they hold at a weekly auction on the interbank credit market. The interest rate on these deposits lies between 100% for short-term and 150% for long-term deposits.[37] Not surprisingly, hardly any money flows into the banking system, unless the market actors can hold their deposits in US dollars. As a result, the traders flying in goods from Moscow and Dubai receive no credit in consumption-starved Ashkhabad.

This situation is highly paradoxical. Through the mid-1990s, Turkmenistan's annual balance of payments had a theoretical surplus of about $500 million. However, one must view Ashkhabad's foreign trade statistics with great care. Because the country officially receives little valuta for its cotton and its natural gas customers are insolvent, its reported surplus really is a deficit. Obviously, the government therefore has a strong interest in rendering murky transactions (especially deals involving cotton) more transparent. Hence, since the beginning of August 1994, all im- and exports have had to be handled via the new commodities exchange in Ashkhabad or at least be registered there. Still, the actual balance of payments situation probably is much worse than officially reported. For example, real imports from Russia don't even appear in published Turkmenian data.

Turkmenistan's de facto balance of payments deficit and its lack of foreign exchange reserves have led it to delay payments to its trading partners. Most affected have been Turkey and Iran, the two countries with the largest volume of trade with Turkmenistan. Fortunately for Ashkhabad, so far neither has been willing to bring legal action before an international settlements court. Apparently, both fear starting a domino effect that well might result in near total losses for all of Turkmenistan's foreign creditors.

Besides external debt problems, Turkmenistan faces an internal debt crisis. Turkmenian enterprises owe one another more than 5,5 billion TMM, but their deposits in commercial banks fall far short of that amount.[38] For its part, the government appears unable to resolve either the external or the internal debt crises.

---

[37]Hermann, *op. cit.*, pp. 8-9.

[38]Hermann, *op. cit.*

ECONOMIC DECLINE: THE STATE BUDGET AND NEEDED REFORMS

In 1992, its first year of independence, Turkmenistan's government budget had a surplus amounting to 14% of GDP. Beginning with a 7% deficit -- excluding off-budget activities -- the state budget has been in the red ever since 1993. Never a reliable information source, the official budget has been particularly misleading in those years when such wealthy ministries as agriculture, oil and gas, and construction have been off-budget. Presumably, that has facilitated plundering their income and assets and thus has accelerated the country's economic decline. For example, the established practice of the state purchasing the entire cotton crop has permitted the government to realize substantial off-budget income. Producers have received about $400 per ton for cotton the government sells at $800 per ton on the world market.[39] The difference has lined officeholders' pockets instead of financing urgently needed economic reforms.

So far, the government has failed to formulate a clear priority list for the country's long-run development, free prices, cut state expenditures and subsidies, deregulate and privatize business, and sharply curtail the state's role in the economy. Indeed, Turkmenistan has been the most reluctant of the Soviet successor states to adopt meaningful economic reform measures. Niyasov apparently has viewed the transition to a market economy as a danger and feared the loss of economic power that such a move would entail.

Accordingly, Turkmenbashi's initial response to the debt crises just described was not to initiate the needed reforms. Instead, he proclaimed the free distribution of bread beginning in 1995. Later, as export earnings continued to dwindle, the government finally approved a package of half-hearted measures. Besides introducing the above mentioned commodities exchange, it provided for sale of the state's retail trade outlets, cafés, and restaurants to private individuals at auction. The real estate involved, though, remained state property.

Furthermore, Ashkhabad has planned the privatization of "larger enterprises". Managers and employees supposedly will be able to buy up to a 49% interest in them, while the state will retain majority ownership. With help from World Bank experts, mass privatization of the state's residual holdings will follow at an unspecified future date.

Privatization in the agricultural sector has been half-hearted too. The relative proportions of agriculture in sovkhozes, kolkhozes, cooperatives, and private farms scarcely have changed since independence. Moreover, to avoid parceling the land, the government has decided against downsizing the sov- and kolkhozes. Instead, it has toyed with the idea of allowing stock companies and leasing associations to operate the larger farms. Whether farms were large or small, operators would be unable to purchase farmland. Official thinking seems to be that long-term leases and the right to retain receipts earned from crop production alone would afford farmers sufficient incentives to increase output.

---

[39]Hermann, *op. cit.*, pp. 4-5.

BUREAUCRACY

For a country with fewer than 5 million inhabitants and an economy based largely on minerals and cotton, the structure of Turkmenistan's governmental bureaucracy is complex. After a period of financial autonomy, both the Agriculture and Oil and Gas Ministries have moved back onto the central budget. So, at present, the government's core administrative apparatus comprises 20 Ministries and 7 state committees with the rank of a Ministry. Within the Cabinet of Ministers/President's Office, there are 13 Deputy Ministers, each with a group of ministerial portfolios under his or her supervision. The most senior is Valery G. Otchertsov, Deputy Prime Minister in charge of Economic Affairs. He also serves as the Deputy Chairman of the Cabinet of Ministers. The Cabinet's Chairman is the ubiquitous President Niyasov.

Following a major workforce reduction in the Agriculture Ministry, Turkmenistan's civil service at the administrative and technical/professional level is relatively small. The 42 central public bodies currently list 2,893 staff members. The top ten employing ministries are: Agriculture (259), Economy and Finance (208), President's Office (194), Prosecutor's Office (172), Trade and Resources (160), Consumers' Association (119), Oil and Gas (117), State Tax Inspection (117), Foreign Affairs (105), and Education (81).[40]

Historically there has been no Turkmenian civil service as a professional corps. Since Soviet times, recruitment, assessment, and promotion have been on an *ad hoc* ministry-to-ministry basis. Low, post-independence salaries and the resultant corruption have affected civil servants' professionalism negatively, caused them to have a bad reputation, and has made coherent policy towards them difficult.

That is not to say that the Turkmenian bureaucracy is altogether incapable. Informal, social relations among officials enable the system to function. However, what technical capability Turkmenistan's civil service possesses pertains to fulfilling centrally planned goals and implementing the communist party line. It has no experience with either democratic government or free enterprise. The country thus has some highly skilled officials, but they lack knowledge in such areas as economic and financial management, human resources, and legal and organizational development. Hence, creating a bureaucracy to support self-sustaining institutions for collective decision making and efficient resource allocation poses a particularly daunting task.

BUREAUCRATIC REFORM AND THE EU

Creating such civil services certainly would help prepare some countries for eventual membership in or close association with the EU (e.g., Estonia, Latvia, Lithuania, and Slovenia). Additionally, it would contribute to stability along the EU's eastern borders

---

[40]Tacis, "Terms of Reference: Public Administration Capacity Building in Turkmenistan", Annex I, p. 2, March 7, 1996.

generally and possibly enable Brussels to enhance its economic and political influence there. In the mid-1990s, the EU therefore began offering countries in eastern Europe and the former Soviet Union financial support to acquire foreign expertise, equipment, and training to modernize their bureaucracies.[41]

Following the study tours undertaken to Western Europe in 1994 and 1995, Ashkhabad and Brussels called for proposals promoting public administration capacity-building in Turkmenistan. The project ultimately approved in 1996 and funded for 18 months with 1 million Ecu had two immediate objectives: (1) development and adoption of legislation firmly anchoring the civil service within the reform process; and (2) erection of an institutional framework to strengthen its effectiveness and professionalism.

With regard to the first objective, the EU furnished technical assistance to the Ministry of Finance and the Ministry of Economy's Labor Department in drafting a civil service law. The law defines the status of civil servants within central and local authorities. It provides for their rights and duties, recruitment, selection, appointment, appraisal, promotion, training, and classification, as well as their conditions of service, including dismissal and retirement. The law's scope includes Parliament (the Medjlis), the President's Office, Cabinet of Ministers, the Ministries, state committees and other national and local bodies financed by the central budget. The EU furthermore is helping to develop subsidiary regulations and structures to implement this legislation.

With regard to the second objective, the project foresaw establishment of both a Center for Civil Service Management (CCSMA) within the government and an Institute for Public Administration (IPA) at Turkmen State University. Patterned on European models, the CCSMA's objectives are to institutionalize and implement the measures embodied in the civil service reform legislation. The IPA, on the other hand, is to develop curricula for updating the skills of senior civil servants and training new midlevel entrants. With these purposes in mind, the curricula emphasize accounting, budgeting, computing, economics, finance, personnel management, and English. Finally, as a "center of excellence", the IPA is to give the government good policy advice.[42]

Presumably, Turkmenbashi accepted this EU project because it had few strings attached. The EU not only supplied all the initial funding, but guaranteed a minimum 10% (later renegotiated to 30%) set aside for the employment of local nationals. Any follow-on, local currency funding, though, would require Niyasov's approval. Moreover, his ministers would make all CCSMA- and IPA-appointments. Consequently, institutionalization of the civil service reforms would legitimize the president's direct and indirect control over the bureaucracy for the foreseeable future. At the same time, a more effective and efficient civil service just might solve some of Ashkhabad's administrative problems, thereby further solidifying Niyasov's rule.

Besides a resident team leader, the project included a legal expert on long-term assignment and numerous short-term consultants. All of these individuals were West

---

[41]The EU program initially funding civil service reform was PHARE.

[42]Katharina Tegeder and Robert C. Rickards, "Proposal for Public Administration Capacity-Building in Turkmenistan," presented to the TACIS Procurement Unit, European Commission, Brussels, Belgium, April 26, 1996.

Europeans. Germans, particularly faculty members from the state College of Public Administration -- North Rhine-Westphalia and the Federal College of Public Administration predominated. The project also employed a sizable contingent of Turkmen.

Due to the difficult conditions in Turkmenistan and the reallocation of substantial project resources to employ more local nationals, project implementation lasted almost a year longer than planned. Nevertheless, by the end of 1998, draft civil service reform legislation and agreement on the CCSMA's structure and functions existed. Likewise, a high-level government committee was ready to appoint the CCSMA's staff,[43] Turkmen State University had received a small library and data processing equipment, new public administration curricula were in place, and Turkmenian faculty members had completed their training workshops. In addition, the Minister of Education, Chairman of the Parliamentary Committee on Legislation, and the Rector of Turkmen State University had committed themselves to founding the IPA.

LONG-RUN PROSPECTS

The project thus appears to have been largely successful in the short-run. To determine whether this success extends into the long-run, additional indicators of achievement are necessary. In the case of the civil service reform legislation, such indicators might include: establishment of a unit to facilitate legislative development; enactment of reform laws and adoption of subsidiary regulations; wide acceptance of the legal changes across ministries and by relevant social partners; agreement on the structure of civil service institutions and their respective mandates; and provision of adequate financing for their operations.

The CCSMA's success indicators might comprise: its actual establishment and functioning as a support unit to advance the reform process; codification of the relationships between the CCSMA and other civil service institutions; development of relevant organizational charts and plans for work flows; formulation of procedures for organisation and personnel management; training of key CCSMA officials and their assumption of responsibilities; and the putting in place of decision making mechanisms spanning the government's entire institutional framework.

Appropriate indicators to measure the IPA's success might cover: the founding of the IPA and appointment of its core staff; regular use of the curricula and training materials developed; and governmental officeholders actively using the IPA as an advisory board.

---

[43]Members of the Commisssion are: Minister of Economy and Finance (Chairman); Deputy Minister of Education (Vice-Chairwoman); Economics Department, Cabinet of Ministers; Senet (network of state enterprise training centers); State Statistics Committee; Turkmen Polytechnic Institute; Academy of Sciences Institute of Economy; Central Bank; Turkmen Institute of National Economy; State Taxation Inspection; Turkmen State University; Cabinet of Ministers Institute of Economy; and Technical Assistance Unit, Cabinet of Ministers.

As this list of indicators suggests, there are considerable grounds for skepticism about the long-run prospects for bureaucratic modernization in Turkmenistan. After all, the EU-sponsored project not only cost Turkmenistan nothing, but in fact brought fresh money to individuals enjoying Niyasov's confidence. Subsequently, no ongoing local financial support for bureaucratic reform has been forthcoming. Instead, Ashkhabad has been sounding out the International Bank for Regional Development, the International Monetary Fund, and the UN about contributing new hard currency resources for this purpose. Were such short-run funding again forthcoming, it nevertheless is highly uncertain that the amount would be sufficient to see the reform process through to completion. So, whether Ashkhabad really has the political will to modernize its civil service remains an important, unanswered question.

Even if new internal or external funding were to go into the reform process, though, at present there are no criteria or priorities for disbursing the money. Furthermore, Niyasov's government still has made no commitments to enact the requisite reform legislation, adopt subsidiary regulations, and actually implement key elements of the modernization process. Given the demonstrated inclination of the Gas and Oil and Agriculture Ministries to go their own ways, lack of cooperation or conflict among the ministries certainly could delay or thwart the reforms altogether.

Similarly, bottlenecks may emerge in crucial phases of reform implementation. For example, insufficient qualified personnel may be available to staff civil service institutions. After all, rather than competitive selection based on merit, the Council of Ministers chose administrators for training in the EU-sponsored project according to other, unspecified criteria. Moreover, the project targeted midlevel, generalist entrants' training needs. Yet, the Turkmenian bureaucracy lacks more specialized expertise in many areas too.

Just within the areas of economic and financial management, these needs include auditing, banking, budgeting, contract negotiation, debt management, fiscal policy, forecasting, information management, national income accounting, privatisation, project appraisal, purchasing, regulatory controls, and tax administration. Turkmenistan's civil service likewise needs greater legal, human resources, and organizational development expertise such as: career planning, commercial law, judicial administration, legal drafting, local government management, manpower budgeting, organisational and job analyses, personnel performance appraisal, policy analysis, program evaluation, remuneration, service delivery, and training needs assessment.[44] It indeed is difficult to imagine any modern governmental bureaucracy functioning well without these skills. For this reason alone, poor administrative decision making probably will continue in Ashkhabad indefinitely.

Besides lack of acceptance of the proposed new laws, insufficient commitment to their implementation, and manpower bottlenecks, bureaucratic modernization in Turkmenistan might not succeed for two more reasons. First, the civil service institutions may either fail to adopt or to practice the management changes taught by the IPA.

---

[44]Tacis, "Terms of Reference", *op. cit.*

Second, although the IPA may give good policy advice, the government simply may choose to ignore it.

CONCLUSIONS

Excepting the Baltic countries, none of the Soviet Union's successor states has improved its nationals' living standards much. In Turkmenistan, President Niyasov has transformed a one-party regime into a one-man government. Furthermore, his retention of the old nomenklatura has impeded the development of market business and democratic political institutions. It also has fostered the widespread corruption and mismanagement that have caused the country's economy to collapse. With agriculture de-mechanized, a looming water crisis, investment resources misallocated to prestige projects, the government budget perennially in deficit, galloping inflation, few meaningful economic reforms, and insufficient cotton and energy exports to prevent national insolvency, the outlook for Turkmenistan is dismal.

Nevertheless, Ashkhabad's strategic location in an unstable area, together with its vast energy reserves, make it an attractive prize in a new round of the "Great Game" among rival powers. The EU is playing a small, but important role in this regard. The EU's project to begin modernizing the Turkmenian civil service exemplifies that role. Although the institution-building task is essential to the country's eventual progress, EU authorities well understand that Turkmenistan cannot accomplish it overnight. Much time, more resources, and a great deal of approbation will be necessary.

However, the ultimate users of market business and democratic political institutions must consider them significant too. In particular, they must be willing to help sustain efforts to build these institutions by committing their own resources. Because Turkmenbashi so far has shunned such commitments, there currently are no grounds for optimism about the country's long-run prospects.

INDEX

A

administrative reform, 1, 4, 11, 13, 14, 15, 16, 17, 18, 21, 22, 23, 24, 25, 29, 30
Afghanistan, 195, 207, 209
Africa, 189
Alcaltel Deutschland, 206
arbitration, 166, 167
Armenia, 207
Asia, 39, 62, 65, 78, 79, 80, 196, 197, 200, 202, 208
Australia, 151
autocracy, 20
automobiles, 77
autonomy, 73, 78, 82, 161, 173, 175, 178, 192, 212
Azerbaidjan, 199, 200, 207, 208

B

balance of payments, 61, 192, 210
bank credit, 182, 184
banking system, 153, 182, 187, 191, 192, 210
banks, 137
banks, commercial, 25, 159, 210, 211
barter, 200, 204
Beijing, 157, 158, 162
Belgium, 214
black market, 185, 210
Brazil, 154
Britain, 67
bureaucracy, 2, 5, 6, 10, 12, 15, 21, 22, 23, 27, 30, 56, 66, 74, 75, 78, 82, 195, 202, 212, 214, 215
business community, 11, 12, 17, 79

business risk, 179, 183
business transactions, 17, 204

C

cabinet members, 3, 4, 5, 6
California, 184, 195
Canada, 199
capital, 71, 152, 174, 175, 186, 190, 191
capital investments, 183
capital outflows, 62
Caspian Sea, 195, 197, 208, 209
Central Asian republics, 197, 203
Central Bank, 58, 59, 60, 61, 62, 81, 182, 202, 214
cereals, 203
Chiang Ching-kuo, 55, 56, 57
Chiang Kai-shek, 56
Chile, 154
China, 57, 58, 59, 60, 61, 62, 65, 66, 73, 75, 76, 79, 81, 137, 151, 154, 155, 156, 157, 158, 159, 160, 161, 162, 164, 165, 166, 167, 168, 169, 170, 173, 174, 175, 176, 182, 183, 185, 188, 189, 190, 193, 197, 209
citizenship, 201
civil service, 195, 201, 203, 212, 213, 214, 215, 216
Civil War, 197
coalition government, 8, 31
coastal cities, 164
Commonwealth of Independent States, 202
Communist Party, 161, 163, 172, 174, 176, 179, 182, 191, 198
communities, 5, 58
compensation, 20, 159, 163, 165
conflicts, 9, 16, 29, 184, 192

confrontation, 16
constitution, 64, 198, 199
constitutional authority, 3, 4
consumer electronics, 78
consumption taxes, 17
cooperation, 27, 202, 215
corporatism, 78
corruption, 66, 67, 201, 204, 212, 216
cotton, 196, 200, 202, 204, 205, 206, 210,
    211, 212, 216
crop production, 212
currency, 187

D

debt, 65
debt service, 66
decentralization, 82
decision-making process, 8, 81
defense spending, 65, 81
democracy, 195, 198
Democratic Progressive Party, 55
democratization, 55, 57, 58, 61, 65, 67, 72,
    73, 75, 80, 82, 198
Deng Xiaoping, 163, 172
devaluation, 153, 184, 185, 186, 187, 188,
    189
diet, 3, 4, 6, 9, 10, 15, 18, 19, 21, 22, 23,
    28, 29
domestic economy, 57, 79, 161, 163

E

East Germany, 203
economic crisis, 188
economic decline, 203, 206, 207, 209, 211
economic development, 57, 59, 70, 73, 74,
    78, 80, 159, 163, 179, 180, 184, 192,
    202
economic growth, 57, 62, 69, 179, 180,
    188, 192
economic policy, 36
economic reforms, 85, 158
economic zones, 161, 164

education, 65, 152, 212, 214
elections, 18
elite bureaucrats, 6
emigration, 200
energy conservation, 78
enterprises, state-owned, 151, 168, 171,
    191
environmental impact, 70
environmental protection, 66, 70, 71, 74,
    78
environmental security, 76
Estonia, 213
Europe, 200, 206, 208, 213
European Bank for Reconstruction and
    Development, 203
European Union, 195, 202, 203, 213, 216
excess liquidity, 62
exclusion, 70
executive branch, 1, 3, 4, 8, 63
exercise, 2, 3, 10, 11
exploitation, 163, 199, 205
export earnings, 66, 201, 211

F

failure, 2, 11, 18, 20, 28, 29, 30, 73, 78,
    207
fairness, 17
family, 199
farmland, 212
Federal Reserve, 58
financial crisis, 62, 153, 187, 188, 189,
    190, 191, 192
financial stability, 59, 61
financial support, 200, 213, 215
floods, 204
foreign capital, 154, 156, 159, 190
foreign competition, 79
foreign direct investment, 151, 153, 154,
    155, 156, 157, 158, 159, 160, 163, 164,
    179, 180, 181, 182, 183, 184, 187, 189,
    190, 192

foreign exchange, 59, 61, 62, 69, 79, 151,
    153, 154, 166, 184, 185, 186, 187, 188,
    189, 190, 204, 205, 210
foreign exchange reserve, 189
foreign investment, 159, 161, 164, 165,
    166, 183, 184, 185
foreign trade, 75, 86, 151, 158, 165, 186,
    210
Foreign-invested enterprises (FIEs), 158,
    183
France, 6, 67
Fujian, 157, 158, 162
Fukuda Takeo, 14, 29

G

General Agreement Tariffs and Trade
    (GATT), 159, 170
Georgia, 207, 208
Germany, 67, 154, 195, 202, 203, 206
global market, 74
goods and services, 209, 210
government, 8, 17, 65, 66, 74, 76, 79, 161,
    177, 178, 182, 184, 187, 197
government policy, 22, 180
government spending, 11, 29, 62, 81
grandstander, 1, 27, 29, 30, 31
Gross Domestic Product, 62, 66, 67, 156,
    158, 203, 204, 208, 209, 211
Gross National Product, 153
Guangdong, 156, 157, 158, 159, 162, 163
Guangzhou, 161
Guizhou, 157, 162

H

Hashimoto Ryutaro, 2, 4, 9, 21, 22, 29
health care, 78
health insurance, 66, 67
heart disease, 199
Hong Kong, 66, 69, 78, 79, 151, 153, 154,
    155, 172, 173, 176, 181, 182, 187, 188,
    191
human resources, 212, 215

human rights, 57, 201
human rights violations, 57
Hungary, 154

I

import duties, 77
import substitution, 73
import tariffs, 170, 171, 183
imports, 156, 189, 204, 205, 210
impoverishment, 201
income, 77, 162, 164, 165
independence, 59, 196, 198, 201, 203, 205,
    206, 208, 211
Indiana, 196
indirect taxes, 17
Indonesia, 153, 154, 188
industrial policy, 55, 56, 58, 72, 73, 74, 78,
    80, 82, 183
industrial sector, 20, 77, 80, 165, 180, 183
industrialization, 73, 74
industrialized nations, 16, 66
inflation, 58, 60, 62, 69, 185, 186, 188,
    193, 196, 201, 203, 209, 216
information technology, 80
infrastructure, 65, 71, 74, 158, 183, 200,
    202, 203
Inner Mongolia, 162
Intellectual Property Rights, 109
interest groups, 13, 18, 28, 68
International Monetary Fund, 182
intervention, 186
interview, 18, 20, 59, 61, 62, 64, 66, 75,
    76, 77, 80
investment, 78, 151, 152, 153, 154, 155,
    157, 158, 159, 160, 164, 165, 166, 172,
    183, 191, 192
investment policy, 168
Iran, 195, 200, 202, 207, 208, 210
irrigation, 196, 205
Italy, 154

J

Japan, 1, 2, 5, 6, 8, 10, 12, 13, 15, 17, 22, 24, 25, 28, 57, 58, 61, 66, 67, 78, 79, 80, 154, 170, 188, 206
Jiang Zemin, 170, 172, 191
Jiangsu, 157, 158, 162, 163
joint ventures, 153, 159, 161, 163, 164, 165, 166, 168

K

Kaifu Toshiki, 11, 29
kamikaze fighter, 1, 28, 29, 30, 31
Kazakh, 196
Kazakhstan, 195, 197, 205, 207
Kishi Nobusuke, 11, 14, 28
know-how, 163
knowledge, 6
kolkhozes, 211
Korea, 50, 61, 66, 67, 78, 79, 80, 153, 188
Kuomintang, 55

L

labor force, 196, 204
labor law, 166
labor shortage, 74
land planning, 76
land reform, 73
Latin America, 79, 189
Latvia, 213
leadership, 1, 9
leadership style, 1, 2, 9, 30
Lee Teng-hui, 56
legal authority, 1, 2, 4, 9, 26, 30, 71
legal restrictions, 6
legislation, 6, 15, 19, 23, 68, 70, 71, 72, 77, 155, 213, 214, 215
Liberal Democratic Party, 4, 17
liberalization, 57, 61, 67, 68, 71, 198
licensing, 69, 153, 167
Lithuania, 213
living standard, 195, 196, 216

loans, 158, 160, 191
local government, 166, 168, 171, 174, 180, 215
low-interest loans, 77
loyalty, 5

M

mainland, 57, 73
Malaysia, 153, 154, 188
manufacturing, 205, 207
Mao Zedong, 67
market access, 108
market economy, 33, 156, 176, 179, 195, 211
market forces, 74
mass media, 15, 25
Mexico, 154
MFN, 112
Miami, 71
Michigan, 2
Miki Takeo, 11
mining, 165, 166
Ministry of International Trade and Investment (MITI), 20
Miyazawa Kiichi, 19, 29
modernization, 65, 67, 73, 163, 195, 202, 207, 215, 216
Monetary Policy, 58, 59, 60
Mongolia, 157
multinational companies, 79, 151
Muslims, 196

N

Nakasone Yasuhiro, 2, 10, 11, 12, 13, 16, 27, 28, 29
National Defense, 65
national interest, 6
national leader, 2, 3, 4, 11, 26
national unity, 201
natural gas, 196, 199, 201, 204, 207, 208, 209, 210
negotiation, 215

Netherlands, 199
New Party, 55
New York, 2, 68, 79
New Zealand, 151
nomenklatura, 207, 216
North Korea, 71, 198

O

Obuchi Keizo, 9
Ohira Masayoshi, 5, 11
oil crises, 62
Open Door Policy, 151, 161, 184, 185
opposition parties, 10, 15, 19, 21, 27, 28, 30, 64

P

Pacific, 39, 170
Pakistan, 209
Parliament, 6, 213
partisanship, 8
party system, 70
peace lover, 1, 29, 30, 31
Pearl River Delta, 162
Peoples Republic of China, 151, 153, 154, 155, 156, 158, 159, 160, 161, 163, 165, 166, 168, 169, 170, 171, 172, 173, 174, 175, 176, 179, 180, 181, 183, 184, 185, 188, 189, 190, 191, 192
personal relations, 6
personality, 26, 198, 201
personnel training, 77
pesticides, 205
Philippines, 78, 153
planned economy, 156, 176, 179
Poland, 154
police, 199, 201
policy decisions, 73
policy goal, 1, 11, 27, 29
policy initiatives, 6, 56
policymaking, 2, 3, 5, 6, 9, 12, 17, 26
Politburo, 198
political insider, 1, 9, 27, 29, 30, 31

political instability, 208
political parties, 5, 22
political reform, 29
political resources, 1, 3, 9, 27, 28, 31
political stability, 55, 155, 161, 163
political support, 25, 30
pollution, 57, 68, 70, 78, 81
population density, high, 66
population growth, 205
poverty, 196
prime minister, 1, 2, 3, 4, 5, 6, 7, 9, 10, 11, 12, 13, 14, 17, 18, 19, 20, 22, 23, 24, 25, 26, 27, 28, 29, 30, 31
privatization, 12, 15, 24, 25, 72, 200, 202, 211
product development, 80
project management, 202
property rights, 168
protest movement, 57
public administration, 213, 214
public debt, 66
public image, 11
public interest, 1, 81, 82
public opinion, 15, 16, 24
public ownership, 177
public sector, 16
public services, 203
public support, 10
public works, 12

R

rate, economic growth, 62
rationality, 188
raw materials, 166, 183, 197, 201, 204
recession, 14
reforms, economic, 151, 158, 172, 176, 180, 207, 211, 216
regulations, price, 209
regulatory policy-making, 55, 68, 69, 82
relatives, 57
Renminbi (RMB), 153, 154, 157, 162, 168, 169, 170, 171, 172, 174, 175, 182, 184, 185, 186, 187, 188, 192, 193

ruling party, 1, 2, 6, 7, 9, 10, 16, 23, 25, 27, 28, 29, 30, 72

Russia, 197, 198, 199, 200, 201, 202, 206, 208, 210

S

sales tax, 17, 18, 19, 20
Saudi Arabia, 209
school curriculum, 200
sectionalism, 4, 6
security threat, 57
Shandong, 157, 158, 162
Shanghai, 153, 157, 158, 159, 161, 162, 173, 174, 175, 181, 182, 192
Shenzhen, 153, 159, 173, 174, 175, 181, 182, 184, 185, 192
Sichuan, 157, 162
Singapore, 66, 78, 154
Slovenia, 213
social assistance, 66
social insurance, 66
social life, 68
social movements, 57
social regulation, 58, 70
social security, 66, 180
social welfare, 65, 66, 67, 81
Southeast Asia, 62, 153
Soviet Union, 28, 195, 197, 202, 204, 206, 213, 216
sovkhozes, 211
Spain, 154
special economic zones, 161, 164, 165
spending cuts, 12
Stalin, Joseph, 198
state property, 211
state-owned enterprises, 67, 73, 79, 153, 156, 159, 166, 168, 169, 170, 171, 172, 173, 175, 176, 177, 178, 179, 180, 181, 182, 183, 191, 192
Suzuki Zenko, 2, 11, 16, 29
Switzerland, 155, 202

T

Taiwan, 55, 56, 57, 58, 59, 60, 61, 62, 63, 64, 65, 66, 67, 68, 69, 70, 71, 72, 73, 74, 75, 76, 77, 78, 79, 80, 81, 82, 154
Takeshita Noboru, 2, 9, 10, 11, 19, 21, 27, 29
Tanaka Kakuei, 9, 10, 11, 27, 29
tax base, 17, 183
tax burden, 17, 67
tax credits, 77
tax incentives, 79
tax Law, 164
tax reform, 1, 2, 17, 18, 19, 20, 21, 27, 28, 29, 153, 192
tax revenues, 67
tax system, 17, 18, 28, 183, 188
technology, 76, 151
technology transfer, 156, 161, 164, 166, 187
telecommunications, 75, 206
telegraph, 69
Telekom, 206
textiles, 111
Tiananmen Square, 141
Tianjin, 157, 158, 161, 162
Tibet, 157, 162
trade balance, 104
trade barriers, 170, 171
trade policy, 168, 179
trade surplus, 60, 61
transportation, 69, 71, 72, 75, 166, 167, 202, 208
troops, 197
Turkey, 200, 202, 206, 207, 208, 210
Turkmenistan, 195, 196, 197, 198, 199, 200, 201, 202, 203, 204, 205, 206, 207, 208, 209, 210, 211, 212, 213, 214, 215, 216

U

U.S. Environmental Protection Agency,
    (EPA), 70, 75
Ukraine, 200, 207, 208
unemployment, 57, 66, 172, 196
unemployment rate, 57
unions, 71
United Nations, 202
United States, 11, 14, 57, 67, 73, 74, 152,
    153, 154, 200, 208
Uno Sosuke, 11
Urals, 209
USSR, 197, 198
Uzbekistan, 195, 197, 205, 207, 208, 209

V

Vietnam, 33

W

water crisis, 216
water supply, 205
wealth, 58
Western Europe, 208, 213
work force, 66
World Bank, 168, 182, 202, 211
world market, 201, 204, 208, 211
World Trade Organization, 111, 153, 159,
    170, 171, 179, 183, 184, 188, 191

Y

Yeltsin, Boris N., 199
Yoshida Shigeru, 11, 28
Yuan, 55, 56, 59, 63, 64, 65, 67, 68, 69,
    71, 73, 74, 75, 81, 153, 170, 184, 185,
    186

Z

Zhao Ziyang, 161
Zhejiang, 157, 158, 162
Zhu Rongji, 168, 179, 180, 182, 188, 192
zoku groups, 7, 16